THE WAY IT WAS
New York, 1850 - 1890

THE WAY IT WAS

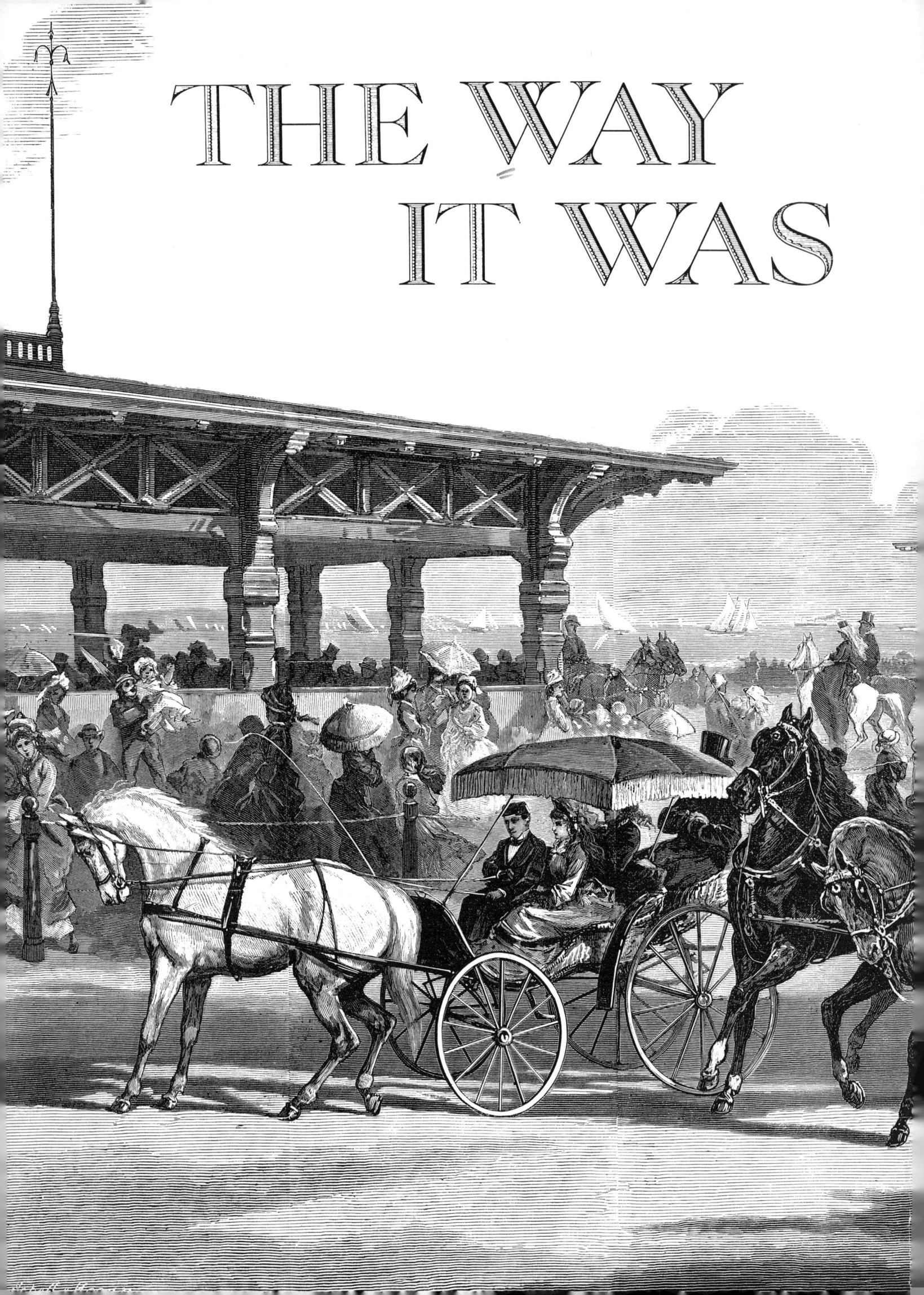

CLARENCE P. HORNUNG

New York, 1850 – 1890

SCHOCKEN BOOKS · NEW YORK

ACKNOWLEDGMENTS

To all whose drawings, engravings and photographic collaboration have contributed to this pictorial essay the author hereby gives generous thanks for the talents that have shaped the face of this volume. Especially, he singles out for highest praise the master artist-journalists who, with their competent engravers, have preserved for us those precious moments that portray the facets of the city, long since gone and all but forgotten. Where words have failed, he has turned to the masters of the written word, Dickens and Whitman, Dreiser and Riis, for their incomparable impressions. Equally, he extends thanks to the reporters of the defunct journals for their vivid descriptions of the contemporary scene. Turning to the twentieth century, grateful acknowledgments are due the authors and publishers for their permission to quote from the sources listed and so to complete this story, a blending of words and pictures into a harmonious ensemble:

Edward Robb Ellis and Coward, McCann & Geoghegan, Inc. for *The Epic of New York City,* 1966. Albert Ten Eyck Gardner and Clarkson N. Potter, Inc. for *Winslow Homer, An American Artist: His World and His Work,* 1961. Henry Hope Reed and Sophia Duckworth, and Clarkson N. Potter, Inc. for *Central Park: A History and a Guide,* 1967. Susan Elizabeth Lyman and Crown Publishers, Inc. for *The Story of New York,* 1964. Alfred Kazin and *Harper's Bazaar* for "Brooklyn Bridge," 1946. Cleveland Rodgers and Rebecca B. Rankin, and Harper & Row, Inc. for *New York: The World's Capital City,* 1948. Kenneth H. Dunshee and Hastings House for *As You Pass By,* 1952. Marshall B. Davidson and Houghton, Mifflin Company for *Life in America,* 1951. Richardson Wright and J. B. Lippincott Company for *Hawkers and Walkers in Early America,* 1927. Frederick Van Wyck and Liveright Publishing Corp. for *Recollections of an Old New Yorker,* 1932. Maxwell F. Marcuse for *This Was New York,* 1969. Lewis Mumford for excerpts from "The Metropolitan Milieu" in *America and Alfred Stieglitz,* 1934, and *Brown Decades,* 1931. Bayrd Still and New York University Press for *Mirror for Gotham,* 1956. Lloyd Morris and Random House for *Incredible New York,* 1951. Robert Greenhalgh Albion and Charles Scribner's Sons for *The Rise of New York,* 1939. John A. Krout and the United States Publishers Association for "The American Stage" in *Yale Pageant of America.*

First published by SCHOCKEN BOOKS 1977

Copyright © 1977 by Schocken Books Inc.

Library of Congress Cataloging in Publication Data
Main entry under title:

The Way it was.

   Bibliography: p. 205
   Includes index.
   1. New York (City) in art.   2. New York (City)—Description—Pictorial works.   3. Wood-engravings, American.   4. Wood-engravers—United States.
I. Hornung, Clarence Pearson.

NE954.2.W39   769'.4'99747103   76-49975

Manufactured in the United States of America

*To the memory of my parents
who made me a proud New Yorker:*

*my Mother, from Heidelberg, Germany,
and my father, from Mulhouse, France.*

CONTENTS

INTRODUCTION viii

PART ONE   *East Side...West Side*   1

South Street wharves... East River and North River... Unloading at the docks... West Side waterfront... Immigrants and customs inspection... Fulton Market and fishing fleets... Washington Market and farm produce... Battery Park and New York Bay

PART TWO   *All Around the Town*   27

Broadway and mercantile districts... Traffic jams at Fulton Street... Wall Street... Times of panic... Stock Exchange... Crystal Palace and Exposition... Panoramic view of New York... Grand Central Depot... Tammany Hall... New Post Office... Newspaper row... Fifth Avenue mansions... Old residences... Athletic clubs... Steam pipes and electric cables

PART THREE   *The Sidewalks of New York*   57

German street bands... Street hawkers... Flower markets... Moving day... East Side tenements... Slums and squalor... Penny lunches... Park visits and matinees... Parades and celebrations... Election returns... Firework displays

PART FOUR   *Across the Water*   81

Staten Island and New York Harbor... East River frozen... Ferries to Brooklyn... Brooklyn Bridge under construction... Opening Day celebration... Views of the bridge... Harlem River bridges... Excursions by boat to Harlem... Statue of Liberty... Unveiling and celebration... Coney Island and Brighton Beach... Iron steamboats to Coney Island

PART FIVE *Manhattan on the Move* 113

> Buses and stages on lower Broadway . . . Footbridge at Fulton Street
> . . . Proposals for traffic relief . . . Overhead railways suggested . . .
> Pedestrians and traffic snarls . . . Experimental subway in 1870 . . .
> Elevated railway system takes shape . . . Rush hour crowds . . .
> Jam-packed horsecars . . . Railroad tracks under Park Avenue

PART SIX *Up in Central Park* 135

> Views in Central Park . . . The Mall and Terraces . . . The Menagerie
> . . . Boating on the lake . . . Squatters in park areas . . . The joy of
> skating . . . Sleigh-bells in the park . . . Coaching and carriage drives

PART SEVEN *Times of Trouble* 153

> City Hall afire . . . Civil War draft riots . . . Fire-fighters at home and
> in action . . . Fireboats on the river . . . Hook-and-ladders . . .
> Horsecar perils in deep snow . . . The Great Blizzard of 1888 . . .
> Bloody strikes of streetcar workers

PART EIGHT *In Pursuit of Pleasure* 173

> Winter sports in the snow . . . Horse market at Bull's Head . . . Racing
> on Harlem Lane . . . Annual Horse Show at Madison Square Garden
> . . . Coaching up Fifth Avenue . . . Jerome Park Race Course . . .
> Smart-set driving four-in-hands . . . Promenade on ''The Avenue''
> . . . Baseball at the Polo Grounds . . . Lawn tennis in the parks . . .
> Cycling by moonlight . . . Riverside Drive and the beauty of the
> Hudson . . . Barnum's Museum and the Academy of Music . . . The
> Rialto and theatre district . . . Hotels and fine restaurants . . . Society
> Balls and Carnegie Hall

SELECTED BIBLIOGRAPHY 205

ARTISTS, ENGRAVERS, AND PHOTOGRAPHERS 208

GENERAL INDEX 209

Introduction

MANY PEOPLE over the years have felt impelled to write their impressions, record their recollections, or present information about New York. Pictorial histories have burgeoned in the twentieth century, illustrated, for the most part, by photographs from archives in private hands or museum collections. A glance at the appended bibliography reveals how extensive this iconography is. The volumes listed, though but a small part of books on the subject, readily indicate how intensively the topic has been explored from every angle. Why, then, another entry?

This native New Yorker believes that, in the pages that follow, certain facts and information, not previously presented, will unfold a picture seen only by those who were here over a century ago, recorded by graphic processes (some no longer in use), and vividly related by on-the-spot reporters or contemporary authors.

Thanks to the illustrated weeklies with their vast store of wood engravings—of portraits, scenes, and current events—all present-day Americans, whether or not they be readers, can gain a vivid understanding of what this glamorous metropolis was like in the second half of the century.

Unlike an adopted son, the native-born is usually permeated with a genuine sense of belonging; he feels inspired to proclaim his city's unique character. I remember my early childhood, the neighborhoods where we lived, the scenes and smells of the streets, though, in my opinion, my family moved far too often. I protested such frequent changes of address, the trials of getting acquainted with new schools and their teachers, the distance from trusted friends; but, to my parents, there was the potent lure: a new landlord who enticed tenants into his building with concessions of a few months' free rent plus, very frequently, an extra ten dollars which in those days covered moving a vanload of furniture.

My West Side story was staged just a few doors from Central Park at Sixty-sixth Street. Sheep nibbled the meadow grass and were housed in a fold that, after many vicissitudes, has become the Tavern-on-the-Green. I rode the carousels, skated in winter, flew kites in summer. At the boat pond, I met a staggering disappointment.

All winter my father had whittled away in our kitchen on a three-foot boat. Both he and I were confident that this would be the envy of all beholders. But, alas, when the great day for launching came, our boat toppled over and would not sail. Apparently my father had no knowledge of the relationship of keel-weight to sail-area, but this was no consolation to me.

There were, however, other compensations. There was Durland's Riding Academy across the street, where I was a frequent visitor. There, now the headquarters of the American Broadcasting Company, I had my introduction to the best of the horse-and-buggy era and the importance of equestrian life in an urban environment. As my father was one of Durland's riding masters, I frequented the stables after school and on holidays. My friends and I were allowed to visit the riding arena and look in the stalls at the superb mounts, while maintaining a respectful distance from their rapier-sharp hooves ever ready to protest our intrusion. More daring, younger boys had a game of running under the horse's belly, as it stood clear of the stall.

Every visit to Durland's held matchless fascination for me—the glistening harnesses of tallyho and park drag—the heady thrill when, on special occasions, I was allowed to ride in a stately coach or four-in-hand through the winding drives of Central Park, as a bonus for having polished carriages until their dark, satiny surfaces reflected my own face, broken only by creamy stripes or the ornate crest of an opulent owner. My early love of a handsome carriage has never rubbed off. I still stand in almost worshipful admiration before a fine vehicle, whether in a museum or on parade.

Later on, when my family had moved to the Upper West Side, I found myself sharing more daring escapades, incurring greater dangers than those from mettlesome horses. There, it was the neighborhood custom to "snitch a hitch"—grab a free ride—on the trolley cars that rattled along Broadway and Amsterdam Avenue.

The fear of being branded a sissy, if one did not conform, developed in each of us an indifference to danger. A stolen ride on the rear platform of an open trolley, even if the ride lasted but a few blocks, was a grand way to cool off in hot weather. We had to hitch behind when the conductor was up front, collecting fares. By the time he had worked his way back, the culprit had already ridden four or five blocks at the traction company's expense. Jealous kids on the street often alerted the irate conductor with cries of "Hitch behind!" But, just as he was about to grab the offender, the free rider went flying into space. Many times I flopped, face down on the rough cobblestones of the street, returning home with bleeding knees and great holes in the long black stockings we wore in those days.

But trolley "hitches" were tame, compared to the thrills of "hopping the freights" down at the New York Central tracks that ran along the Hudson River edge below Riverside Drive. Those long lines of moving freight cars fascinated us—box cars of red, yellow, and brown, emblazoned with trade-marks and logotypes from all four corners of our land. Many had traveled thousands of miles to reach Manhattan. The least we could do in welcome was a trip aboard. This required hopping from one car to another, often travelling in the opposite direction. Many a youngster learned that his trapeze skill was not equal to the leap of five or six feet. I remember one bloody incident when "Smitty" was carried off in an ambulance to St. Luke's Hospital where he had a close call from a threatened amputation.

Living in a crowded neighborhood, a boy had to follow the herd or be ostracized. It was the law of the street jungle—each gang member faced the terrors that were borne by all. The leader set the tune when "having fun" meant upsetting the vendors' push-carts and stealing their apples and bananas. Election night called for a huge bonfire; boxes stored for weeks were piled to the height of three-story houses and set ablaze. Invariably, the fire engines arrived, but only when the flames seemed to reach the sky, and the pavement had softened under the heat.

I had my own special interests. My instincts for collecting old magazines, catalogs, and prints go back as far, or so it seems, as memory itself. At one time when the far West for me was as far off as Mars, I specialized in brochures extolling the wonders of golden California, its fruit farms and vineyards, promotions issued by the railroads. This forced me to roller skate five miles downtown on Saturday mornings, to the railroad offices along Broadway and about Twenty-eighth Street, where I collected armloads of colorful catalogs over which I drooled for days.

During World War I, the beauty of the war posters inspired me to build a large collection which, later, was presented to the New York Public Library. At about the same time, motivated both by patriotic fervor and my needs as a young commercial artist accumulating reference materials, clippings and magazine covers on the American eagle became the focus of my collecting activities. These acquisitions over a span of five decades have grown to such staggering proportions that with this nucleus of memorabilia I have recently compiled a book, soon to be published under the title "The American Eagle in the Arts."

It is difficult to name the date when I first began to collect old magazines. The rich pictorial content of *Harper's, Leslie's,* and *Scientific American* spurred me on to collect them eagerly. I made cross references to their engravings to facilitate my future work. But I never did foresee that, fifty years later, the illustrations from these ancient periodicals would be the basis of this book.

Obviously the period herein treated, 1850 to 1890, spans but a small fraction of the four centuries of Gotham's history. But this particular half-century has not been chosen arbitrarily. It corresponds to a specific period when people for the first time were kept abreast of daily happenings and news events by means of clear and vivid engravings, the work of a handful of talented men.

At the halfway point of the nineteenth century, many city dailies carried current events, political and local news. But their news columns were enlivened only occasionally by a trade cut or a logotype, which Ben Franklin early advocated to add spice and liveliness to a dull page. The enterprising firm of Currier & Ives, and a few others, issued topical lithographs to commemorate outstanding events or record a national disaster. But there was a considerable time lag before a color print could be produced and offered for sale and, consequently, a loss of newsworthiness.

In this vacuum of prompt communication, a few publishers saw and seized their opportunity. Boston and New York City were the nation's established publishing centers. These cities offered the needed elements for launching the illustrated weeklies, especially the giant printing presses essential to handle large editions. The wood engravers, of whom there were fewer than two dozen in the country, had been attracted to New York because the publishers offered the best hope for utilizing their talents.

Credit for the nation's first weekly must go to Frederick Gleason, Boston's successful publisher of the story-paper *Flag of Our Union*. In 1851, Gleason founded a copiously illustrated family miscellany called *Gleason's Pictorial Drawing-Room Companion*. Gleason chose as his editor Maturin Murray Ballou. More important, Gleason's good judgment dictated the selection, as head of his engraving department, of an English-born engraver who had arrived in New York in 1848 before venturing to Boston. Under the guidance of this man, Henry Carter, who had changed his name to Frank Leslie, the Gleason weekly did well, due chiefly to its profusion of illustrative matter. Leslie's name, as engraver, appears on many of these early pictures, but his ambition to publish his own magazine soon lead him to seek backing elsewhere. In 1852, Leslie appeared at P. T. Barnum's home in Bridgeport, Connecticut, proposing a new magazine which he, Leslie, would edit. Apparently Barnum approved of the idea. Soon, a new magazine called the *Illustrated News* was published in New York, its controlling interest divided between Barnum and H. D. and A. E. Beach of the *New York Sun*. Frank Leslie was appointed managing foreman.

In a short time, Barnum's promotional efforts helped boost circulation above seventy thousand. By 1855, Leslie had sufficiently mastered the technique of publishing to launch his own weekly, titled *Frank Leslie's Illustrated Newspaper*. It consisted of sixteen pages, illustrated with large and striking woodcuts, and sold for ten cents a copy. The pictures usually were devoted to important news events, and the paper appeared within a fortnight of the reported happenings. Such speed in illustrative reporting had been hitherto unknown, and was unmatched by any competitor.

Frank Leslie's scoop in publishing prompt, pictorial accounts of newsworthy events was the first step toward tabloid journalism. It enabled him to report murders, fires, railroad and steamship disasters, lynchings and morgue scenes. The element of sensationalism made an instant appeal. Circulation figures soon reflected nationwide interest. To achieve the speed essential in news reportage, Leslie's innovative genius enabled him to achieve an important breakthrough in publishing history. To prepare large engravings with great speed, he divided the wood block into as many as 32 sections, assigning separate parts to a staff of trained engravers who often worked through the night to meet publication deadlines. The separate sections of each plate were then bolted together by another expert who checked the joints for defects and reduced them to a minimum.

Many of the large engravings in this book were made by this method. The illustrations became larger and larger for special events, until they had spread to an enormous gatefold measuring over forty inches. Simultaneously, while *Leslie's* was prospering, Gleason up in Boston, the originator of the illustrated weekly, had "realized an ample competence" and retired from the scene. He sold out to his editor, Ballou, who promptly changed the publication's name to *Ballou's Pictorial Drawing-Room Companion*. This continued publication until 1859. Some of the first views of New York to appear in a periodical reached wide readership through the pages of *Gleason's* and *Ballou's* of Boston. They pioneered in supplying the reading public with pictures of New York City.

The publishing scene shifted back to New York, with the appearance of a weekly that was to achieve high standards and a large, well-merited circulation. This was *Harper's Weekly* and, fortunately for New Yorkers, the city was *Harper's* home base. The periodical presented many aspects of our home life, its mysteries and miseries, its highlights and shadows, its success stories and its squalor. With its lively and alert editorial policy and its employment of the finest illustrators, *Harper's Weekly* was able to document the New York story in great detail from the publication's inception in 1859 until the 1890s. Fletcher Harper, one of the four brothers whose book-publishing empire was preeminent in this country, conceived the idea of the weekly after observing the success of *Gleason's, Ballou's,* and *Leslie's.* "It became his pet enterprise," says his grandson, J. Henry Harper, "and until within a few months of his death the best energies of his controlling mind were devoted to it."

Harper's Weekly: A Journal of Civilization became a strong social and political force, doing much to advance the cause of American magazines in this country. By its prominent use of large illustrations at the hands of the finest artists, its vivid pictorial journalism, its thorough news coverage and editorial comment, plus its feature articles, *Harper's Weekly* may well be called the precursor of today's pictorial and news magazines.

Each of the illustrated weeklies employed a staff of trained engravers, chosen to achieve competence and speed as each picture was fitted into its place in the magazine layout. These men had behind them a historic legacy of four centuries of wood engraving, dating back to the earliest block books printed as impressions carved on a single wood plank even before the days of Gutenberg. Successive developments in the many schools of European and British engravers had brought the art to a superlative state. But the need for speed had never been present in previous centuries.

When *Harper's* and *Leslie's* began their weeklies, it was found that, to produce a modern news publication, its art department must be organized to meet any emergency, from the creative conception to final mechanical production. At the apex of this pyramid were the outside illustrators, some of whom sketched directly on the wood block, or on paper from which the sketch was transferred to wood by a corps of lesser craftsmen functioning chiefly as tracers. Frequently the outside illustrator wrote special instructions on his sketch. By following these notes, the "re-drawers" were able to interpret the effects desired by the original artist.

The surface to which the drawing was transferred was a highly polished block of fine-grained boxwood, its face coated with a white, satiny sizing receptive to pen and ink, pencil, and India ink washes. The many gradations of fine lines and cross-hatchings took on a variety of tonal qualities, textures that could best be indicated by varying tones of wash from dark to light. With an engraving staff of different degrees of skill, the manager of an art department had to assign the work accordingly. Some men excelled at figure work; others, the "grainers," were best at interpreting textures in endless variety. Later, certain mechanical devices were employed, the results of which are revealed in the grain treatment of skies and cloud effects.

Where the press run was large, often exceeding one hundred thousand, the wood engravings could not withstand the tremendous pressures. The constant pounding eroded the delicate lines of the picture. An electrotyped version of the printing plate, which retains every minute hairline of the original, is the final achievement of the staff enterprise: from illustrator to art director, to wood engraver, to electrotyper, to printing press, and the eventual impression on the printed page.

Reproductive wood engraving, as exemplified on the pages of the illustrated weeklies, had its heyday during the 'Seventies and 'Eighties. The best examples are the work of such artists as Homer, de Thulstrup, Frenzeny, Tavernier, Waud, Abbey, Reinhardt, Graham, Gibson, and Gray-Parker. Often, in addition to crediting the original illustrator, the engraver's name was listed to share the honor, but this practice was by no means general. Their glamorous years of success were brief.

In the late 1880s, Stephen H. Horgan invented the half-tone process. With this, a wash drawing or photograph could be translated into a printing plate photomechanically. Half-tones appeared very slowly in the weeklies; their initial printing quality was weak and lacking in contrast, a poor substitute for the sharp, crisp quality of the wood engraving. But the half-tone offered speed and economy, and as its quality gradually improved it brought an end to the era of wood engraving. Its demise was deplored in print and in speech. A valuable art form, the process of wood engraving had given employment to hundreds. The invention of the metal half-tone plate ended a period that gave us a precious treasure of graphic records.

You have only to turn these pages to appreciate the legacy left by the artist-journalists who worked in close harmony with the celebrated illustrated weeklies, now but memories.

C.P.H.

PART ONE

East Side...West Side

From *Gleason's Pictorial Drawing-Room Companion*, 1855.

VIEW OF SOUTH STREET, NEW YORK CITY

South Street, more than any other New York thoroughfare, symbolized the bustling activity of a maritime city. Extending along the East River waterfront on "made land" beneath which the tides had ebbed and flowed until about 1800, its busy wharves berthed packet ships landing spices from far-off Cathay, or ivories from Madagascar. Gilded figureheads nestled under bowsprits, and jibbooms thrust their sharp harpoons across cobbled streets. A hundred carts and drays, heavily laden, wobbled with wares from the Seven Seas. Facing the docks were the countinghouses and ship's brokers, the sail lofts, chandlers, and provision stores. Above the drone and clatter of dense traffic one could hear the screeching sea gulls as they swooped down beside the fishermen to rescue remnants of the day's catch.

East Side...West Side

WHEN GIOVANNI DA VERRAZANO, in 1524, first entered the mouth of the lower bay, sailed between "two small but prominent hills" (the Narrows), crossing the broad expanse of water to behold the long, golden tongue of Manhattan, what a wondrous world lay before his eyes! What unlocked portals to welcome all from across the sea . . . "the homeless, the tempest-tossed" . . . destined as a haven for all nationalities. As if to presage the melting pot that was to become New York, here was an Italian adventurer sailing for a French patron, Francis I. Before him had come another proud son of Italy, Cristoforo Colombo, promoting the interests of the Spanish King and Queen. And yet another Genovesan, Giovanni Caboto, better known as John Cabot, had been granted letters patent to lay claim to lands in the name of Henry VIII, of England.

As yet no attempts had been made by Italian, Spanish, and British claimants to follow up their early discoveries in the New World. European wars and rivalries kept their countries in a state of turmoil, and the discovery of this sea-girt isle with its superb setting was but a minor incident in their wild dreams: expansion of trade, establishment of empires beyond the Seven Seas, and especially the elusive search for spices of the Indies. It was three-quarters of a century later when Henry Hudson, an Englishman employed by Dutch interests, entered New York harbor and continued his voyage up the Mauritius (Hudson River), to the neighborhood of present-day Albany. "A very good land to fall in with, and a pleasant land to see!" was the report of the stout and staid old explorer to his backers. The Dutch West India Company soon acted upon Hudson's enthusiasm, and negotiated for the purchase of this coveted piece of real estate at the mouth of the two rivers. The Indians seemed equally pleased, having traded over seven thousand skins—beaver, otter, mink, and wildcat—and even threw in some logs of oak and nutwood to seal the bargain. Thus, in 1626, did Peter Minuit take possession of the island and its adjacent lands and waters.

For the millions who followed these early navigators, their first glimpse of Manhattan bared the lower tip (the Battery); the two flanking arms of water were to shape the future metropolis. The island extended generally in a northward direction some fourteen and a half miles, from a mere breadth of a half mile to about two miles wide, and from low flatlands and swamps in its southern regions to rocky cliffs and headlands in the north. Long before the city adopted its grid plan, in 1811, the natural formation of its geography predetermined its "East Side, West Side" makeup. For more than half its length, Fifth Avenue became an arbitrary longitudinal divider between East and West, but the real character was determined by its waterfront and the commerce that developed around slips, wharves, and ferries. South Street, facing the East River, with its forest of packet-ship masts, its sailmakers' lofts, its cordage and tannery shops, was redolent of the maritime trade in every inch of its cobbled stones. Here at the wharves and ferry slips, the confusing traffic of hundreds of drays and wagons created a bewildering scene. Here, too, close to the river's edge where the fishermen unloaded their catch, was the Fulton Market, where fish, clams, and oysters for an entire city could be bought.

Similarly, the West Side repeated this scene of waterfront activity with but slight variations. West Street was the principal thoroughfare running north and south. Here the Atlantic liners, in latter years, had their berths because of deeper water and larger, covered docks and wharfage facilities. The confluence of oceangoing ships and riverboats differed in character from that of the East River trade. Washington Market became the center for meats and produce, arriving by ferry and canal boat from the rich, adjacent farmlands to the west and north.

Nature had endowed the port of New York with an abundance of natural advantages, a shoreline that extended for miles, protected from the full fury of the seas by harbors that interceded to break the violence of winter storms. But it was the energy of the first settlers and traders and the human initiative of later generations that built New York into the Empire City as we now know it.

Between two rivers stands mighty Manhattan,
heart of the greater metropolis.

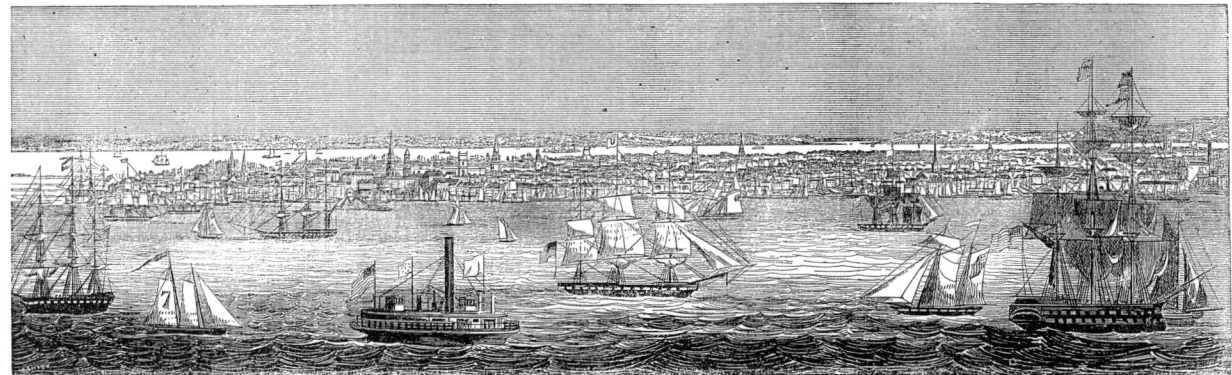

From *Gleason's Pictorial Drawing-Room Companion,* March 26, 1853.

THE CITY OF NEW YORK, AS SEEN FROM THE EAST RIVER

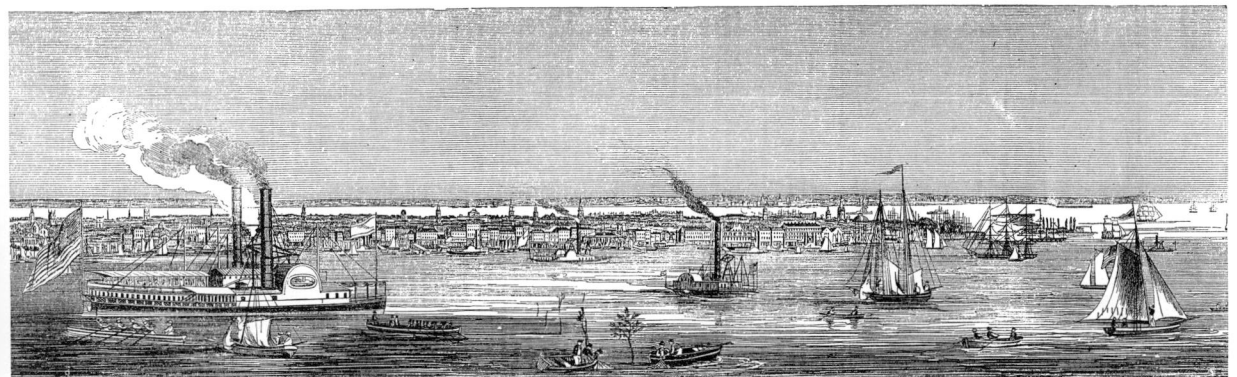

From *Gleason's Pictorial Drawing-Room Companion,* March 26, 1853.

THE CITY OF NEW YORK, AS SEEN FROM THE NORTH RIVER

"The harbor of New York is determined by three islands, Manhattan, Long, and Staten, and a small part of New Jersey. The upper bay, about seven miles long and about three miles in its greatest width, and thence it broadens into the noble expanse of the lower bay. With Long Island on the east, separated from Manhattan by the East River, the throat of Long Island Sound, and New Jersey on the west across the Hudson River, we have Staten Island on the south, separated by the Narrows from Long Island. West of Staten Island is separated from New Jersey by the Kill van Kull and Arthur Kills. The system of rivers, bays, and channels extending from the Raritan River in New Jersey to Yonkers on the Hudson, and from the Narrows to Fort Schuyler where the East River enters the Sound about eight miles from New York, constitutes the great port of New York, and the city's future will ultimately use this vast expanse with its contiguous shores. No harbor in the world has such a magnificent and varied congeries of outlets and inlets, such extended possibilities of wharfage and dockage if intelligently treated."

From *Harper's Weekly,*
August 31, 1889.

From *Ballou's Pictorial Drawing-Room Companion,* June 6, 1857.

VIEW OF BROOKLYN, FROM THE FOOT OF WALL STREET, NEW YORK

In all kinds of weather, fighting wintry storms, ice floes, or summer heat...

"A new type of floating population developed in the 'canallers' who lived aboard the boats throughout the season from the breaking up of the ice in spring until the canal finally froze over in November. Families, not always bound together by matrimony, made their homes on these freighters, as admirably depicted by the historical novelist who has recreated so ably the conditions attendant upon the building and workings of the Erie Canal. In 1830, a convention of delegates from the towns along the canal gathered at Syracuse. Alarmed by the 'gambling, drinking, blasphemy, licentiousness of every kind' and 'the actual pillage of property transported on the canal,' they sought, without much effect, to 'promote the moral and religious improvement of the canallers.'"

From *The Rise of New York Port*, by Robert Greenhalgh Albion, 1939.

From *Harper's Weekly*, February 8, 1862.

THE "COLD SNAP" IN 1862—ICE IN THE EAST RIVER

The severe winters that visited New York over a century ago created extreme shipping hazards for both sailing vessels and ferry boats, and untold hardships for rivermen and canallers. At the height of the worst winter, in 1862, the East River was so solidly frozen that thousands of citizens marched across from Brooklyn to New York. When the river thawed a bit, the ferry boats went into action after a long lay-up, but ice floes continued to pose dangerous problems. Several venturesome captains had their vessels crushed by sharp, jagged "ice-picks."

LAID UP FOR WINTER—CANAL-BOAT COLONY IN COENTIES SLIP, EAST RIVER

...an army of boatmen, canallers, and dockhands brought produce and supplies to the city.

Engraving from sketches by C. A. Keetels, *Harper's Weekly,* November 15, 1873.

SCENE ON THE GREAT FLOUR DOCKS, COENTIES SLIP, EAST RIVER, NEW YORK

"The hustle and bustle of New York's busy port and its ever-increasing terminal facilities owes its growth in no small measure to the linkage with the Erie Canal, and its system of upstate feeders. The canal and its construction was due to the genius and energy of Governor De Witt Clinton, and the same may be said of the Champlain Canal. Together, they constitute a network of waterways extending from the Great Lakes down to saltwater. The canal floats about 2000 boats, each with a capacity of 8000 bushels of grain or a corresponding bulk of other products, and the round trip between Buffalo and New York consumes about a month. The canal boat thus becomes the residence for the boatman and his family. It is a common sight to see lines of wash drying aboard deck, indicating families with three or four children of all ages growing up without proper schooling but with an innate love for life on the water."

From *Harper's Weekly,* August 31, 1889.

From *Harper's Weekly,* December 23, 1877.

GRAIN ELEVATOR TRANSFERRING CARGO FROM A CANAL-BOAT TO A SHIP   SHIPMENT OF GRAIN AND FLOUR

"The canal-boat in great measure does its own lighterage and storing. Again, the inducements which stimulate the enterprise of the boatman are deadened by heavy tolls at the elevator, which stands, in his estimation, at the very gateway of commerce, like the castles of the robber-barons of the Middle Ages to which the fat and peaceful burghers had to pay tribute.... The boating interests have made a stubborn fight against the owners; and a bill passed the Legislature recently reducing the tax.... The contest between the canal men and the elevator trust rests on these conflicting claims: The former assert that a bushel of grain can be handled at the elevator for from one-eighth to a quarter of a cent per bushel while the actual charges prior to the passage of the bill was one and one-eighth of a cent per bushel."

From *Harper's Weekly,* August 31, 1889.

The arduous job of loading and unloading clipper ships was
so much sweat and grime to truckers and longshoremen . . .

CITY of ships! (O the black
  ships! O the fierce ships!
O the beautiful sharp-bowed
  steam-ships and sail-ships!)
City of the world! (for all races
  are here,
All the lands of the earth make
  contributions here;)
City of the sea! city of hurried
  and glittering tides!
City whose gleeful tides
  continually rush or recede,
  whirling in and out, with
  eddies and foam!
City of wharves and
  stores—city of tall facades
  of marble and iron!
Proud and passionate
  city—mettlesome, mad,
  extravagant city!
Spring up O city—not for
  peace alone, but be indeed
  yourself, warlike!

    From "City of Ships,"
      by Walt Whitman.

Engraved from a drawing by I. Pranishnikoff, *Harper's Weekly*, April 20, 1878.

VIEW IN SOUTH STREET, NEW YORK

... but to Walt Whitman, the poet's voice celebrated and proclaimed "O the beautiful sharp-bowed steamships and sail-ships!"

"The most numerous personnel associated with the wharves were the laborers who came to be known as longshoremen, the counterpart of the English dockers, who worked under the supervision of stevedores. Some firms had their own permanent personnel of stevedores and longshoremen—the house of Grinnell, Minturn & Co., for instance, had seventy at one time. For the stevedore himself, and for the first mate who was responsible for the stowing of the cargo, the work required a considerable amount of skill. For the ordinary longshoremen, however, it was largely a matter of muscle, necessary for hoisting freight into or out of the hold. The longshoremen came to realize their strategic position, for they could delay a vessel's sailing if they refused to work. As early as 1825, they staged a strike:

> Yesterday the wharves were thronged with crowds of labourers standing out for higher wages. Nearly all the ships in port were deserted by their men, to join in the general combination; several vessels nearly ready for sea are delayed for want of hands. Two very active and noisy individuals who employed themselves in going about and preventing those disposed to work from doing so, were taken up and committed to Bridwell."

From *The Rise of New York Port,*
by Robert Greenhalgh Albion, 1939.

Engraved from a drawing by I. Pranishnikoff, *Harper's Weekly,* July 14, 1877.

SCENE ON A NEW YORK DOCK—STEVEDORES UNLOADING A SHIP

Nothing could match the hustle and bustle of the waterfront scene along the West Street docks . . .

. . . Rich, hemm'd thick all around with sailships and steamships, an island sixteen miles long, solid-founded,
Numberless crowded streets, high growths of iron, slender, strong, light, splendidly uprising toward clear skies,
Tides swift and ample, well-loved by me, toward sundown,
The flowing sea-currents, the little islands, larger adjoining islands, the heights, the villas,
The countless masts, the white shore-steamers, the lighters, the ferry-boats, the black sea-steamers, well model'd,
The down-town streets, the jobbers' houses of business, the houses of business of the ship-merchants and money-brokers, the river-streets,
Immigrants arriving, fifteen or twenty thousand in a week,
The carts hauling goods, the manly race of drivers of horses, the brown-faced sailors . . .

From "Mannahatta," by Walt Whitman.

ALONG THE DOCKS, NEW YORK CITY—VIEW FROM WEST STREET

... where every type of vessel and vehicle served the commerical needs of full-time maritime activity.

From *Harper's Weekly*, September 4, 1869.

A full forty years after this setting depicted in the wood engraving, the confusion of vehicular traffic continued unabated, but with the addition of cabs, cars, and trolleys:

"West Street is quite out of the ordinary. Every conceivable kind of vehicle—dray, expresswagon, mail-wagon, furniture-van, butcher-cart, garbage-cart, beer-skid, beam-reach—is there. Sandwiched in among them or dashing across them are cabs, carriages, hansoms, automobiles. Dozens of trolley cars run across the street to the different ferry-houses; two car tracks run the full length of it, and down these tracks, perhaps in the busiest portion of the day, will come a long train of freight-cars of the New York Central Railroad. . . . No one can hear himself talk during traffic hours, except the cabbies and the truck drivers. Even they are usually purple in the face from trying to outroar the rumble, though sometimes they get blue and green with wrath when a collision takes place, and they exchange compliments about each other's driving."

From *The New New York*, by John C. Van Dyke, 1909.

To Americans far from coastal cities, the mass circulation of the illustrated weeklies brought pictures of New York's huge seaport trade.

"Never since the close of the war has business been so brisk as it is this fall; and the prosperity of the commercial metropolis as evidenced by the bustling waterfront activity is an index of the general prosperity of the country. All over the land, from Maine to Texas, from the Atlantic to the Pacific coast, abundant harvests have rewarded the labor of the farmer and the planter; the hum of busy factories is heard where a few months ago the silence of stagnation brooded; railroads and canals are crowded to their utmost capacity with freight; and fleets of steam-ships and sailing vessels carry our products and manufactures to all the countries of Europe.

"The contrast presented by the Old World is very striking. While peace and plenty reign in our country, disturbed only by trouble with the aborigines on our Western middle lands, Europe is distracted by apprehensions of wars, impoverished by immense standing armies, disheartened by bad harvests, and in terror of domestic convulsions.

"Thousands of industrious . . .

A BUSY SCENE AT A FERRY SLIP.

LOADING COTTON.

FREIGHT FOR EUROPE.

A JAM ON W

THE DAWN OF BETTER DAYS—BUSY SCENES IN THE STREETS OF NEW YORK

Editors assigned roving artist-reporters, repeatedly, to depict these scenes, as "hunger from the hinterlands" cried out for news from the waterfront.

AN EVERY-DAY INCIDENT—WEST SIDE.

THE QUITTING HOUR—HOMEWARD BOUND.

GRAIN-ELEVATOR—UNLOADING A CANAL-BOAT.

Pen and ink drawing by A. B. Shults, *Harper's Weekly,* November 8, 1879.

... people forsake her shores, in despair of better times at home, and seek a refuge within our hospitable borders, where there is room and livelihood for all. Thus we not only supply the Old World with our products, receiving millions of dollars in exchange therefor, but afford more than ever before a hopeful outlet for her distressed surplus population. "The return of better times in this country is marked by many encouraging features. There is little of that wild spirit of speculation which has been dreaded by some of our contemporaries as a probable result of renewed prosperity. Advices from every part of the Union show that business men perceive the wisdom of conducting their affairs on a sound and safe basis, and are not misled by the craze for becoming suddenly rich, which a few years ago precipitated disasters all over the land. The revival of prosperity in all branches of industry is in every respect a healthy one, and promises to be as substantial and lasting as it is vigorous."

From *Harper's Weekly,* November 8, 1879.

Castle Garden, where Jenny Lind performed, in 1850, was the receiving point for incoming foreigners "systematically bled by licensed runners and touters waiting for the immigrants."

"Misery, disease, and shameless exploitation featured one major branch of the port's business during the years of the 70's and 80's. Along with the textiles and hardware brought westward across the stormy Atlantic came millions of Irish, German, English, and other European immigrants to seek their fortunes in the New World. Some close parallels may be drawn between the traffic in living and inanimate freight. The same ports participated in each in about the same proportion. In this country, New York received the overwhelming share of immigrants as of manufactures. There was, however, one significant difference. Whereas New York became the nation's richest city by managing to disperse most of its commercial imports throughout the country, it increased its lead as the nation's biggest city by keeping a much larger share of its human imports within its own environs. . . . The flow of newcomers fluctuated much more violently than did the importations of commodities, being extremely sensitive to economic conditions on either side of the Atlantic. Economic factors in the United States affected this volume noticeably; both in boom periods when the newcomers swarmed to this side, and in times of depression, when the arrivals fell off sharply and many, already here, actually returned home. On the other hand, there were constant complaints, particularly from New Yorkers, that Europe was using this country as a dumping ground for its paupers, criminals, and other undesirables, with many a prince, parish, or landlord paying the passage to be rid of the burden."

From *The Rise of New York Port*, by Robert Greenhalgh Albion, 1939.

THE LABOR EXCHANGE—EMIGRANTS ON THE BATTERY IN FRONT OF CASTLE GARDEN, NEW YORK

Engraved from sketches by Stanley Fox, *Harper's Weekly,* August 14, 1868.

THE LABOR EXCHANGE—INTERIOR VIEW OF THE OFFICE AT CASTLE GARDEN, NEW YORK

On the other hand, returning American travelers were beset by eager custom officials who terrorized them with baggage examinations designed, it would seem, to discourage future travel.

From *Frank Leslie's Illustrated Newspaper,* November 27, 1880.

NEW YORK CITY—THE TERROR OF OCEAN TRAVELERS—A DAY WITH A CUSTOM HOUSE INSPECTOR

The hordes of immigrants entering the New York port area, the main point for almost 90 per cent of European travelers, taxed the customs inspectors to irritable degrees. It has been estimated that between 1880 and 1884 some two million people headed for the United States. During the mid-year months of greatest activity, there were weeks when well over 15,000 were handled on Ellis Island, in New York harbor. Customs officials, in their processing on the docks, had to bear the brunt of this wild disorder, as resultant scenes of confusion with disgruntled passengers were commonplace. Generally, arrivals fell into four main categories: 1) immigrants, who made up the vast majority; 2) commercial travelers with interests abroad; 3) returnees, those who had come a few years before and made return visits to the homeland; 4) the wealthy, whose European junkets meant the Grand Tour and profligate spending. Inspectors were alerted to spot contraband carried by immigrants, and this meant minute inspection of clothes and personal effects. Temper flare-ups were frequent when zealous inspectors pried into every nook and cranny of trunks and carpetbags stuffed with assorted belongings.

Joyous memories of a glorious trip abroad came to an abrupt end as travelers faced the rigors of custom inspection.

"Most of this ostentatious class go to Europe for no better purpose than to *say* they have been, or to gather ideas for making the grandest display on their return home. Numbers of ladies visit Paris with no desire beyond that of seeing the fashions, and taking home something newer than their neighbors have got. . . . A proud husband, on his return, glorifying himself and his better half: 'quite an elegant lady. These sixteen boxes are her luggage. She spent in Europe thirty thousand dollars on dress.' I could have sworn that they lived in a 'brown stone front,' and that the wife would display her diamonds at the cabin dinner, and so it turned out. Of course, there are Americans—both men and women—of talent and genius who visit European cities for the study of art and of science, and who wish to contemplate the marvellous works of bygone ages, while others seek general improvement or the mere excitement of travel. The greater part, however, visit Europe for the 'say' of the thing, and because it denotes that they have wealth to squander."

From *Teresina in America,* by Thérèse Yelverton, 1875.

Engraved from a drawing by I. Pranishnikoff, *Harper's Weekly,* March 29, 1879.

HOME FROM THE OLD WORLD—EXAMINATION OF BAGGAGE BY CUSTOMS-HOUSE OFFICERS ON A NEW YORK STEAM-SHIP WHARF

Those who could not afford a return to the "old country" had to content themselves with a longing sight of the sea.

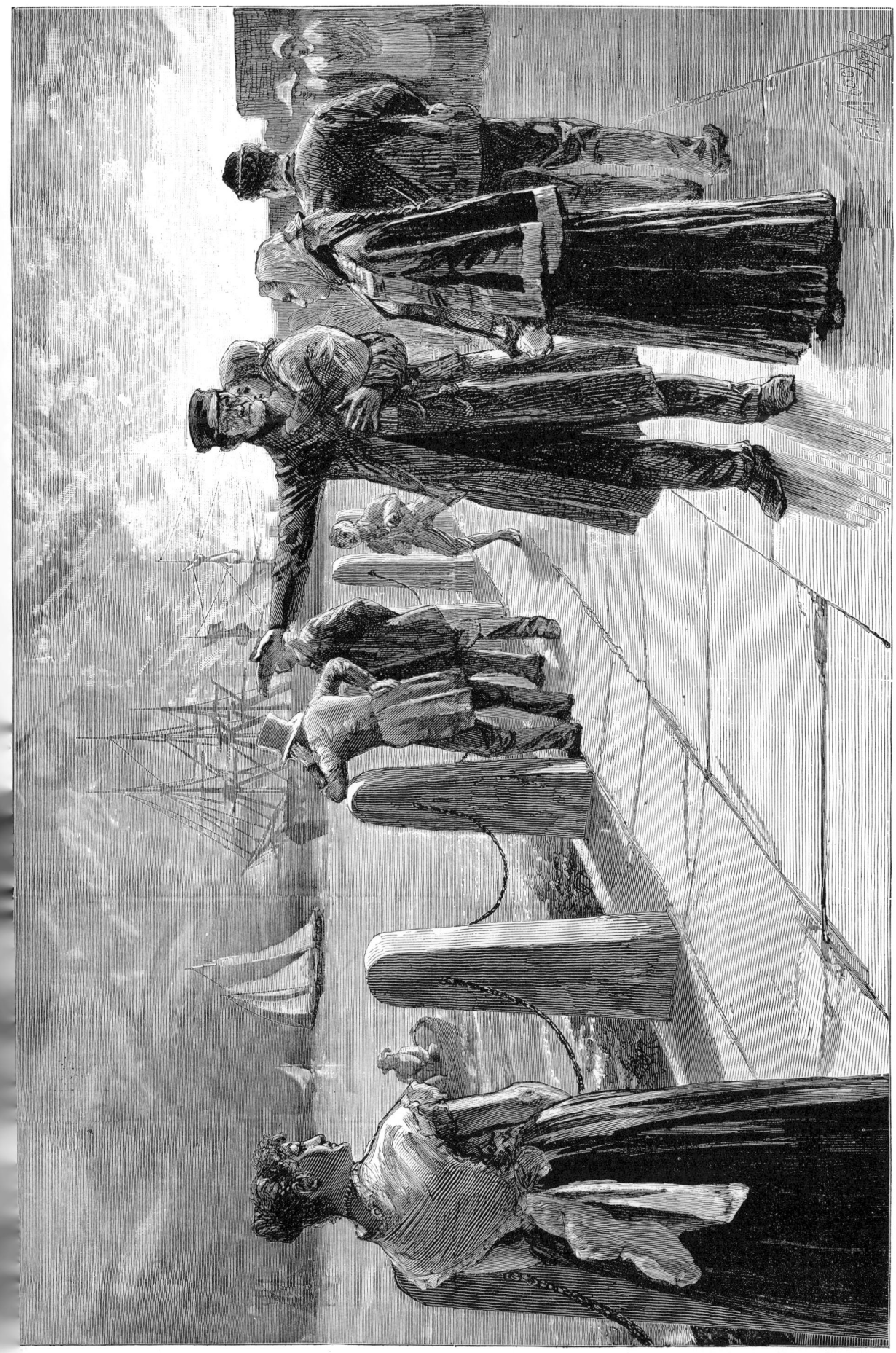

Engraved from a drawing by E. A. Abbey, *Harper's Weekly,* April 6, 1878.

EVENING ON THE BATTERY

"'The New York waterfront, Battery included, was lined by dreaming landsmen as well,' wrote Herman Melville, 'posted like silent sentinels all around the town . . . thousands upon thousands of mortal men fixed in ocean reveries. Some leaning against the spiles; some seated upon the pier-heads; some looking over the bulwarks of ships from China; some high aloft in the rigging, as if striving to get a still better seaward peep. But all these landsmen, of week days pent up of lath and plaster—tied to counters, nailed to benches, clinched to desks. . . . Strange! Nothing will content them but the extremest limit of the land. . . . They must get just as nigh the water as they possibly can without falling in. And there they stand—miles of them—leagues. Inlanders all, they come from lanes and alleys, streets and avenues—north, east, south, and west. Yet there they all unite.'

"When Melville wrote, New York was a city of ships, hemmed by masts and ever conscious of the salty lick of the sea at the end of every short crosstown street."

From *Life in America,* Vol. I, by Marshall Davidson, 1951.

Newer and larger ferryboats transported thousands of commuters from New Jersey and Brooklyn to their places of business in New York . . .

THE NEW HOBOKEN FERRY-BOAT "BERGEN" COMPLETED

THE "BERGEN" ON THE WAYS

THE HOBOKEN FERRY-BOAT "ORANGE"

CABIN OF HOBOKEN FERRY-BOAT "ORANGE"

Long before Manhattanites managed river crossings by bridge or tube, there were innumerable ferries to Brooklyn, Jersey, and Staten Island. On the Hudson and East rivers they crisscrossed to opposite sides, at times proceeding several miles upstream to some strategic ferry point. Earliest records trace the first right of ferriage on the East River to the year 1659, when Cornelis Dircksen, a farmer, came, at the sound of a horn hung on a nearby tree, and ferried passengers over for "three stivers wampum." That veracious chronicler Diedrich Knickerbocker refers to the thrifty village of Communipaw, on the Jersey side, as the "egg from whence was hatched the mighty city" of New York. "It is within but a half-hour's sail by ferry of the latter place, provided you have a fair wind." It was doubtless to accommodate "foreign trade," the transportation of oysters, buttermilk, and cabbages, that the first ferry on the North River from Communipaw was established in 1661. William Jansen was the first licensed ferry man, authorized by the governor-general and Council to charge certain established rates for service. With the coming of steam, the pioneering efforts of John Stevens, in 1811, put the first "team-boat" on the Hudson. It was reported to have "three manifest advantages: it was independent of wind and tide; it could accommodate from six to eight loaded wagons and nearly one hundred persons; and to crown all, one could drive a horse and wagon on the boat without unhitching the team." Accordingly, the advent of this new type of boat was announced with some pardonable pride, and the boats were duly inspected by the city authorities, and "pronounced by the public all that could be desired for comfort and safety." In design, they were similar to the catamaran, with double hulls (called by the farmers "Buck and Bright"), yoked . . .

. . . and at the same time, carts and trucks crammed the boats carrying farm produce and other wares on countless ferry crossings daily.

CABIN OF THE NEW HOBOKEN FERRY-BOAT "BERGEN"

Pen and ink sketches by Fred S. Cozzens, Hughson Hawley, and F. H. Schell, *Harper's Weekly,* August 23, 1890.

PROJECTED IMPROVEMENTS IN THE TERMINAL FACILITIES OF THE PENNSYLVANIA RAILROAD

. . . together by deck beams, with knees and braces. Between these two hulls, aft of the center, was the paddle wheel, which was geared to a kind of treadmill on which one or two horses walked, and thus propelled the boat. These early team-boats had a covered cabin, and were in all respects superior to the early scows and piraguas. Following the first paddle-wheelers, named the *Fairy Queen* and *Pioneer,* much larger boats were built to accommodate the rapidly growing river traffic, as shipments of produce and commuting workers from Jersey seemed to grow in staggering numbers. The North River boats now ran "every hour by St. Paul's clock" to Barclay Street, with a boat to Christopher Street three or four times a day, weather permitting. In winter, the ferry trips were more uncertain, and frequently the boats abandoned all attempts to make their regular landings; often an entire day was needed to navigate a round trip when the ice floes were heaviest. Gradually, as new boats were constructed, the design was improved: broader beams, placing the engine and pilot house in the center, thus enabling teams to have double gangways for speedier loading and unloading. Commodious cabins were equipped with more comfortable seating, and double deck features and stairways added for the comfort of ever-increasing numbers of passengers. Rest rooms, refreshment stands, and bars were introduced, and steam heating replaced the old cabin stoves. The old oil lamps gave way to gas lighting, as interior decoration of the spacious cabins were paneled in oak, cherry, and maple, with bent wood arms for seating dividers. The largest of the ferryboats in the 1880s could carry five hundred persons and as many as forty or fifty wagons, loaded with all manner of produce and manufactured goods for New York's hungry markets.

Often an artist sent to sketch a market scene lost himself in romantic aspects, introducing sailors or other colorful characters to enliven pictorial interest.

"Other cities may boast of finer edifices, under the shelter of which scaly inhabitants of our coasts and our rivers tempt the appetite of the epicure; but no city in the world can show so great a variety of fish as is daily displayed on the stands in Fulton Market, New York. Especially is this the case during the Lenten season, when a stroll through the avenues of the Market early on a bright spring morning is positively refreshing; the eye is gratified by the elegant outline and color of many of our fishes, and the sense of smell is not offended. A visitor to the Market at this season will find, offered for sale, halibut, cod, haddock, striped bass, smelt, and shad, just taken from their briny element. Of fresh-water fishes he will be offered white-fish, brook-trout, pickerel, and salmon—this latter, kept by the new process of cold-air refrigeration."

From *Harper's Weekly*, April 3, 1869.

From *Ballou's Pictorial Drawing-Room Companion*, September 28, 1856

VEGETABLES AND PRODUCE, WASHINGTON MARKET, NEW YORK CITY

Engraved from a sketch by Stanley Fox, *Harper's Weekly*, April 3, 1869.

FISH STANDS IN FULTON MARKET, NEW YORK

The Fulton Fish Market, just south of the Brooklyn Bridge, provided a slip where fishing boats could conveniently unload their fish at the point of sale.

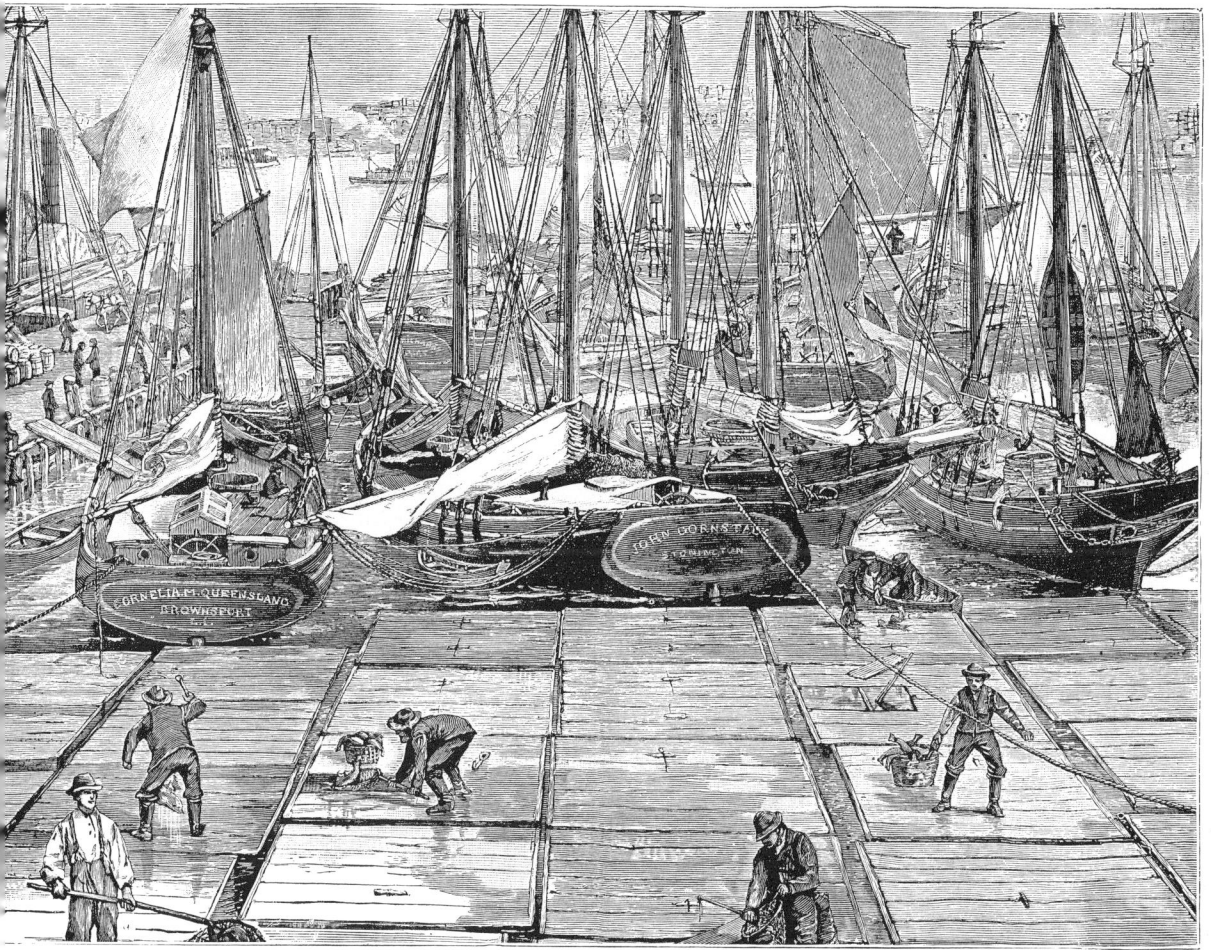

Engraved from a drawing by D. C. Beard, *Harper's Weekly,* April 30, 1887.

THE FISH LANDING SLIP AT FULTON MARKET, NEW YORK

When the city decided to modernize its two largest markets—Washington Market in 1872, and Fulton Market in 1882—it was responding to popular demand as well as urgent need. The old, dilapidated buildings had long been condemned as obsolete and considered firetraps of great peril.

"Perhaps no feature of city life is so picturesque as that of the street markets, some of them busy daylight markets and some being markets at night. There is the Fulton Fish Market where the daily catch is landed from the vast fleet of fishing boats. Nearby, under the first arches of Williamsburg Bridge, a fish market is open two evenings a week: the stalls, roofed by the bridge itself, and lighted by flambeaux, might be a market in an archway of ancient Florence. There are street markets, with long lines of pushcarts lined along the curb, just outside of the sidewalk, on Bleecker Street, off Tompkins Square, and in many streets of the Jewish quarters on the lower East Side. Here, not only fish, fruits and vegetables are for sale but cloth, hosiery, kitchenware and a host of things."

From *The Book of New York,* by Robert Shackleton, 1917.

Engraved from a drawing by Charles Graham, *Harper's Weekly,* March 11, 1882.

THE NEW FULTON MARKET, NEW YORK CITY

Bringing fresh produce to the city dwellers who lived some distance from the large municipal markets, the cries of the peddler rang out, announcing his arrival . .

"The street vendors of fruits and vegetables are chiefly patronized by the poorer classes in New York, partly because of the scarcity of large markets, and partly because they generally manage to undersell the regular market-men. It is not always an advantage, however, to buy of them, for sometimes they load their wagons with stock left over a day or two at the large markets, and sold cheap rather than thrown away, and there is danger of its being already unfit for use when it reaches the purchaser. A great deal of the sickness that prevails in summer among the poor of this city results, no doubt, from this cause. There should be many more large markets in New York than now exist, placed under strict superintendence, so that the poorest might have the opportunity to obtain food at cheap rates and of good quality. Until this is accomplished the street vendors will continue to make the air hideous with their loud, uncouth cries."

From *Harper's Weekly,* September 22, 1877.

Engraved from a drawing by W. M. Cary, *Harper's Weekly,* September 22, 1877

STREET VENDORS OF FRUITS AND VEGETABLES

. . . but those who lived nearby or could manage some means of conveyance preferred to shop at the market, for better selection and assurance of fresh goods at every stall.

"This is the time of the year when the Washington Market's stalls are crowded with almost every description of foreign and domestic fruits and vegetables. The scene as depicted by our artist, Granville Perkins, is a busy one, especially early in the morning, when the market wagons come in from the country, loaded with fresh produce; and even to a late hour in the forenoon the streets and sidewalks are blocked by wagons, carts, and a crowd of porters and buyers. Both Washington and Fulton markets are a disgrace to New York. In their place there ought to be erected handsome and commodious stone and iron structures, with accommodations for the wagons and teams that now present such impediments to passing through the adjoining streets."

From *Harper's Weekly*, September 14, 1878.

Engraved from a drawing by Granville Perkins, *Harper's Weekly*, September 14, 1878.

AT WASHINGTON MARKET, NEW YORK

A typical market day provided enough interest and confusion to inspire this on-the-spot pictorial report by the artist-journalist.

Washington Market on the lower West Side waterfront was the scene of bedlam, of struggling masses, carts and drays tangled together, and the cacophony of shouts and sounds creating a din that was indescribable. It was the largest point of entry for fish and fowl, meats and produce, that poured in from across the river daily to provision a hungry city. Established on this site since 1813, it replaced the original Bear Market. During the dark hours of early morning the heavily laden wagons arrived by nearby ferry from Jersey, choking the thoroughfares for blocks around. A fee of twenty-five cents was charged each waggoner, but many avoided the payment due the clerk of the market. As reported in *Harper's Weekly:* "The tax is often exacted at the expense of ugly language freely spilt by the elusive brutes who man the trucks. They have to be pursued in many cases into the lowest dives before the reluctant quarter satisfies the toll. When the waggoner cheats the city it costs his employer nothing and means drink-money." The entire market site has been cleared only within the last decade.

WASHINGTON MARKET—NEW YORK—THANKSGIVING TIME

For graphic detail and anecdotal reportage such an illustration conveyed, by judicious composition, its message proving that "a picture is worth ten thousand words."

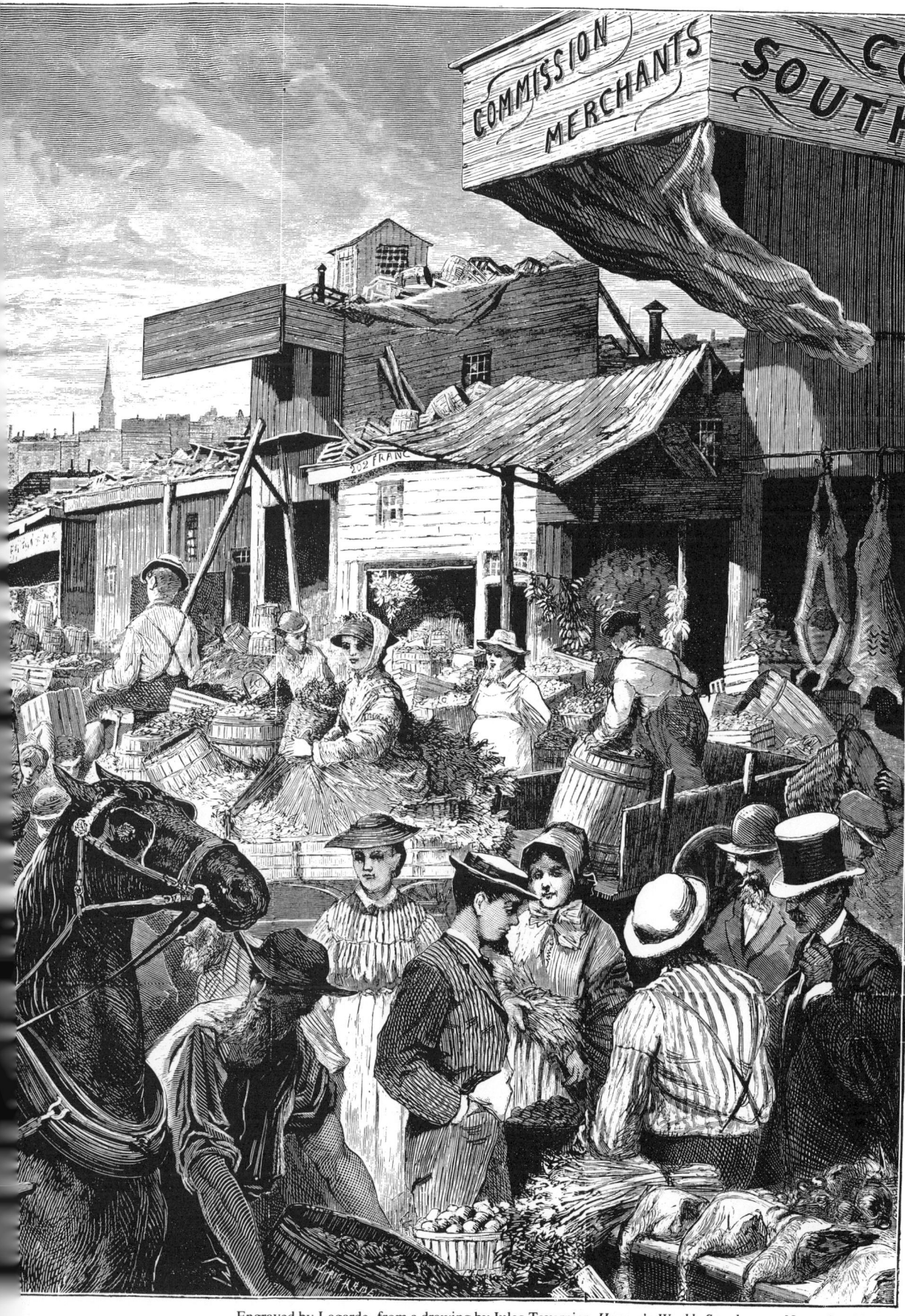

Engraved by Lagarde, from a drawing by Jules Tavernier, *Harper's Weekly Supplement*, November 30, 1872.

The reportorial talents of the magazine illustrators were often at their best when called upon to depict a scene of melée and confusion. While the early photographer had to set his cumbersome box camera and tripod at a given spot and then hope for a lucky moment, the artist, employing his best judgment, could arrange his people and setting for the composition that best told his story. Only through the artist's innate sense of journalism could such a scene be made available to the public. His drawing was then transcribed onto a block of wood for an engraver (in this case Lagarde) to prepare for printing in the illustrated weeklies. Their vast circulation reached out to every corner of the country, the only medium of communication then available to all.

There was a popular song of the day: "He went to the Washington Market one day, And there he stole a big ham. He got three months in the penitentiary, Along with the rest of the gang."

After years and years of continuing protest, the city finally took heed and made plans to replace the dilapidated stalls that were threatening to tumble down . . .

"Every day, except Sunday, is a market-day in New York. Meat is cut up and sold by the joint or in pieces, by the licensed butchers only, their agents, or servants. Each of these must sell at his own stall, and conclude his sales by one o'clock in the afternoon, between the 1st of May and the 1st of November, and by two o'clock in the winter months. Butchers are licensed by order of the mayor, who is the clerk of the market. He receives for every quarter of beef sold in the market six cents; for every hog, shoat, or pig above 14 lbs. weight, six cents; and for each calf, sheep, or lamb, four cents; to be paid by the butchers and other persons selling the same. To prevent engrossing, and to favour housekeepers, it is declared unlawful for persons to purchase articles to sell again in any market or other part of the city before noon of each day, except flour and meal, which must not be bought to be sold again until four in the afternoon: hucksters in the market are restricted to the sale of vegetables, with the exception of fruits. The sale of unwholesome and stale articles of provision; of blown and stuffed meat, and of measly pork, is expressively forbidden. Butter must be sold by the pound, and not by the roll or tub. Persons who are not licensed butchers, selling butcher's meat on commission, pay triple fees to the clerk of the market. . . ."

From *Travels through Canada and the United States of North America,* by John Lambert, 1814.

Engraved from a drawing by Stanley Fox, *Harper's Weekly,* May 26, 1866

WASHINGTON MARKET, NEW YORK CITY

... building in their place stone and brick structures joined by arched gateways of modern design, and restricting wagons to an outer plaza to relieve congestion.

Engraved from a photograph, *Harper's Weekly,* December 29, 1888.

THE NEW WEST WASHINGTON MARKET, NEW YORK CITY

"The New West Washington Market was overhauled and completely modernized in 1888, replacing old sheds with stone and brick stalls, separated by arches, and leading to avenues of shops. The new plan included endless lanes of stalls where meats, fish, fruits, vegetables, groceries and specialties were sold in sections apart from one another. During the dark hours of early morning, as hundreds of wagons of all descriptions converge upon the market regions, pandemonium reigns as traffic chokes the thoroughfares for blocks around. *Harper's Weekly,* in its December 29, 1888 issue, reported 'the downtown streets were taken possession of, from this rustic invasion, which was as relentless as the grip of an octopus. The mayor's office was for years bombarded with complaints and reproaches that such important avenues of traffic should be choked up by the huge produce vans, even for a limited period in the morning.' Life in the marketplace begins to seethe shortly after midnight as the wagons approach. Each driver is anxious for the pick of the best place and the desire to unload and be gone, and in this aspect rivalry often leads to bloody noses. Many of the vans are bulky, measuring twenty-five feet long and ten feet high. Such a load is drawn by four horses, with several farm hirelings on hand to unload in jig time."

From *Wheels Across America,* by Clarence P. Hornung, 1959.

Nothing seemed more inviting than the neat butcher's stall, yet the boxes of decaying fruits and vegetables created a stench that permeated the nostrils.

"And then into Washington Market, with its stands grouped by subject, like the classified books in a public library: butchers in one section, fish dealers in another, and so on. What sights to tickle the appetite! One could then buy venison quite easily and casually. A place where, as mother said, a friend of hers used to go, about 1860, for carps' livers, a delicacy much favored by her husband. People went to the market carrying their baskets, or, if they had servants, having them carried. In the pocket-books two-dollar bills were familiar, and silver dollars not unseen. . . . The boy's observations were made before the days of telephone orders and having everything sent; life was simpler. The basket had not been replaced by the paper bag. There were however in those eighteen-seventies, sheets of rough, straw-colored paper in which grocers wrapped your purchases, often deftly turning the sheet into a cornucopia, or 'toot,' as the children of the East Side called those paper cones."

From *Manhattan Kaleidoscope,*
by Frank Weitenkampf, 1947.

Engraved from a drawing by Schell and Hogan, *Harper's Weekly,* December 29, 1888.

THE NEW WASHINGTON MARKET, NEW YORK

PART TWO

All Around the Town

NEW YORK IN 1855

From *Ballou's Pictorial Drawing-Room Companion*, April 21, 1855.

"What Threadneedle Street is to England, Wall Street is to America. It is a narrow street, in the lower part of Manhattan, running from Broadway to the East River. At the head of Wall Street stands the massive Trinity Church, the Cathedral of the city. It lifts its tall steeple to heaven, amid the din and babel of business. From its tower magnificent bells strike out the quarter and half hours of the day, and chime, with mellifluous peals the full ones, telling the anxious, excited, and rushing crowd how swiftly life passes. The great moneyed institutions of the country are in Wall Street. Here stands the elegant granite building devoted to the United States Treasury in New York."

From *Sunshine and Shadow in New York*,
by Matthew Hale Smith, 1868.

All Around the Town

OVER A SPAN of two centuries, from the primitive, pioneer settlement of New Amsterdam at the lower tip of the island, Manhattan slowly developed into a sprawling urban community before the middle of the nineteenth century. The Netherlanders, under Peter Minuit and Peter Stuyvesant, through discipline, thrift, and industry, had fashioned a substantial trading center through dint of hard labor, only to lose their foothold on the American continent to the British, in 1664. The take-over was complete, and New York was firmly established under the laws and statutes of England. During the next hundred years, however, the overlords overseas looked upon their American colonies as a vehicle for trade and commerce. Violent differences and the Revolution that followed gave New Yorkers their opportunity, at long last, to fashion a democratic government—the outgrowth of oppressive measures and total misunderstanding.

From an enclave of several hundred houses within the walled fortifications of Dutch days, the colony's limits pushed steadily northward. By the early 1880s when a new City Hall was to be relocated, its present site was considered so far "out of town" that its northern exterior was faced with inferior stone because, as it was said, "nobody would see it anyway." The city, which owed its very existence to natural, physical advantages at the head of the harbor and estuary of the Hudson, now turned to internal development. The commissioners' gridiron street plan of 1811 was an extension of its hopes for the future. For many decades the long north and south thoroughfares and their cross streets intersecting at regular block intervals represented just so many lines on the city map. Gradually, the prominent avenues took shape. Broadway, originally Bloomingdale Road, was preeminent. From Bowling Green and the Custom House, it headed north past Trinity Church, St. Paul's, City Hall Park, and Madison Square. Its direction was northwesterly; when it reached the vicinity of Fifty-ninth Street, in the 1850s, this was the limit of urban concentration and it became known as the Western Boulevard as it continued for three or four miles past Manhattanville and open country. Through its many periods of glory and glamour, Broadway always maintained a special aura.

The lower regions of this all-important street have experienced many phases of constant change; in fact its expansive development may be said to epitomize the growth of the city. First, from a strictly residential area for prominent citizens, it became mercantile, housing shops and stores in great variety before giving way finally as a citadel of finance. The Buttonwood Agreement of 1792, signed under the tree that gave it this name, stipulated the terms under which brokers in stocks, bonds, and produce could operate as a trading group. It is generally considered the forerunner of the Stock Exchange. Wall Street, just off Broadway, had been the seat of municipal government. As this was transferred to the new building a half mile to the north, the city fathers moved out and the bankers and brokers took over the entire area, then familiarly referred to as "the Street." Periodically, as economic tremors shook the nation, Wall Street was the scene of many panics, particularly in the years 1837, 1857, and 1873. Some of these financial setbacks reached cataclysmic proportions from which recovery, at times, was a matter of years.

Throughout the nineteenth century, but especially in the middle and latter decades, the constant shifting of business and mercantile areas, and their progression in response to urgent needs, meant that older buildings were razed to make room for the new. Historic importance of a structure was never a consideration in delaying its demolition. Scarcity of building sites and skyrocketing land values were the only desiderata, particularly in that compact section below City Hall known as the "financial district." It applied, as well, to Park Row and Nassau Street where most of the city's newspapers were published along "newspaper row." Witness the location of the giant new Post Office at the southern tip of City Hall Park, viewed by many to have been a costly mistake from the start. Throughout its lifetime, from 1875 until 1939, it had been the butt of jokes and quips until finally public pressure to clear the park area succeeded, and once again New Yorkers could enjoy the unobstructed vista restored to gracious City Hall.

What was true of commercial buildings and their constant replacement was equally true farther uptown where the demand for newer residential sites doomed houses that stood in their way. The need for land in the lower Fifth Avenue section was keenly felt, as fortunes grew with good times for the industrialists and railroad tycoons. The wealthy planned ever-larger mansions, pushing developed areas farther northward. "Upper Fifth Avenue" was once a term applied to the Murray Hill section; now it applied to streets above Forty-second and eventually streets in the seventies and eighties. Change in New York was a well-established tradition. Growing pains assumed two distinctly different aspects: In the downtown districts, confined and inflexible, soaring towers could only point skyward, darkening the streets below into dismal canyons; in residential districts, expansion could move northward where shacks and shanties could be eliminated to clear the land for expansion.

When lower Broadway was a shopper's paradise, Dickens, on his first visit in 1842, had noted: "Heaven save the ladies, how they dress!"

Engraved from a drawing by W. S. L. Jewett, *Harper's Weekly,* February 15, 1868.

BROADWAY, FEBRUARY, 1868

"The great promenade and thoroughfare, as most people know, is Broadway; a wide and bustling street which, from the Battery Gardens to its opposite termination in a country road, may be four miles long . . . Was there ever such a sunny street as this Broadway! The pavement stones are polished with the tread of feet until they shine again; the red bricks of the houses might be yet in the dry, hot kiln; and the roofs of those omnibuses look as though, if water were poured on them, they would hiss and smoke, and smell like half-quenched fires. No stint of omnibuses here! half-a-dozen have gone by within as many minutes. Plenty of hackney cabs and coaches too; gigs, phaetons, large-wheeled tilburies, and private carriages . . . Heaven save the ladies, how they dress! We have seen more colours in these ten minutes, than we should have seen elsewhere, in as many days. What various parasols! what rainbow silks and satins! what pinking of thin stockings, and pinching of thin shoes, and fluttering of ribbons and silk tassels!"

From *American Notes,* by Charles Dickens, 1842.

The vast and rapidly changing panorama of New York, of constant interest not only to city dwellers but citizens throughout the nation . . .

From the days of early Nieu Amsterdam when an Indian pathway followed along the ridges of dry land in swampy lower Manhattan, Broadway soon became the principal thoroughfare to which flocked the city's crowds and mercantile establishments. Visitors from abroad, in presenting their impressions of America, seldom failed to describe Broadway in all its kaleidoscopic splendor, as well as its sordid sidelights. In this three-part panoramic view of downtown Broadway, from the Astor House near Vesey Street, and extending about a half mile northward, *Gleason's Pictorial Drawing-Room Companion* presented to its readers, nationwide, this graphic picture of some fifty stores and buildings on the west side of the avenue facing City Hall Park and above. The commercial houses included a wide variety of shops and goods to tempt the passerby: stores of clothing, haberdashery, hosiery, gloves, and other articles of apparel; merchant tailors, jewelers, bookstores, daguerreotype salons, pianofortes, sewing machines, and many more, all carrying signs unmistakably emblazoned on their storefronts for all to see. The stores lining the street were generally four and five stories high, with spacious underground vaults serving as extra warehousing. The mercantile aspect of this area continued until the latter years of the nineteenth century when the growth of the financial district broke out of Wall Street, the taller structures replacing the small, unprofitable buildings that for a long period had characterized lower Broadway.

ASTOR HOUSE   BARCLAY STREET

WARREN STREET

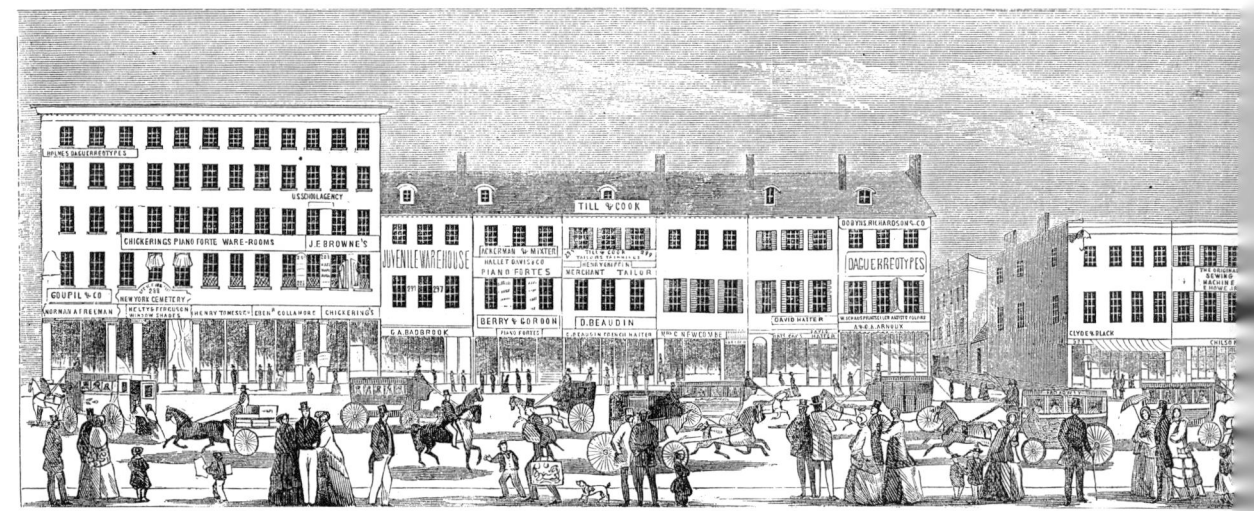

LAFARGE BUILDINGS   DUANE STREET

A PANORAMIC VIEW OF BROADWAY, NEW YORK CITY, COMMENCING AT THE ASTOR HOUSE

... proved a boon to publishers of views, in portfolio form as well as in magazine pages, and a challenge to graphic artists in their delineation of building facades.

DWAY BANK   PARK PLACE   MURRAY STREET

CHEMICAL BANK   CHAMBERS STREET   IRVING HOUSE

HOSPITAL

From *Gleason's Pictorial Drawing-Room Companion*, March 11, 1854.

"Broadway stands for an idea—a romantic identification with the gay and sophisticated world which touches everybody. In terms of responses it commands, Broadway is the greatest of all the evocative avenues, *the* street which the world holds in common. Robust, monumentally vulgar, and durable is Broadway. Like humanity, it survives, swinging its earthy hips athwart the neat geometry of Manhattan, twisting along the hard high backbone of the island from one corner to the other. Almost barren of graces, and with none of the endearing intimacies of other famous streets, yet it produces a bizarre nostalgia of its own. . . . And it has its lyric moments: unexpected, unfamiliar vistas, so unlike the views taught the eye by right-angled streets. Columbus Circle in the summer twilight, or the whirling snow. The foot of Wall Street on a Saturday afternoon, where Broadway tips its hat to Trinity, that dowager of churches, so self-possessed among the banks. And for some, the furious cacophony of sound and color and multitudes around Times Square holds a barbaric magic that amounts to poetry. . . . The famous Astor House, between Vesey and Barclay Streets, was the first of the great New York hotels, and from 1836 onward it maintained its dominance for half a century as a meeting place for celebrities, long after the center of social life had moved north."

From "Broadway," by Edward Stanley, in *Holiday Magazine*, 1951.

By nightfall, illuminating gas, first introduced to the city in 1823, provided an added note of excitement to Broadway as the only gaslit thoroughfare...

"Give me Broadway with the soldiers marching," wrote Walt Whitman, the keenest observer New York ever had. Elsewhere, in his *Leaves of Grass*, he wrote his "Broadway Pageant":

When million-footed
Manhattan unpent
descends to her
pavements,
When Broadway is
entirely given up to
foot-passengers and
foot-standers, when the
mass is densest,
When the facades of the
houses are alive with
people, when eyes gaze
riveted tens of thousands
at a time,
When guests from the
islands advance, when the
pageant moves forward
visible,
When the summons is
made, when the answer
that waited thousands of
years answers,
I too arising, answering,
descend to the pavements,
merge with the crowd,
and gaze with them.

Gaslight had first been introduced to the streets of New York in the mid-twenties, and was making houses more comfortable and livable. Visitors from abroad were thrilled with the excitement of downtown Broadway. "An evening stroll along Broadway," wrote an Englishman, "when the lamps are alight with gas, will please more than one at noon-day. The shops then look rather better; . . . though their proprietors, of course, remain the same, with their cold indifference."

From *Ballou's Pictorial Drawing-Room Companion*, December 13, 1856.

BROADWAY, NEW YORK, BY GASLIGHT

... By daylight, New Yorkers flocked to downtown Broadway like teeming hordes of lemmings, making pedestrian crossing extremely hazardous.

"Broadway is a noble street, eighty feet wide and straight as an arrow, extending from the Battery northward nearly two miles. But broad as Broadway is, it is now quite too narrow for the immense travel, business, and locomotion of various kinds, of which it is the constant scene. This is particularly the case with that part below Canal Street; and more particularly so south of the Park. Here the attempt at crossing is almost as much as your life is worth. To perform the feat with any degree of safety, you must button your coat tight about you, see that your shoes are secure at the heels, settle your hat firmly on your head, look up street and down street, at the self-same moment, to see what carts and carriages are upon you, and then run for your life. We daily see persons waiting at the crossing places, for some minutes, before they can find an opening, and a chance to get over, between the omnibuses, coaches, and other vehicles, that are constantly dashing up and down the street; and, after waiting thus long, deem themselves exceedingly fortunate if they can get over with sound bones and a whole skin. . . ."

From *A Glance at New York*, by Asa Greene, 1837.

Engraved from a photograph by Rockwood, *Harper's Weekly*, June 8, 1867.

THE LOEW BRIDGE ACROSS BROADWAY, AT FULTON STREET, AND THE NEW HERALD BUILDING

The Loew footbridge, built as an overhead pedestrian crossing for the busy thoroughfare at Fulton Street, near St. Paul's Church, afforded but temporary relief from dangerous traffic conditions. It was erected at the instigation of hatter Genin who complained about loss of business from those unable to reach his store and other nearby merchants, on Broadway's east side. But after only two years of service, Knox, on the opposite side, organized merchants to petition for the demolition of the bridge. The experiment proved a failure for other reasons, too. Pedestrians enjoyed watching the spectacle of congestion from above, making it virtually impossible, at times, to cross.

There is a relative serenity to the average day on Wall Street that hardly reveals the changing fortunes of the nation's speculators...

"Wall Street is a narrow, six-block canyon overshadowed by towering buildings that many call the counting-house of the American nation. Today, this makes it the financial heart of the free world. From nightfall to daybreak, Wall Street is deserted, except by policemen and the scrubwomen who clean its offices. From Saturday noon until Monday morning it is mainly left to sight-seeing tourists and resident pigeons. But on weekdays, from nine to five, Wall Street collects a population greater than that of many large cities. Bankers, brokers, lawyers, insurance companies, and a vast force of clerical workers crowd its buildings. Evangelists preach on its sidewalks, unheeded by the throngs that scurry by. Vehicular traffic makes the canyon ring with the din of its incessant noises and honking. In the great domain of American business, the Street, as it is familiarly called by many of its workers, is a separate realm—a society that has its individual history, unwritten laws, and particular language. Wall Street is the only thoroughfare in New York that emerges from a graveyard to end in a river. It begins at Broadway, opposite Trinity Church erected more than a century ago. Trinity is the third church to be built on this site, and it remains a quiet sanctuary in the citadel of high finance. Clerks and office girls flock there during lunch hour, but on warm days many more eat box lunches amidst the crumbling gray tombstones of the churchyard. 'Sitting on Gravestones Is Not Allowed,' a sign warns. But pigeons can't read, and apparently the pretty girls won't."

From "Wall Street: Men and Money," by Gene M. Brown, in *Park Magazine*, 1952.

Engraved from a photograph by William B. Austin, *Harper's Weekly*, June 23, 1866.

WALL STREET, NEW YORK

... but when financial panic strikes the atmosphere is charged with turbulence as plunging prices spell doom for the less fortunate.

LOST

THE PAYING TELLER

GAINED

The history of Wall Street is marked by periodic breakdowns in security values, resulting all too often in cataclysmic depressions of nationwide consequences. There have been at least a dozen such major calamities starting with the Panic of 1837, just a few years after New York's great fire that destroyed vast areas of the downtown district. There were many business failures and bank closings which resulted in great unemployment. Twenty years later, disaster again struck as a result of crashes throughout the nation. As business after business closed, and bank runs followed, George Strong, noted diarist, recorded this dismal note: "We are a very sick people just now. . . . This is far the worst period of public calamity and distress I've ever seen, and I feel it is but the beginning." The great Panic of 1873 delayed reconstruction for many years. It was brought on by the collapse of Jay Cooke & Company, railroad speculators, and a condition of overexpansion throughout the nation. Fortunes were lost, as empires crumbled in the financial district. The depression that followed was very extensive, but it brought hordes of buyers to New York for the purpose of picking up bargains, as huge stores and wholesalers offered entire stocks at reduced prices for spot cash. To walk down Broadway during the height of the panic was a scene never to be forgotten. Scores of business houses were closed, and notices posted about receivership. As reported in *Valentine's Manual:* "It seemed as if the end of all things had come, but New York rose like a phoenix from the ashes and began its new career of prosperity which has brought us to our present wonderful development."

JAY COOKE & COMPANY'S OFFICE

RUN ON THE UNION TRUST COMPANY

THE EXCITEMENT ON THE STREET

AROUND THE STOCK INDICATOR

From *Harper's Weekly*, October 11, 1873.

SCENES IN WALL STREET DURING THE PANIC

As brokers executed customers' "buy and sell" orders, the trading floor of the Stock Exchange was a scene of constant turmoil...

"Here is the building of the New York Stock Exchange, which has an ornate, pillared facade on Broad Street. The Stock Exchange is the financial heart of the nation, and it has transformed trading into a science. It is the direct descendant of a group of men who met daily under an old buttonwood tree on Wall Street to trade in securities.... Trading on the Exchange today is a highly formalized, complicated activity. To become a member, one has to buy a 'seat'—probably the most costly chair in the world, since it has no physical existence. The main trading floor is a huge, domed hall, with a grove of 'trading posts' which are a modern equivalent for buttonwood trees. From the visitors' gallery, the floor makes a bewildering impression. Men are running about without apparent direction. Clacking noises issue from two great call boards at the north and south ends of the hall. There is a constant flashing of ticker tape on large screens, recording the latest transactions. Every company listing its securities on the Exchange receives a coded designation, and to read the ticker you have to master the Exchange's codebook."

From "Wall Street: Men and Money," by Gene M. Brown, in *Park Magazine*, 1952.

Engraved from a drawing by Graham and Thulstrup, *Harper's Weekly*, September 10, 1881.

THE NEW YORK STOCK EXCHANGE

... yet nothing to compare with the frenzy that struck the Street at times of severe depression, throwing trading into a tailspin.

Engraved from a drawing by Schell and Hogan, *Harper's Weekly,* May 24, 1884.

THE PANIC—SCENES IN WALL STREET, WEDNESDAY MORNING, MAY 14

The narrow canyon of Wall Street was ill prepared to handle the huge crowds and traffic that accumulated during periods of sudden stress on the securities market. When the news circulated that commodity values were plunging, thousands of brokers and bankers as well as the frenzied citizenry descended upon the financial houses to learn of their fate. Caught up in the milling throngs were the horse-drawn omnibuses that turned off Broadway at Trinity Church to make their way through the street. The favorite vantage point, as always, for viewing the tumult, was the steps of the Sub-Treasury Building as crowds hovered around the statue of Washington. On this very site (now called Federal Hall) stood the first seat of the United States Government. From its steps the Declaration of Independence was first read to New Yorkers, and from its balcony George Washington took his oath of office when inaugurated as the country's first president, in 1789. The huge bronze statue was the work of John Q. A. Ward, who modeled this likeness from portraits by Gilbert Stuart and the head by Jean Antoine Houdon. It was unveiled in 1883, just a year before the tumultuous scene depicted herewith.

The great Crystal Palace exposition, erected in Bryant Park in 1852, inspired by a similar international display in London the previous year . . .

Around a palace, loftier,
  fairer, ampler than any yet,
Earth's modern wonder,
  history's seven outstripping,
High rising tier on tier with
  glass and iron facades,
Gladdening the sun and sky,
  enhued in cheerfulest hues,
Bronze, lilac, robin's-egg,
  marine and crimson,
Over whose golden roof shall
  flaunt, beneath thy banner
  Freedom,
The banner of the States and
  flags of every land,
A brood of lofty, fair, but
  lesser palaces shall cluster.
Somewhere within their walls
  shall all that forwards
  perfect human life be
  started,
Tried, taught, advanced,
  visibly exhibited.

> From "Song of the
> Exposition,"
> by Walt Whitman.

Engraved by J. W. Orr from drawings by S. Wallin and W. Wade, *Gleason's Pictorial Drawing-Room Companion*, January 1, 1853.

A BEAUTIFUL REPRESENTATION OF THE NEW YORK CRYSTAL PALACE

... provided an American showcase for the review of the nation's progress alongside the best of what foreign governments had to exhibit.

From an engraving by J. Wells, *Gleason's Pictorial Drawing-Room Companion*, January 1, 1853.

You shall see hands at work at all the old processes and all the new ones,
You shall see the various grains and how flour is made and then bread baked by the bakers,
You shall see the crude ores of California and Nevada passing on and on till they become bullion,
You shall watch how the printer sets type, and learn what a composing-stick is,
You shall mark in amazement the Hoe press whirling its cylinders, shedding the printed leaves steady and fast,
The photograph, model, watch, pin, nail, shall be created before you.

In large calm halls, a stately museum shall teach you the infinite lessons of minerals,
In another, woods, plants, vegetation shall be illustrated—in another animals, animal life and development,
One stately house shall be the music house,
Others for other arts—learning, the sciences, shall all be here,
None shall be slighted, none but shall here be honor'd, help'd, exampled.

From "Song of the Exposition," by Walt Whitman.

For the thousands who thronged to visit the fair the countless foreign displays gave them their first taste of European culture...

A full year before completion of New York's Crystal Palace building, the weekly illustrated journals were busily promoting the wonders of the coming fair. *Scientific American,* in October 1852, reported: "In remote districts of this great and growing country, young men, and old, too, have begun to lay by a few shillings weekly or monthly that they may be enabled to come from the far prairie and backwoods to see the Crystal Palace in New York.... We now hope that our countrymen of every art and trade are preparing themselves to exhibit machines and apparatus which will make us proud of their genius and artistic skill. We have seen it stated that England will do everything to decry our effort; such language exhibits a silly fear, in which there is not the least necessity for indulging.... We do not expect to see royalty carried to the fair in carriages drawn by cream colored Arabian horses, but in the royal cars of the Sixth Avenue railroad which will take as many passengers as choose to go, from Chambers Street to the Palace, the fare is only one five-cent piece." On July 14, 1853, when President Pierce opened the exhibition, thousands thronged to the fairgrounds at Forty-second Street (the present Bryant Park) to see not only this country's products but some of the best that Europe had to offer. There were Gobelin tapestries, Sèvres vases, the finest English silver, Bohemian glassware, silks and satins from France, Italy, and India. The nearby Latting Tower, 350 feet high, provided an unsurpassed view of the city, which at the time was gradually sprawling northward.

From an engraving by Pilliner, *Gleason's Pictorial Drawing-Room Companion,* February 4, 1854.

A PANORAMIC REPRESENTATION OF THE INTERIOR OF THE CRYSTAL PALACE, NEW YORK

. . . until a most unfortunate blaze destroyed the entire exhibition building, thought to have been fireproof, and the valuable contents in a matter of fifteen minutes.

From *Harper's Weekly*, October 16, 1858.

DESTRUCTION OF THE NEW YORK CRYSTAL PALACE BY FIRE, OCTOBER 5, 1858

"Bryant Park became the scene of a great disaster October 5, 1858, when the famed Crystal Palace was destroyed by fire. Opened July 14, 1853, for the 'Exhibition of the Industry of All Nations,' this glass and iron 'fairy palace' vanished in smoke in the short space of half an hour, burying a tremendous collection of art and manufactured products from all over the world. Armor from the Tower of London, Sèvres china, Gobelin tapestries, jewelry, Marochetti's statue of Washington and innumerable other works of art perished in a molten mass of ruins. Firemen repeatedly rushed into the building in an attempt to save the fire apparatus that was on exhibition but their efforts were unsuccessful. . . . There were well over 2,000 persons in the building when the fire started but not a life was lost, though one man was rescued just a few seconds before the dome fell. The work of incendiaries who ignited papers in the lumber room, the fire resulted in a total loss of two million dollars.''

From *As You Pass By*, by Kenneth Holcomb Dunshee, 1952.

The ever-popular panoramic views of the city, invariably drawn from church steeples as the only high vantage points towering above the streets..

Where the city stands with the brawniest breed of orators and birds,
Where the city stands that is belov'd by these, and loves them in return and understands them,
Where no monuments exist to heroes but in the common words and deeds,
Where thrift is in its place, and prudence is in its place,
Where the men and women think lightly of the laws,
Where the slave ceases and the master of slaves ceases,
Where the populace rises at once against the never-ending audacity of elected persons,
Where women walk in public processions in the streets the same as the men,
Where they enter the public assembly and take places the same as the men,
Where the city of the faithfulest friends stands,
Where the city of the cleanliness of the sexes stands,
Where the city of the healthiest fathers stands,
Where the city of the best-bodied mothers stands,
There the great city stands.

From "Song of the Broad-Axe,"
by Walt Whitman

NEW YORK CITY AND ENVIRONS FROM THE SPIRE OF DR. SPRING'S NEW BRICK CHURCH, FIFTH AVENUE

... shows the monotony of rows of four-story buildings, their facades and rears facing narrow gardens, in the regular grid pattern of cross streets, looking south on Fifth Avenue.

Engraved by Anthony from a drawing by Hitchcock, *Harper's Weekly*, April 23, 1859.

Accompanying this bird's eye view of Manhattan from the steeple of Dr. Spring's new Brick Church, at Thirty-seventh Street and Fifth Avenue, is a diagrammatic chart labeling the various church steeples to be seen in lower New York. Looking southward along tree-lined Fifth Avenue, we see the Upper Bay and the distant hills of Staten Island, and just to the left the Narrows and nearby Brooklyn. At the right is the Hudson River and the distant shores of Jersey City and Hoboken. *Harper's Weekly* in which the panoramic view was featured, acknowledges credit to Matthew Brady for photographic assistance in the production of this fine engraving, drawn by Hitchcock and engraved by Anthony.

Dr. Spring's Church was erected in 1857, built on a site that had previously been occupied by the Murray Hill residence of W. C. H. Waddell, a castellated "Suburban Gothic Villa." The Brick Presbyterian Church survived for over eighty years and was demolished in 1938.

The new Union Depot at Grand Central proved a great convenience for travelers and commuters, and at the same time sparked a building boom in this area.

"One of the most imposing buildings in the city is the new Grand Central Depot, on Forty-second Street and Fourth Avenue. It was projected by Commodore Vanderbilt and ground was broken for it on the 15th of November, 1869; it was ready for occupancy by October 9th, 1871. The depot is constructed of red brick, a mansard roof, with iron trimmings painted white, in imitation of marble. The south front is adorned with three and the west front with two massive pavilions. The central pavilion of each front contains an illuminated clock. The entire building is 696 feet long and 240 feet wide. The train shed is 610 feet long, and 200 feet wide, and is covered with an immense circular roof of iron and glass. The principal entrance is on Forty-second Street. There are included accommodations for offices, waiting rooms, baggage rooms, etc. The Hudson River and New York Central using the depot are the only lines entering the city, and they are provided with a common terminus in the very heart of the metropolis. The waiting rooms and offices are finished in hard wood, are handsomely frescoed, and are supplied with every convenience. The height of the roof of the main depot is 100 feet from the ground. It is lighted from the roof by day, and at night, large reflectors, lighted by an electrical apparatus, illuminate the vast interior. About eighty trains enter and depart from this depot every day. The running of these is regulated by the depot-master, who occupies an elevated position at the north end of the car-house, from which he can see the tracks for several miles. A system of automatic signals governs the running of the trains through the city."

From *Lights and Shadows of New York Life; or the Sights and Sensations of a Great City*, by James D. McCabe, 1872.

EXTERIOR VIEW OF THE NEW UNION DEPOT (NOW IN THE COURSE OF CONSTRUCTION)

From *Frank Leslie's Illustrated Newspaper*, November 26, 1870.

FOR THE NEW YORK CENTRAL AND HUDSON RIVER AND NEW HAVEN AND HARLEM RAILROADS, FOURTH AVENUE, NEW YORK CITY

The powerful, political forces of Tammany, an influential governing group in the city, built themselves a handsome new headquarters in the busy district just off Union Square.

Engraved from a photograph by Rockwood, *Harper's Weekly,* July 11, 1868.

NEW TAMMANY HALL, EAST FOURTEENTH STREET, NEW YORK CITY

On the north side of East Fourteenth Street, between Irving Place and Third Avenue, was located the "new Tammany Hall," as depicted in this engraving appearing in *Harper's Weekly,* July 11, 1868. It was a handsome, red brick building located in a popular section of the city at a time when Tammany became a synonym for Democratic rule and later a euphemism for political bossism under the notorious Boss Tweed. The hall contained many fine spacious facilities which were rented out for theatrical purposes, similar to the London music hall variety shows. Lloyd Morris, in his *Incredible New York,* describes the entertainment features "with bars, a restaurant, a 'conversation saloon fitted up in Turkish style,' a theater, a basement oyster saloon and a promenade hall. In the theater, a variety show held the stage. In the restaurant, entertainers performed. In the hall, an orchestra played popular concerts. Between the hours of seven and midnight, you could enjoy all these attractions for an admission fee of fifty cents."

The choice of City Hall Park as the site for the new post office was a most unfortunate decision, robbing the city of a fine natural setting for its municipal capitol...

In a city where new construction is constantly in progress, demolition of the old and the excavation of the site are a commonplace to which New Yorkers have long become accustomed. Nowadays, to accommodate the curious passerby, the boardings are prepared with peepholes so that "sidewalk superintendents" may watch every step in the construction process. But this huge tract at the southern tip of City Hall Park attracted more than the customary interest; it was being prepared for a new federal post office. "In 1869 the Federal government decided to depart from its niggardly policy, and take steps toward the erection of a Post-office adequate to the needs of a great and growing community. It was decided to erect an edifice which should be an ornament to the city, and capable of rendering postal service for generations to come. The municipal authorities offered to sell the land to the government for a half million dollars. The corner stone was laid in June, 1869. The new building was expected to cost about four million dollars. In the background may be seen the City Hall."

From *Harper's Weekly,* October 23, 1869.

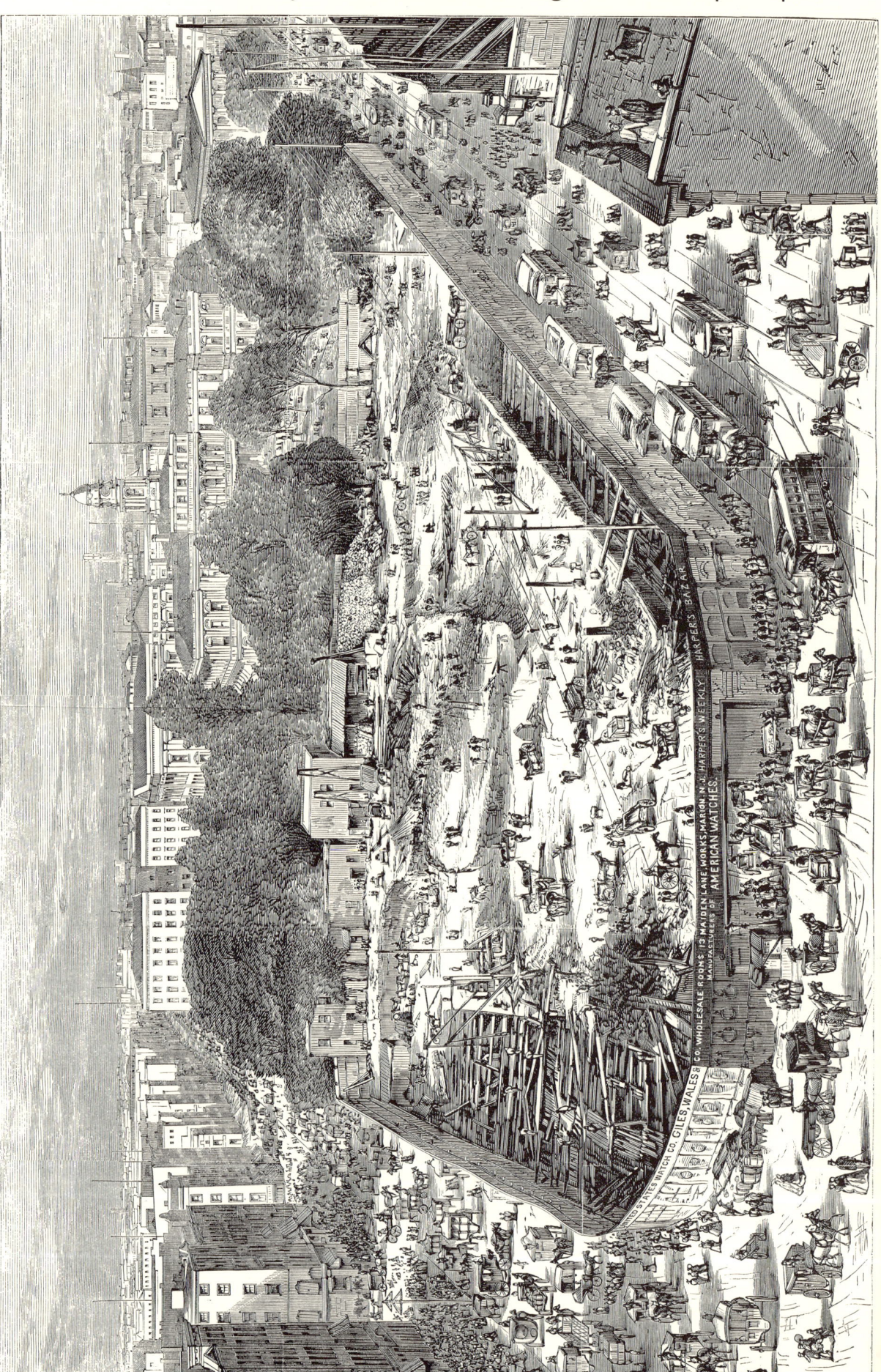

Engraved from a photograph by Rockwood, *Harper's Weekly,* October 23, 1869.

EXCAVATING FOR THE FOUNDATION OF THE NEW YORK CITY POST-OFFICE BUILDING

... but the completed structure, a busily fragmented design of columns, arches, and architraves, convinced the citizens they had been cheated with a costly monstrosity.

From an engraving in *Harper's Weekly*, November 12, 1870.

VIEW OF THE NEW YORK POST-OFFICE, NOW ERECTING IN THE CITY HALL PARK

The new post office building erected at the intersection of Broadway and Park Row was designed in the Italianate manner, with characteristic French influence, particularly the prominent mansard roof treatment. It was the largest single building in this style erected in New York, when the great post-Civil War depression of 1873 curtailed most construction. An elaborately detailed description appears in McCabe's *Lights and Shadows of New York Life:* "The Mansard roofs of the corner pavilions, rising 107 feet above the sidewalk, are covered with an ironclad cornice and metallic cresting. The irregular angles imposed by the shape of the lot are marked by semi-hexagonal pavilions. The roof, square-domed, rests on the arms of a Greek cross, out of the centre of which rises a heavily buttressed cupola, carrying pediments, with detached columns on its four faces. One hundred and fifty-nine iron columns in the basement, and 117 in the first story support the walls and floors. The fronts on Broadway and Park Row are broken by central pavilions with pyramidal roofs, of which the first and second stories are faced with detached colonnades of coupled columns." After six long years of construction the post office was finally dedicated in 1875. From the very beginning, the structure was maligned by architectural critics and others who considered it to be an eyesore, intruding upon the stately beauty of the much-overshadowed City Hall, seen at the left background. In 1939, after a never-ending controversy, the building was razed, and the original park approach to City Hall was restored.

Printing House Square at the junction of Nassau Street and Park Row, across from City Hall Park, was the home of New York's newspapers, presided over by Ben Franklin, in effigy...

Our view looking south shows the intersection of Nassau Street on the left and Park Row on the right, forming an area that, since 1861, has been known as Printing House Square. The offices of most New York newspapers were located here: at the left, the *Sun* offices, and beyond, the tall building of the *Tribune*, built in 1875. Just left of the *Sun* building, now shown in this picture, were the offices of the *New York World,* the *Staats Zeitung,* the Associated Press, and others. The *New York Times,* whose new building was completed in 1888, had occupied this same site in previous years. First organized in 1851, it had completely outgrown its 1858 offices only thirty years later. In its opening editorial it proclaimed: "We shall be conservative in all cases where we think conservatism essential to the public good; and we shall be radical in everything which may seem to us to require radical treatment and radical reform." With this clear definition of its policies, the paper had prospered and grew steadily, with both the city and the nation. In a detailed statement of the *Times*'s history, *Harper's Weekly,* October 27, 1888, said: "The *Times* has never ceased to maintain its reputation for enterprise and liberality in the collection of news. The promptness, fullness, and accuracy of its election returns have also given it a recognized supremacy on the day following any important election."

Engraved from a drawing by Charles Graham, *Harper's Weekly,* October 27, 1888.

THE NEW BUILDING OF THE NEW YORK "TIMES"—GEORGE B. POST, ARCHITECT

... while a block to the north the new structure called the Pulitzer Building housed the offices and plant of another titan of the press, the *New York World*.

Engraved from a drawing by Charles Graham, *Harper's Weekly,* January 18, 1890.

THE PULITZER BUILDING, THE NEW HOME OF THE NEW YORK "WORLD"

For years the Pulitzer Building, home of the *New York World,* stood as a landmark among the younger generation of towers erected in downtown New York. Joseph Pulitzer had acquired the *World,* after his success with the *St. Louis Post Dispatch*. He was the first newspaper publisher to grasp the idea of featuring pictures in his pages. The newly improved process of photoengraving, attributable to Benjamin Day, appealed to Pulitzer, who was more fully alive to the advantages of the new idea than any of his contemporaries; furthermore, the *World* was desperately in need of circulation. Beginning with portraits, he soon added pictures of wrecks, fires, and, in fact, anything that could add spice to his paper. The lively features attracted new readers, and circulation figures boomed. Pulitzer, facing blindness, wanted to build himself a monument to perpetuate his name. He engaged George B. Post, who had also designed the nearby *Times* building, to plan a fifteen-story structure to outshine them all. The gleaming, golden dome atop his building could be seen from all directions. Facing City Hall, and easily seen from the Brooklyn side as well, his new "monument" was soon surpassed by a crop of newer towers, following the principle of "steel-cage construction" devised by Bradford Lee Gilbert, a young architect who had gained fame with his Tower Building, at 50 Broadway. Pulitzer's World Tower, erected in 1889, stood at the strategic entrance to the Brooklyn Bridge. It was demolished in the early 1950's to facilitate the flow of traffic at the busy bridge approach.

Nothing quite symbolized the growing prosperity of the wealthy class more than the stately mansions built in regal splendor along upper Fifth Avenue.

"The Vanderbilt fortune, the greatest ever amassed in America, represents modern New York's financially expansive facilities, as manipulated by the machinery of corporations and the Stock Exchange, and is the accumulation of two generations, a father and son, within the present century. On the west side of Fifth Avenue at Fifty-first and Fifty-second Streets are two elaborate brownstone dwellings with ornamental fronts and having a connecting covered passage, which contains the doorways of both. These are the homes of William H. Vanderbilt's daughters, and are only exceeded in magnificence by his own house, a castellated drab-stone structure, at the upper corner of Fifty-second Street. These palaces were built, decorated, and furnished to outshine any other dwellings in New York, and it is said that three million pounds were expended upon them. . . . ."

From *The London Times*, 1887.

The prevailing vogue for many of the prestigious palaces was inspired by the epoque of François Première, typified by so many of France's noted chateaux. Upper left is the home of William K. Vanderbilt, by Richard M. Hunt. Upper right is the house of Cornelius Vanderbilt II, after designs by George B. Post and certain details by Richard M. Hunt. Below are the twin houses of William H. Vanderbilt, completed in 1884 from designs by Gustav and Christian Herter. These were built for Vanderbilt's daughters, Mrs. William D. Sloane and Mrs. Eliot F. Shepard.

HOUSE OF WILLIAM K. VANDERBILT
DESIGNED BY R. M. HUNT

HOUSE OF CORNELIUS VANDERBILT
DESIGNED BY GEORGE B. POST

Engraved from photographs by Pach, *Harper's Weekly*, January 21, 1882.

HOUSES OF WILLIAM H. VANDERBILT—DESIGNED BY THE MESSRS. HERTER

THE VANDERBILT HOUSES

Cooper Union was built by philanthropist Peter Cooper to provide free educational facilities to students in the arts and sciences.

Cooper Union occupies the full block between Seventh and Eighth streets, and Third Avenue and Astor Place. Foundations for the building were laid in 1854, notable for its early use of rolled-iron sections in its construction. The rolled beams were produced at Cooper's own mill in Trenton, New Jersey. Cooper had amassed a fortune in various enterprises, many the result of inventions of his own making. But this building and Cooper Institute represented the crowning glory of a life devoted to philanthropy, which he personally administered throughout his long lifetime. "The Union for the advancement of science and art" enabled many thousands who could not afford higher education to develop their skills and talents. In addition, the Cooper Union auditorium became a forum for discussions on matters of national and civic interest. Most notable was the meeting held on February 27, 1860, at which Abraham Lincoln was the principal speaker. "He was a little-known figure to Easterners, and the audience of fifteen hundred did not fill the auditorium. It was a select audience, however, including many leading citizens, and Lincoln laid before them the fact that the federal government had the power to control slavery, stressed the urgent need to prevent its extension, and appealed for understanding of the South. 'No man,' reported the *Tribune* next day, 'ever before made such an impression on his first appeal to a New York audience.'"

From *The Story of New York*, by Susan Elizabeth Lyman, 1964.

Cooper Union, from *Leslie's Illustrated Newspaper*, April 14, 1883.

NEW YORK CITY—THE MONUMENT OF A PHILANTHROPIST: THE COOPER UNION AND ITS SCHOOLS OF ART

There were already nostalgic reminiscences as long ago as 1889 when these sketches were published, regretting the inevitable passing of some noted homesteads...

When *Harper's Weekly,* back in October, 1889, featured this group of "Historic Homes," in pen-and-ink renderings by Hughson Hawley, it was already aware that the immutable forces of change would doom many of these structures. Today, of the ten dwellings shown, only four have survived: Fraunces Tavern at Pearl and Broad streets, Colonel Smith's Mansion on East 60th Street, Jumel Mansion on West 160th Street and Jumel Place, and Van Cortlandt Manor in the park of that name. The urgent need for the preservation of these dwellings is the province of the Landmarks Preservation Commission as well as the Historic American Buildings Survey. This need is expressed by Nathan Silver, in his *Lost New York:* "Whatever the reasons for cherishing them, many of the most valuable elements of a city are those buildings which are wonderful for their own sakes. They may be so bound up with the city's history, or so representative of the spirit of a certain time, or so beautiful as buildings alone, that their loss is unthinkable. Such buildings certainly deserve to be defended as objects in their own right. They should be sorted out from the rest, protected and preserved for their singularity. . . . Preservationism must be a component of protecting a city's essential form."

Pen and ink sketches by Hughson Hawley, *Harper's Weekly,* August 31, 1889

HISTORIC NEW YORK HOUSES

... at the same time wealthy sportsmen were indulging in favorite diversions at their country clubs and city athletic houses.

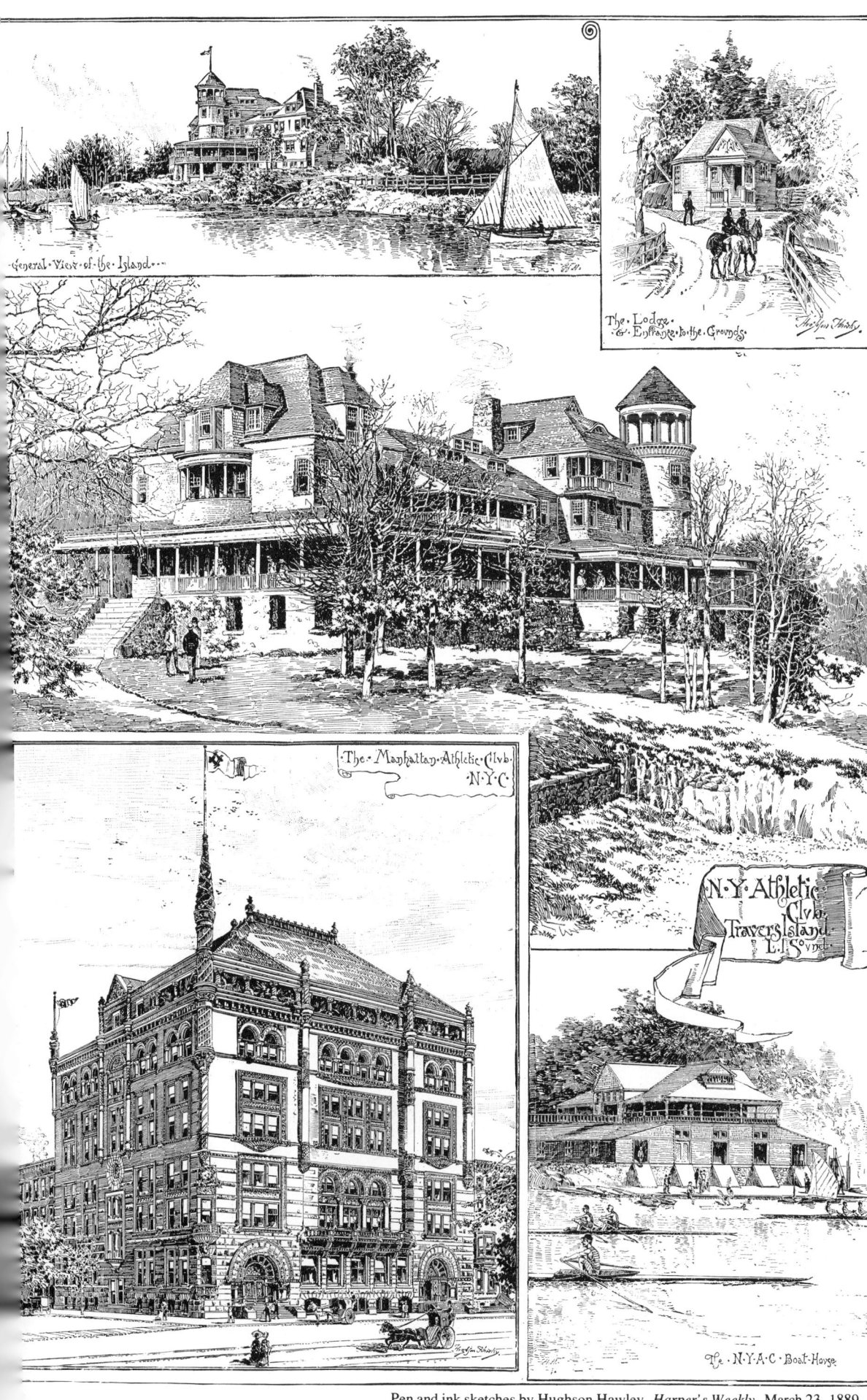

The affluence of many of New York's leading families, and others who shared with them a newfound wealth during the latter part of the nineteenth century resulted in the formation of a number of exclusive clubs. Membership rosters were carefully tailored to admit only those who "qualified." There were clubs for purely social aspirations, literary and artistic societies, pseudo-cultural fraternities, and those catering to the sports-minded. Most prominent among the athletic clubs were the New York Athletic Club and the Manhattan. The Manhattan Athletic Club built itself a handsome structure of Richardsonian design near Madison Square. The NYAC's pride and joy was its country club in Westchester, at least an hour's drive to Travers Island on the Sound. Here, sailboating, tennis, cricket, and riding on the estate's many trails were among the favorite attractions for which members paid handsome dues annually.

Pen and ink sketches by Hughson Hawley, *Harper's Weekly*, March 23, 1889.

HOUSES OF THE NEW YORK AND THE MANHATTAN ATHLETIC CLUBS

In the downtown districts of New York steam was delivered via subterranean pipes from giant steam stations to commercial buildings.

It has been said that the ditches, cuts, and culverts of the city are a sign of steady progress, and that their absence would signal a sure state of decay. In 1882, as depicted in the group of vignettes herewith, a new reason for digging street ditches in downtown New York was occasioned by the laying of pipelines for a central steam system. "Difficulty is experienced in laying street mains on account of the numerous lines of pipes which already undermine the city. A diagram shows twenty-seven systems of pipes, sewerage, and catch-basins. It is obviously difficult to penetrate this network at certain points, and this has slowed the work so far. The New York Steam Company already supplies a number of factories with motive power for elevators, and the buildings will want more steam for heating purposes this winter. In several restaurants the cooking is done over stoves heated by the company. . . . To avoid danger of explosion along the mains, there is never more than eighty pounds of pressure in the pipes, although they are tested for double that amount."

From *Harper's Weekly*, September 9, 1882.

Engraved from a drawing by W. P. Snyder, *Harper's Weekly,* September 9, 1882

HEATING NEW YORK BY STEAM

Workmen were constantly digging ditches, laying cables and conduits, as each new facility had to be accommodated in the network of underground complexities.

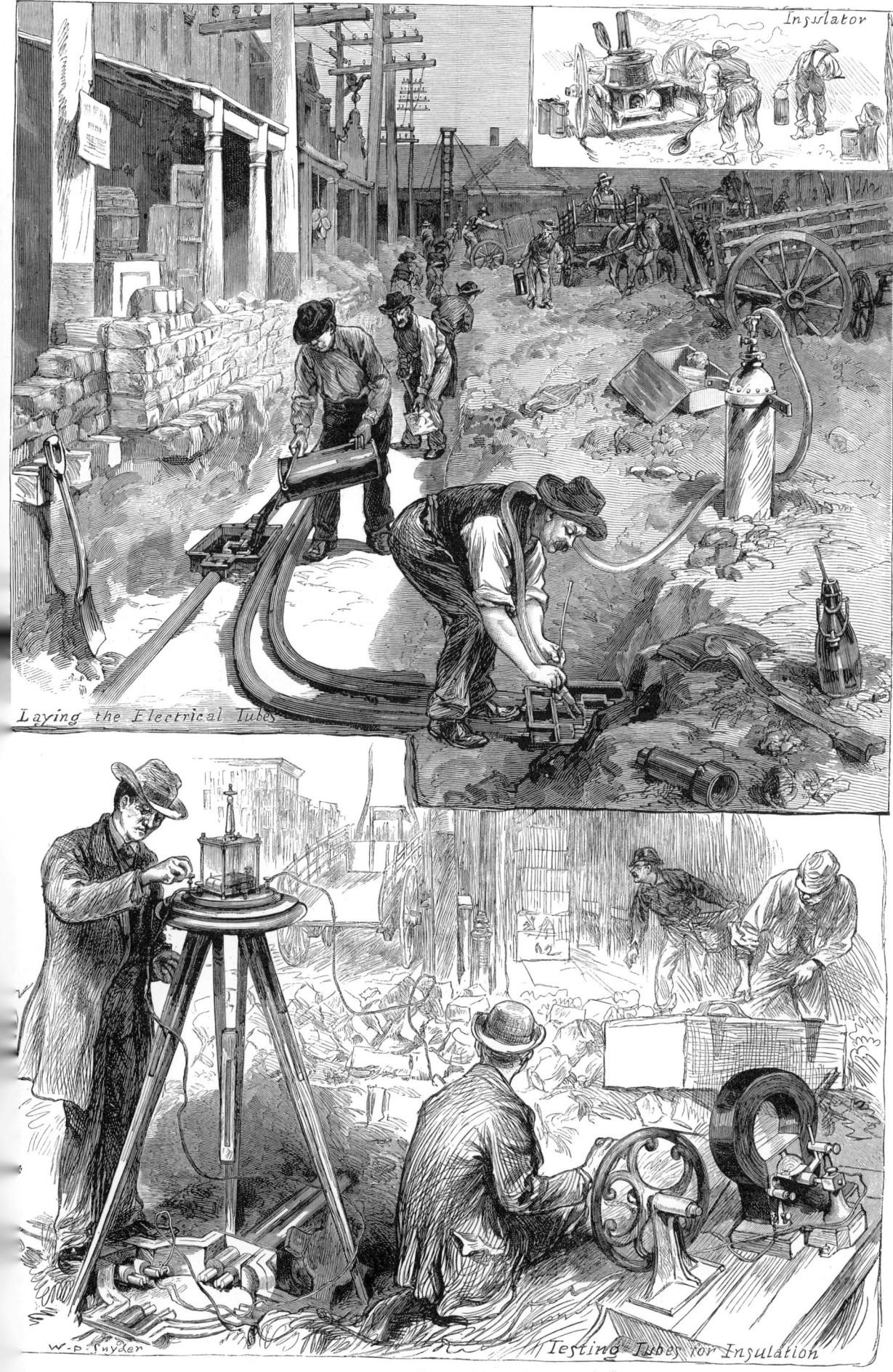

Thomas Edison was convinced that the Brush arc lamps being installed in Union and Madison squares were "not yet entirely satisfactory." He had labored feverishly, experimenting for over a year with various filaments for his incandescent light bulb. Finally, with the reluctant approval of the city's aldermen, the laying of conduits was begun. "Edison was constantly on the go, supervising each detail of his monumental project, watching as each connection was made, and trusting no one to do things right. At night he stretched out on piles of pipes in the growing power station and fell asleep instantly. By October 1, 1882, he had strung wires into the homes of 59 customers, and although the power had not yet been turned on, there was a great demand for securities in his company. . . . Having postponed the premiere many times and fearful that it might be a fiasco, Edison shunned any fanfare that great day. He stayed up all the previous night to rehearse his men in their new jobs after the first switch had been thrown. . . . At 3 P.M., September 4, 1882, with summer sunlight smiling on downtown Manhattan, Edison signaled his chief electrician, John W. Lieb, to pull the master switch and thus light offices and homes with his electricity. The effect was anticlimactic, like striking matches in the glare of a bonfire. Not until the descent of velvet dusk could the radiance of this man-made illumination be appreciated."

From *The Epic of New York City,*
by Edward Robb Ellis, 1966.

Engraved from a drawing by W. P. Snyder, *Harper's Weekly,* June 24, 1882.

THE ELECTRIC LIGHT IN HOUSES—LAYING THE TUBES FOR WIRES IN THE STREETS OF NEW YORK

56

A startling innovation that greeted New York's eyes in the 1880s was the illumination by electric light of Union and Madison squares, followed by Broadway.

"On one of the warmest days of July, at about noon, Madison Square was cleared by the police, and an enormous 160 foot mast was gradually raised from the ground, swung into position, and dropped into its place. From the top of this pole, there shines down the great electric lights in a battery of four arc lamps. They are part of the Brush system, by which a portion of the city— say a mile of Broadway, a mile of Fifth Avenue, Fourteenth and Thirty-fourth Streets, as well as Union and Madison Squares—are to be lighted. This is what is called the 'combination plan,' such as is in use in Cleveland and other Western cities. For the street proper lamps of 2000 candle-power each, on posts from twenty to thirty feet high, set at intervals of a block, are used whereas in open squares the taller masts are used. This street lighting, as well as that for hotels and stores, is performed by the Brush Electric Illuminating Company."

From *Harper's Weekly,* January 14, 1882.

A British visitor to these shores, in 1882, wrote, "The effect of the light in the squares of the Empire City can scarcely be described, so weird and so beautiful is it." From the tall masts "erected in the centre of each square," light was "thrown down upon the trees in such a way as to give a fairy-like aspect."

Engraved from a drawing by Charles Graham, *Harper's Weekly,* January 14, 1882.

THE ELECTRIC LIGHT IN MADISON SQUARE, NEW YORK

PART THREE

The Sidewalks of New York

Engraved from a painting by J. G. Brown, N.A., *Harper's Weekly,* April 26, 1879.

"THE GERMAN BAND"

Everywhere on the sidewalks of New York one could hear strains of music, sometimes from the itinerant Italian organ grinder and his hurdy-gurdy, or the ubiquitous German band playing for pennies on the streets or often in the tenement backyards. From a painting by J. G. Brown, this engraving is "a faithful study from the streets of New York. The German bands are becoming a feature here, and there can be no doubt in the minds of our citizens that if we are to be compelled to listen to music whether we will or no, at almost any hour of the day or evening, the brass-band is a great improvement on the Italian hand-organ."

From *Harper's Weekly,* April 26, 1879.

The Sidewalks of New York

IN EVERY URBAN METROPOLIS, the visible signs of progress are marked by wide contrasts in the ways of life lived by different classes. But nowhere is this more manifest than in New York City, where every phase of the city's social strata is more marked than anywhere in the land. It is a place of peculiar opposites where for every viable way there's always the antithesis, a condition that is hardly new. Theodore Dreiser observed, when he wrote in *Color of a Great City:* "The thing that interested me . . . about New York was the sharp, and at the same time, immense contrast it showed between the dull and the shrewd, the strong and the weak, the rich and the poor, the wise and the ignorant."

As the capital city of commerce and finance, New York can boast of the wealthiest and greatest philanthropists, whose mansions on upper Fifth Avenue are unmatched in any other city; while in extensive sections of lower Manhattan and upper Harlem live some of the poorest, most underprivileged in the country. For these latter, the sidewalks are their recreational areas, in the ghettos of cramped quarters and restricted opportunities. No other city in the world houses so many types of differing ethnic backgrounds, in such vast numbers, so many miles of crowded streets and yet so much loneliness. For many of these, though not homeless, live in solitary confinement, not knowing their neighbors down the hall. For them, the streets provide an inadequate outlet, totally lacking in social compensations.

Broadly speaking, the Lower East Side was synonymous with the tenement districts where the sordid life of the slums assumed its most degrading aspects. Permanent pauperism seemed the lot of too many. Jacob Riis, in his celebrated study of these conditions, wrote in *How the Other Half Lives:* "More than one-half were destitute because they had no work and were unable to find any, and one-sixth were frauds, professional beggars, training their children to follow in their footsteps—a veritable 'tribe of Ishmael,' tightening its grip on society as the years pass. . . ."

The intermingling of races and creeds that created a "melting pot" in the tenement districts is readily understandable, when one recalls that millions from abroad who poured into the crowded city chose to remain where they had landed. The first great influx started with the Irish, after the potato famine of 1848. Then the Italians arrived in great numbers, establishing a "Little Italy" around Mulberry and Carmine streets and a large section of Greenwich Village. Immediately to the south was a small enclave that became Chinatown, while up in Yorkville Germans, Hungarians, and Czechs congregated. A sizable portion of the Lower East Side was solidly settled as the Jewish quarters, speeded in its development by a series of pogroms in Russia and Poland. Grand Street and the Bowery became principal thoroughfares where an active shopping district featured a wide variety of merchandise and foodstuffs prepared for European tastes. Street bazaars made up of hundreds of peddlers and pushcarts formed the bustling markets on the side streets where vehicular traffic was made impassable. Litter and garbage from the pushcarts created a stench that permeated vast areas before strict enforcement of sanitation codes eliminated the unhealthy atmosphere. Violent crime was rampant in sections where the overcrowding reached excessive proportions. One of the most notorious danger spots was the "Five Points" district, and another, close-by, was the equally infamous Mulberry Bend. The trouble spots were not limited to the East Side. On the West Side, a most turbulent area was called "Hell's Kitchen," a tenement district of squat and squalid shanties, saloons, and slaughterhouses not far from the docks and railroad yards that ran up and down Eleventh Avenue. Here, as the police reported, not all the blood that ran in the gutters came from the abattoirs.

But for all the violence that was a feature of depressed areas, the streets and sidewalks of New York had their gayer moments. Military parades in celebration of civic and national events were frequent; workers' processions and political turnouts were a popular sight for the sidewalk watchers. At night, as torchlights glared in the marchers' ranks, festal fireworks were a common sight. The historical drama of pyrotechnic displays was a treat that New Yorkers never tired of. The Fourth of July was always an occasion for brilliant displays; Washington's Birthday was celebrated in spectacular style with the blaze of Roman candles, pinwheels, and dazzling fireworks of every kind. For one such celebration the City Hall cupola and upper story were set ablaze, a near disaster for the historic building, averted only because fire equipment was on the scene at the time.

Political rallies and the reportage of election night returns were occasions that often took on a dramatic turn. Huge bonfires featured all election night festivities regardless of victories or losses. Fire fighters were kept on the run as boys threw boxes, crates, and old furniture, often piled to second-story height, into the flames with impartial enthusiasm.

Strolling peddlers and street criers, offering wares and services, and the itinerant beggar were a common sight on the streets of New York.

From *Ballou's Pictorial Drawing-Room Companion,* December 13, 1856.

SKETCHES FROM THE HIGHWAYS AND BYWAYS OF NEW YORK

"The business of the street vendor and huckster was protested against in many cities and towns. The trade of the established market found unfair competition coming from these itinerants who, by peddling through the streets, or by appearing at the stalls of the markets before the local merchants and farmers could set up their goods, would forestall profitable trade. Many cities passed ordinances against them. In New York City, as early as 1691, a city ordinance forbade hucksters selling their wares until the market had been open for two hours. This law, however, did not apply to persons selling fish, fruit, or victuals, or to those who were selling 'wares of his or their own manufacture . . . nor any Tinker, Glasier, Cooper, Plummer, Taylor or other person usually trading in mending or making Cloaths, Kettles, Tubs, or Hoashould goods.' Despite his bad name, the huckster served a useful purpose as he brought his wares to the housewife's door, and that he served the poorer classes. He was a true itinerant, although his field of wandering was limited to the city and its immediate environs. Moreover, he was a picturesque figure, for he called his wares, and his street cries were among the pleasant (or unpleasant) noises of our early cities and towns."

From *Hawkers & Walkers in Early America,* by Richardson Wright, 1927.

Scattered throughout the city were several flower markets, one at Union Square and another at the west end of Canal Street, popular with both rich and poor.

"Over at the gay and colorful flower market, at the west end of Canal Street near the North River docks, the pre-Decoration Day ceremonies are in full swing days before the holiday. There is ceaseless dickering and chaffering, and the talk and laughter of the people who crowd each other on the thronged sidewalks, and the cries of the rival dealers calling attention to their wares, and the shouts of the children who are playing and dodging about, fill the air with discordant pandemonium. There are potted plants in great variety: roses, fuchsia, lilies, marigold, poppies, phlox, coleus, and many others . . . all contributing to a blaze of many hues and colors. The rich come to select needed varieties to add to their gardens; the poor are happy to choose a few inexpensive plants for their window boxes. By late afternoon the market is gone as stocks are depleted, only to be replaced at an early hour the next day."

From *The Book of New York*, by Robert Shackleton, 1917.

From *Frank Leslie's Illustrated Newspaper*, June 12, 1880.

NEW YORK CITY—PREPARING FOR DECORATION-DAY CEREMONIES—
EARLY MORNING SCENE AT THE FLOWER MARKET ON CANAL STREET

"Taking the air"—as relief from the crowded tenement districts—was a necessary diversion and social outlet.

Engraved from a drawing by Charles Stanley Reinhart, *Harper's Weekly*, September 13, 1873.

TOMPKINS SQUARE, NEW YORK—OUT FOR A BREATH OF FRESH AIR

Tompkins Square was named after Governor Daniel D. Tompkins who held the rank of major general during the War of 1812, and called up the militia to protect the city. The large, verdant area was situated from Seventh to Tenth streets, along Avenue A. In the mid-fifties this had been a noted parklike region famed for fresh air, so much so that it had been called the "White Garden." Most of the residents in this general area, in the latter decades of the nineteenth century, were of German descent. But then, in 1904, a major disaster struck the Tompkins Square section: the sinking of the excursion steamer the *General Slocum,* which went down in the East River with a loss of twelve hundred lives, mostly from this vicinity. Thereafter, to avoid the gloom that pervaded the neighborhood, many families moved uptown to Yorkville where an extensive Germany colony resided. A fountain erected to the memory of the *Slocum* victims stands at the southwest corner of Tompkins Square park.

"May 1 was known to most New Yorkers as "moving day," a condition that persisted throughout the city from generation to generation. In these days of costly movability, it may be difficult to understand why there was a veritable exodus from tenements at the time. Granted that many leases expired on this date, if indeed tenants of those days were bound by legal restrictions, there were mitigating circumstances to account for frequent changes of address. To move the entire contents of a five- or six-room flat, one could readily engage the services of an expressman for from five to ten dollars, plus the customary gratuity paid a helper, a growler of beer from the corner saloon. Concessions of a month or two of free rent, and in bad times, three or four, proved an inducement too tempting to overlook. It was not uncommon for the average family to pick up stakes several times a year. When severe hardship struck, and the attractive moving bargain no longer was a temptation, the modest monthly rent problem was sometimes solved by taking in boarders. Hardly an immigrant family did not harbor newly arrived relatives; often a total stranger could be given a floor mattress in an empty corner.

Because rents were low, moving cheap, and the granting of concessions common practice, the sidewalks of New York were often jammed with household goods at moving time.

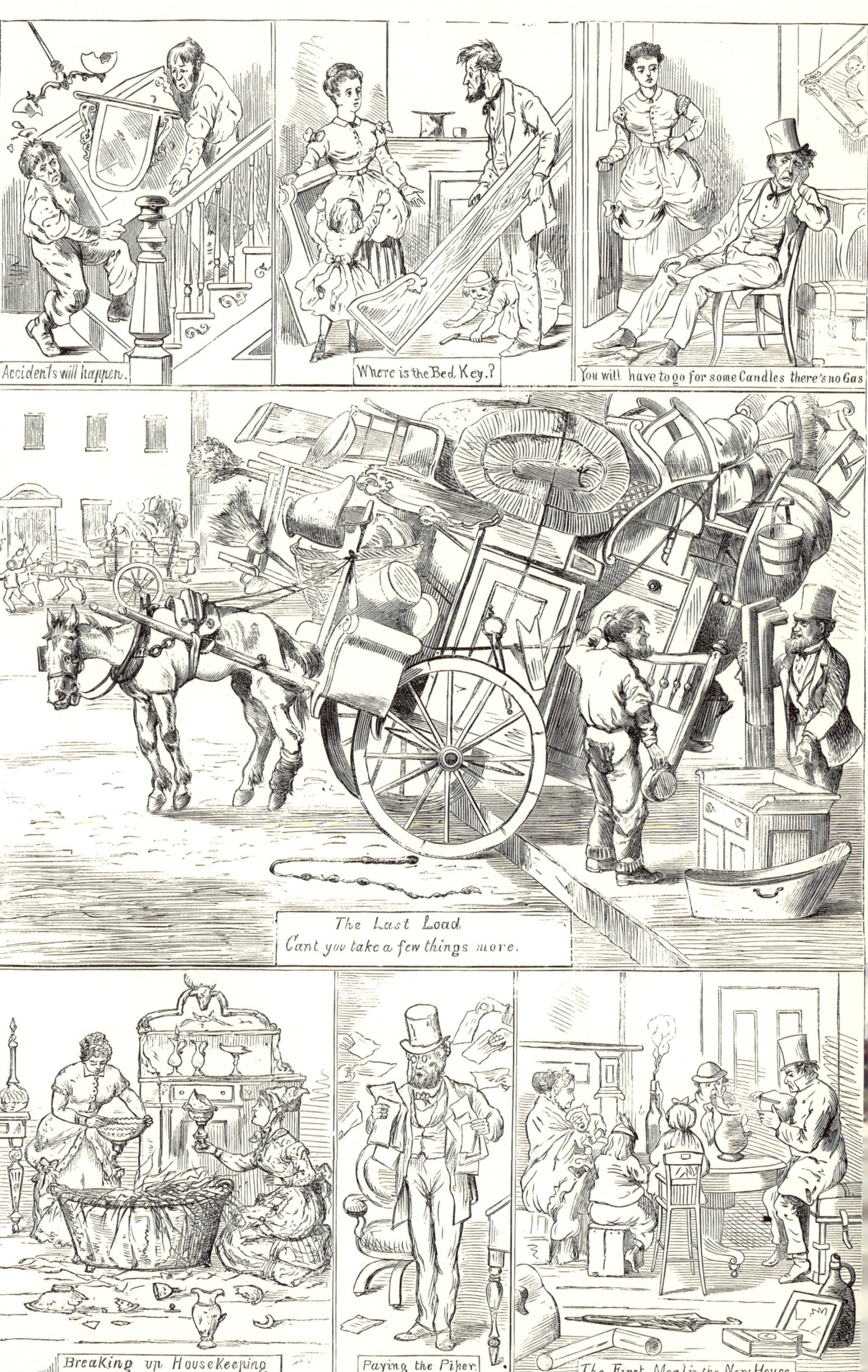

Engraved from a drawing by Thomas Worth, *Harper's Weekly,* May 8, 1869.

THE FIRST OF MAY IN NEW YORK CITY

The Bowery held a lure and fascination that attracted oldsters and street urchins alike, by day or night the year round.

"Walk the Bowery under the elevated railway at night and all you feel is a sort of cold guilt. Touched for a dime, you try to drop the coin and not touch the hand, because the hand is dirty; you try to avoid the glance, because the glance accuses. This is not so much personal menace as universal—the cold menace of unresolved human suffering and poverty and the advanced stages of the disease alcoholism. On a summer night the drunks sleep in the open. The sidewalk is a free bed, and there are no lice. Pedestrians step along and over and around the still forms as though walking on a battlefield among the dead. In doorways, on the steps of the savings bank, the bums lie sleeping it off. Standing sentinel at each sleeper's head is the empty bottle from which he drained his release. Wedged in the crook of his arm is the paper bag containing his things. The glib barker on the sight-seeing bus tells his passengers that this is the 'street of lost souls,' but the Bowery does not think of itself as lost; it meets its peculiar problem in its own way—plenty of gin mills, plenty of flophouses, plenty of indifference, and always, at the end of the line, Bellevue."

From *Here Is New York*, by E. B. White, 1949.

Engraved by Lagarde, *Harper's Weekly*, February 26, 1881.

A NIGHT SCENE IN THE BOWERY, NEW YORK

Typical of the squalor that housed the "huddled masses" were the shacks and shanties of Lower East Side tenements...

"This is the place, these the narrow ways diverging to the left and right, and reeking everywhere with dirt and filth. Such lives are led here, bear the same fruit here, as elsewhere. The coarse and bloated faces at the doors have counterparts at home and all the world over. Debauchery has made the very houses old . . . Open the door of one of these cramped hutches full of sleeping Negroes. Bah! They have a charcoal fire within, there is a smell of singeing clothes on flesh, so close they gather round the brazier; and vapours issue forth that blind and suffocate. From every quarter, as you glance about in these dark streets, some figure crawls half-awakened, as if the judgment hour were near at hand, and every obscure grave were giving up its dead. Where dogs would howl to lie, men and women and boys slink off to sleep, forcing the dislodged rats to move away in quest of better lodgings. Here, too, are lanes and alleys paved with mud knee-deep; underground chambers where they dance and game; the walls bedecked with rough designs of ships, of forts, and flags, and American Eagles out of number; ruined houses, open to the street, whence through wide gaps in the walls other ruins loom upon the eyes, as though the world of vice and misery had nothing else to show . . . all that is loathesome, drooping and decayed is here."

From *American Notes*, by Charles Dickens, 1842.

WEST GOTHAM COURT, CHERRY STREET.

STAGE OF THE OLD CHATHAM STREET THEATRE, NOW USED AS A STABLE.

Engraved from drawings by Charles Graham, *Harper's Weekly,* March 20, 1879.

TENEMENT LIFE IN NEW YORK—SKETCHES IN THE FOURTH WARD

... where, as Dickens reported, "vapours issued forth that blind and suffocate . . ." and crowding into tiny hovels was a staggering sight to behold.

Engraved from drawings by William A. Rogers, *Harper's Weekly,* March 22, 1879.

TENEMENT LIFE IN NEW YORK—SKETCHES IN "BOTTLE ALLEY"

"Bottle Alley is around the corner in Baxter Street; but it is a fair specimen of its kind, wherever found. Look into any of these houses, everywhere the same pile of rags, of malodorous bones and musty paper, all of which the sanitary police flatter themselves they have banished to the dumps and the warehouses. Here is a 'flat' or 'parlor' and two pitch-dark coops called bedrooms. Truly, the bed is all there is room for. The family tea-kettle is on the stove, doing duty for the time being as a wash-boiler. By night, it will have returned to its proper use again, a practical illustration of how poverty in 'the Bend' makes both ends meet. One, two, three beds are there, if the old boxes and heaps of foul straw can be called by that name; a broken stove with crazy pipe from which the smoke leaks at every joint, a table of rough boards propped up on boxes, piles of rubbish in the corner. The closeness and smell are appalling. How many people sleep here? The woman with the red bandanna shakes her head sullenly, but the bare-legged girl with the bright face counts on her fingers—five, six!"

From *How the Other Half Lives,*
by Jacob A. Riis, 1890.

Poverty and rags could hardly be termed picturesqueness, yet such was the task of the artist-reporters, who, along with photographer and reformer Jacob Riis...

"New York life among the poor has one central distinguishing feature—namely, the fact that all live in tenements or in houses built on much the same principle. This principle is about as bad as it can possibly be. In the typical tenement house the staircase passes up a well in the centre of the house. It has no light from the open air, no ventilation; it is absolutely dark at midday, except for such glasses over the doors of the flats, and possibly from a skylight at the top of the house. It is a well for all the noxious gases to accumulate in; it cannot be aired; the rays of the sun never penetrate to it; in the worst houses it is foul with the coming and going of the innumerable denizens of the tenements. On its steps play the pale, unhealthy children who, even allowing for the enormous death rate, still swarm in these horrible dwellings. Can a more frightfully unwholesome system be imagined? Yet this is not the worst. The tenements, opening in flats off these stairs, may be constituted of more or fewer rooms, but as a rule the bedrooms never have direct access to the open air. They open into the living rooms, and their windows open on to the stairs, so that not alone can the bedrooms never be properly aired, but they are so constructed that they receive all the impure gases that accumulate in the central well."

From "The Emigrant in New York," by Charlotte G. O'Brien, in *The Nineteenth Century,* October 1884.

Engraved from a drawing by William A. Rogers, *Harper's Weekly,* August 5, 1879.

TENEMENT LIFE IN NEW YORK—RAG-PICKERS' COURT, MULBERRY STREET

... did much to call attention to the wretched living conditions of the impoverished living in the Italian, Jewish, and Irish quarters of downtown New York.

"Where Mulberry Street crooks like an elbow within hail of the depravity of the Five Points, is 'The Bend,' foul core of New York's slums. Long years ago the cows coming home from pasture trod a path over this hill. Echoes of tinkling bells linger there still, but they do not call up memories of green meadows and summer fields; they proclaim the home-coming of the rag-picker's cart. In the memory of man the old cow-path has never been other than a vast human pig-sty. There is but one 'Bend' in the world, and it is enough. The city authorities, moved by the angry protests of ten years of sanitary reform effort, have decided that it is too much and must come down. Another Paradise Park will take its place and let in sunlight and air to work such transformation as at Five Points, around the corner of the next block. Never was change more urgently needed. Around 'the Bend' cluster the bulk of the tenements that are stamped as altogether bad, even by the optimists of the Health Department. Incessant raids cannot keep down the crowds that make them their home. In the scores of back alleys, of stable lanes and hidden byways, of which the rent collector alone can keep track, they share such shelter as the ramshackle structures afford with every kind of abomination rifled from the dumps and ash barrels of the city. Here, too, shunning the light, skulks the unclean beast of dishonest idleness. 'The Bend' is the home of the tramp as well as the rag-picker. The whole district is a maze of narrow, often unsuspected passage-ways—necessarily, for there is scarce a lot that has not two, three, or four tenements upon it, swarming with unwholesome crowds."

From *How the Other Half Lives*, by Jacob A. Riis, 1890.

VIEW OF "MULBERRY BEND"—
ARRIVAL OF CONTRACT LABORERS FOR THE COAL MINES

THE GARLIC-VENDER

AN ITALIAN RESTAURANT

THE PADRONE

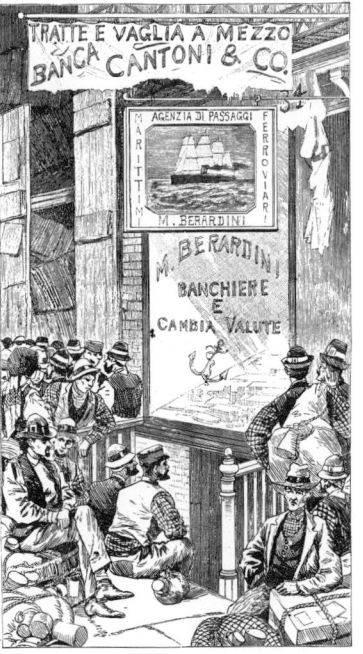

A BANKING-HOUSE IN THE ITALIAN QUARTER

Engraved from drawings by a staff artist, *Frank Leslie's Illustrated Newspaper*, August 11, 1888.

THE CONGRESSIONAL INVESTIGATION INTO THE EVILS OF IMMIGRATION—SCENES IN "MULBERRY BEND," THE ITALIAN QUARTER IN MULBERRY STREET, NEW YORK

At the Penny Restaurant on Grand Street "a fair appetite could be appeased for five cents, and a ravenous one for ten," reported the press at the time.

"A novel enterprise in the restaurant business was recently started at 413 Grand Street, in this city, on the basis of giving good and wholesome dishes at a price so low that nobody with a cent in his pocket need go hungry. 'One cent a plate' is the rule, and though two cents will buy a larger portion, the quantity given for one is quite generous, and the quality excellent. 'Cheap and nasty' does not apply to this establishment. The regular bill of fare gives the following prices: A small cup of tea or coffee, one cent; bread and butter, one cent; soup, one cent; a slice of corned beef, one cent; a baked or boiled potato, one cent; cabbage, one cent; baked beans, one cent; boiled rice, one cent; a quarter of a pie, three cents; apple dumplings, oyster stew, mutton-chops, lamb pot-pie, five cents. The quality of all these things, as already said, is excellent; the one cent portions are small, yet a fair appetite could be appeased for five cents, and a ravenous one for ten."

From *Harper's Weekly*, December 8, 1877.

Engraved from drawings by William A. Rogers, *Harper's Weekly*, December 8, 1877

THE PENNY RESTAURANT

In a day when most householders swept their refuse into the gutter for the "nourishment of local fauna," the city's sanitation department was slowly being organized.

Engraved from drawings by W. P. Snyder, *Harper's Weekly*, November 24, 1877.

HOW THE STREETS OF NEW YORK ARE CLEANED

"The Street Cleaning Department was a temperamental Government function that existed principally for the reward of the 'Boys.' Only the principal thoroughfares received any systematic attention. Perhaps the personal habits of the citizenry in general were largely responsible for the unsavory condition of the highways. The genial custom of householders in the poorer districts of depositing refuse in the gutters for the nourishment of peripatetic pigs, dogs, goats and other local fauna, still persisted. Ragged small boys, such as have been perpetuated by Horatio Alger, swept the crossings for penny perquisites and these, aided and abetted by the kindly elements and by occasional spasmodic municipal exertions, made the streets tolerable for the passage of humanity."

From *Valentine's Manual of Old New York,* edited by Henry Collins Brown, 1926.

For those who could afford the theater, afternoon matinees
were popular as children were often in attendance...

"If you visited New York during the 'seventies or 'eighties, you inevitably went to the theatre, for certain playhouses were nationally famous and you could scarcely face your friends at home unless you could talk about them. Serious drama now had the highest moral sanction; everybody knew that one of the most successful theatres in New York, the Madison Square, was owned by the brothers Mallory, one of whom was publisher of *The Churchman* and the other a clergyman. Union Square had already been superseded as the theatrical center. The stretch of Broadway between Madison Square and Forty-second Street—the 'Rialto,' as it was called—was a street of legend, and it had a romantic attraction for all Americans across the continent. This mile of the wide avenue was lined, on both sides, with luxurious hotels, glittering bars, the city's principal theatres."

From *Incredible New York,* by Lloyd Morris, 1951.

People attending the matinee performances constituted special groups, usually charitable or benefit occasions, and particularly family get-togethers. Children were much in evidence, admitted at reduced prices in those days. Avoiding exposure at night, they could sidestep the terrors that sometimes attended late-evening performances, as thugs and pickpockets were always loitering about the theater lobbies.

From *Harper's Weekly,* February 10, 1866.

LEAVING THE MATINEE

. . . but most popular were the afternoon band concerts in Central Park, an occasion for formal attire as the "stovepipes" clearly show.

71

From *Harper's Weekly*, October 9, 1869.

SATURDAY AFTERNOON IN THE NEW YORK CENTRAL PARK—MUSIC ON THE MALL

"To the Park, accordingly, and to the Park only, hitherto, the aesthetic appetite has had to address itself, and the place has therefore borne the brunt of many a peremptory call, acting out year after year the character of the cheerful, capable, bustling, even if overworked, hostess of the one inn, somewhere, who has to take all the travel, who is often at her wits' end to know how to deal with it, but who, none the less, has, for the honor of the house, never once failed of hospitality. That is how we see Central Park, utterly overdone by the 'run' on its resources, yet also never having had to make an excuse. . . . It has had to have something for everybody, since everybody arrives famished; it has had to multiply itself to extravagance, to pathetic little efforts of exaggeration and deception, to be, breathlessly, everywhere and everything at once, and produce on the spot the particular romantic object demanded, lake or river or cataract, wild woodland or teeming garden, boundless vista or bosky nook, noble eminence or smiling valley. . . . You are perfectly aware, as you hang about her in May and June, that you *have*, as a travelled person, beheld more remarkable scenery and communed with nature in ampler or fairer forms. . . ."

From *The American Scene*, by Henry James, 1907.

> Parades, regardless of those in the line of march and whether they celebrated or protested, were a spectacle that all of New York seemed to enjoy...

Early in the life of the Republic parades of tradesmen, guild workers, and craftsmen became a symbol of strength and solidarity, long before unionization took place. The Christmas holiday was the scene of the annual demonstration of the expressmen of New York. The massing of vans and express delivery wagons, packed with as many workers as the four-horse teams could manage, brought out crowds even in the worst wintry weather.

"Parades. What a part they play in the memories stored by a young boy. Generally they went up Broadway, and it was long before the route was switched to Fifth Avenue. 'Give me Broadway, with the soldiers marching,' wrote Walt Whitman. What a wealth of such affairs we boys had on the Fourth of July and Decoration Day—now more generally known as Memorial Day—and on various special occasions. . . . The St. Patrick's Day parade was probably the most notable repeated emphasis on the immigrant element, and it remains so today. On occasions the butchers turned out, wearing silk hats and white aprons, bravely mounted on their horses. There was evidently quite an esprit de corps in their organization which went back to General Thomas F. Devoe, himself a butcher."

From *Manhattan Kaleidoscope,* by Frank Weitenkampf, 1947.

Engraved by J. A. Bogert from a drawing by A. R. Waud, *Gleason's Pictorial Drawing-Room Companion,* February 12, 1853

ANNUAL CELEBRATION OF CHRISTMAS HOLIDAY, BY THE EXPRESSMEN OF NEW YORK

. . . and often the cause was a step in the organization of member unions out to declare their grievances or agitate for higher wages.

Engraved from a drawing by C. D. Weldon, *Harper's Weekly*, July 8, 1882.

THE PARADE OF THE NEW YORK FREIGHT HANDLERS

Not all of the city's parades were marked with uniformed marchers, gaily colored floats, and dozens of fife and drum corps bands. Often, when a particular group of workers wished to congregate and make their demands known to the people, the ranks were filled with men in their regular workaday clothes. The procession never was at a loss for an audience, and, as always, the streets were lined with watchers and the usual sprinkling of hawkers offering flags, buttons, or more generally victuals.

"Parades furnished organized picturesqueness at intervals. . . . The streets were alive with numerous vendors, some with cries and other means of attracting attention and advertising their wares or activities. The old Irish applewoman at the street corner, often smoking a short clay pipe, sold not only apples but those large, round, fluted-edged gingerbread cakes known as 'bolivars' and St. John's bread. How good it all tasted! She gave way in time to the Italian's fruit stand. On summer days there came the long-drawn call 'hot co-o-orn,' on Sixth Avenue and elsewhere. There were others supplying food, such as the hot-tamale man, the one who sold hot waffles done on the spot, the frankfurter man. All those, usually peripatetic, purveyors of delicacies are now rare. . . ."

From *Manhattan Kaleidoscope*, by Frank Weitenkampf, 1947.

For many years following the close of the Civil War, every able-bodied veteran marched in the Decoration Day parade to pay tribute to fallen comrades...

"A particular zest was given the impressive ceremonies of Decoration Day this year by the appearance of the various posts of the Grand Army of the Republic in their new parade uniform. According to the custom observed since the institution of the memorial ceremonies, there was a parade of the State militia, local and visiting posts, and battalions of the Fire Department. The military statues were decorated with flowers, the graves of the dead soldiers and sailors in the city cemeteries were appropriately honored, and detachments of the veteran organizations visited the suburban cemeteries, and rendered the annual tribute to the commanders and comrades long since laid away. The early procession of the active and veteran soldiery on Monday, May 31st, deserved the hearty commendation it received. Brief services were held at principal monuments; the flag on the red fort in Central Park was hoisted at sunrise; Trinity's chimes rung out upon the clear air their appropriate salutes to the dead and the day; while in the evening the visiting posts and troops from Philadelphia were entertained by their respective hosts."

From *Frank Leslie's Illustrated Newspaper,* June 12, 1880.

From *Frank Leslie's Illustrated Newspaper,* June 12, 188

NEW YORK CITY—THE DECORATION-DAY PROCESSION—THE PENNSYLVANIA STATE FENCIBLES AND G.A.R. POSTS, WITH BATTLE-FLAGS, TURNING FROM UNION SQUARE INTO BROADWAY

... joining his infantry brigade or cavalry squadron as they marched past the President's special reviewing stand in Union Square.

Engraved from a drawing by Thure de Thulstrup, *Harper's Weekly*, June 13, 1885.

DECORATION DAY IN NEW YORK—PRESIDENT CLEVELAND REVIEWING THE PROCESSION

On this Decoration Day in 1885, President Grover Cleveland traveled to New York to watch the annual parade from the reviewing stand at Union Square. The fine squadrons of cavalry officers always presented a striking picture of order and discipline, as the well-groomed mounts pranced about.

The city's time-honored tribute to the dead has always been an occasion for large turnouts of the nation's soldiery marching to the rhythmic beat of drums and much fanfare. This author, in his youth, well remembers witnessing countless parades on Broadway, Fifth Avenue, and Central Park West. As late as the 1920s he recalls standing on the curb at Riverside Drive as the procession approached the Sailors' and Soldiers' Monument at Eighty-ninth Street. The loudest cheers rang out as the thinning ranks of Civil War veterans hobbled by in their faded uniforms and tattered hats, chests covered with medals and campaign ribbons, each proud to be counted in with the handful of survivors. These weary footsoldiers were generally followed by carriages carrying those who no longer could trudge the distance on foot; and again, the applause and hand-clapping reached thunderous heights. There were many teary-eyed bystanders, visibly touched by the drama of their passing. It was difficult not to mentally count the remaining few and compare their smaller numbers with marchers of the year before.

Night demonstrations were favored as both workers and viewers were on hand, and the flares and glowing lanterns added greatly to the spectacular displays...

"The night was propitious, clear and cold, succeeding a bright, bracing autumnal day—dark withal, though the stars shone brilliantly. The hour of half-past six had been fixed as the time for the line to form. It did not, however, prepare to move until about eight, when the companies fell into position without disorder. Early in the evening the crowds began to collect, and at the appointed hour they seemed to grow to a boundless extent. The avenues, the streets and squares were one dense sea of life, and it must be confessed the good humor displayed was as remarkable as the colossal mob.... The police arrangements were excellent, but with such masses of humanity their efforts were almost negative.... The spectacle was grand and exciting. Each company, as it passed, discharged a volley of fire-crackers and candles, followed by a thundering peal from the throng around.... Powder was continually being burned, cannon thundered forth in many places, calcium lights flamed out their dazzling radiance, and rockets rose high in the air and burst in beautiful variegation."

From *Leslie's Illustrated Newspaper,* October 27, 1860.

From *Harper's Weekly,* October 24, 1868

GRAND DEMONSTRATION OF THE DEMOCRACY IN NEW YORK CITY

. . . and for election night returns, figures from the ballot box were projected onto a huge white screen as the street crowds watched and cheered.

Engraved from a drawing by Charles Graham, *Harper's Weekly,* November 17, 1888.

MADISON SQUARE, NEW YORK, ON ELECTION NIGHT

This seething hemisphere's humanity, as now, I'd name—*the still small voice vibrating*—America's choosing day,
(The heart of it not in the chosen—the act itself the main, the quadriennial choosing,)
The stretch of North and South arous'd—sea-board and inland—Texas to Maine—the Prairie States—Vermont, Virginia, California,
The final ballot-shower from East to West—the paradox and conflict,
The countless snow-flakes falling . . .

From "Election Day, November, 1884," by Walt Whitman.

In the 1880s election returns were projected by stereopticon upon a huge screen on top of the two-story building at Broadway and Twenty-third Street, where the north end of the Flatiron Building now stands. The congestion of dense crowds and vehicular traffic kept dozens of policemen on hand until past midnight when most returns were in, and Harrison's election was announced.

Nocturnal festivities for which New Yorkers turned out in great numbers were not considered a success unless accompanied by spectacular fireworks displays...

"New Yorkers celebrated Washington's birthday in a manner worthy of themselves and the noble spirit whom they commemorated. From an early hour, a large number of independent companies and societies were conspicuous from their great force, paraded through the principal thoroughfares with flags flying. At noon, national salutes were fired from the Battery and Hamilton Square. At night the windows of the building were all lit and, as if by magic, in a sudden flash the immense structure was illuminated. The main piece of the pyrotechnic display in front of the Hall was a figure of Liberty, seated. The side pieces were mostly composed of fancy work, such as scrolls, stars, and wheels of various colors. The central transparency, over the portrait of Washington, bore 'Born Feb. 22, 1732,' and all were lit up at the same time with the windows. The fine art of pyrotechny has not until recently been brought to any degree of perfection. In China, it has long been superior to this country; but as if to keep pace with railroads, telegraphs, and other developments of science and art, powder has at last consented to burn as brilliantly and in as many beauteous ways as it has heretofore done among the inhabitants of the Celestial Empire."

From *Gleason's Pictorial Drawing-Room Companion,* March 20, 1852.

From *Gleason's Pictorial Drawing-Room Companion,* March 20, 1852.

DISPLAY OF FIREWORKS, AND ILLUMINATION OF CITY HALL, NEW YORK, ON WASHINGTON'S BIRTHDAY

... whether designed to honor George Washington or to celebrate the formal opening of the Brooklyn Bridge after thirteen long years a-building.

From *Harper's Weekly*, June 2, 1883.

THE GREAT BRIDGE—FIRE-WORKS AND ILLUMINATION, FROM THE BROOKLYN SIDE

"The bridge, as a work of engineering, is so distinct an advance upon anything that has been done before, and its influence will be so important upon the relations of the communities which it unites, that it is worthy of the great pageant with which it was opened to the public. The completion of such a work justifies the most gorgeous rites which the simplicity of our civic organization can command. The official presence of the President, of the Governor of the State, of the dignitaries of the army and navy, and of a squadron of saluting men-of-war, in addition to whatever pomp and circumstance could be given to the occasion by the militia, were all required by the intrinsic importance of the event they were to celebrate. . . . There is always some mixture of tragedy in the memories of a great work that has been continued for many years. The victims of the 'caisson disease' have left their lives under these massive towers. The most illustrious of the sacrifices is that of the great engineer who designed this work, the crowning achievement of his laborious life. But scarcely less pathetic is the fortune of his son and successor, who was only permitted to participate in the ceremonies which celebrated the completion of the bridge as a distant spectator, instead of being the hero of the hour, and receiving in person the honors and gratulations he had earned."

From *Harper's Weekly*, June 2, 1883.

The sidewalks of New York and the frivolities of the weather combined to inspire Winslow Homer to limn this bit of artistic observation.

Only on rare occasions did the weekly magazines depart from their main province: pictorial journalism based, for the most part, on events of local and national importance. This, in itself, formed such a vast field for coverage that seldom was the illustrator allowed the liberty of following his personal preference, as shown in the two illustrations herewith. Winslow Homer's interests were allowed free rein, and this, a few years before he had established his reputation as a wartime reporter. "As an artist Homer was always so independent, so self-centered he never was eager to work in subordination to an author. Even in his work as a reporter of news events there is plain evidence that work of this sort never won his deeper respect. He always looked at things from his own point of view. His best illustrations, therefore, are always those with subjects independently selected by the artist. . . . When left to himself to choose a subject for a picture he invariably selected something simple, something with a timeless human appeal."

From *Winslow Homer, An American Artist: His World and His Work*, by Albert Ten Eyck Gardner, 1961.

MARCH WINDS

Engraved from drawings by Winslow Homer, *Harper's Weekly*, April 2, 185

APRIL SHOWERS

PART FOUR
Across the Water

From *Scientific American,* August 11, 1877.

THE GREAT SUSPENSION BRIDGE BETWEEN NEW YORK AND BROOKLYN— VIEW LOOKING FROM BROOKLYN

"The bridge is an organism of nature. There was no question in the mind of the designer of 'good taste' or of appearance. He learned the law that struck its curves, the law that fixed the strength of the relation of its parts, and he applied the law. His work is beautiful, as the work of a ship-builder is unfailingly beautiful in the forms and outlines in which he is only studying 'what the water likes,' without a thought of beauty. . . . Where a more massive material forbade him to skeletonize the structure, and the lines of effort and resistance needed to be brought out by modelling, he has failed to bring them out, and his structure is only as impressive as it needs to be."

From *American Architecture,*
by Montgomery Schuyler, 1892.

Across the Water

WHAT THRILL CAN COMPARE with a foreigner's first glimpse of Manhattan, that indescribably dramatic moment experienced and best known to millions of newcomers! Supreme among the seaports of the world, its shores washed by many waters—the Upper and Lower bays, the Hudson and East rivers, Hell Gate, the Harlem, the Spuyten Duyvil—New York would be incomprehensible without the continuous flow of ebb and tide that has given it life since early days of discovery. The French sculptor, Frederic Auguste Bartholdi, by his own account, knew this thrill the morning he sailed into New York Harbor, in 1871. He had only the faintest glimmering of an idea for a monument, had made many sketches while crossing the Atlantic. On his arrival, he wrote: "It is indeed the New World, which appears in its majestic expanses with the ardor of its glowing life. Yes, in this very place shall be raised the statue of Liberty." Discarding all previous doodles, he at once drew a sketch of a new goddess holding a torch and in his own words talked of enlightenment to follow, envisioning it "casting radiance upon two worlds." He explored the city, met its many peoples, but mostly he navigated the waters, by launch and sailboat, studying Bedloe's Island, where some fifteen years later his symbolic colossus would finally be dedicated.

Earlier, during the days of Dutch settlement, even as the shores hummed with maritime activity, the lands across the waters beckoned to the burghers for better living. Down the bay from Nieu Amsterdam's tip of land was a vast area ideal for farming, Staten Island, with gentle rolling hills and a headland that commanded the highest point on the long coastal stretch from northern Maine to the tip of Florida. Here, David De Vries established Oude Dorp (Old Town) near South Beach, in 1641, but the settlement was destroyed by Indians.

The low, swampy lands of lower Manhattan caused many of the officials of the Dutch West India Company to cast their glances in the direction of Long Island, to the east. As early as 1636 William Bennet and Jacques Bentyn purchased 930 acres of rich land from the Indians, establishing the first white settlement at Gowanus, named for a Mohawk who planted corn around the bay. A second group followed near Wallabout Bay, and before long, in 1646, Governor Kieft authorized that these settlements be absorbed into the growing village of Breukelen (Brooklyn). Already, a ferry service was in operation from Peck Slip in Manhattan to a point across the river called Ferry Road, later to become Fulton Street. Hundreds followed the trek to the rich and fertile fields across the water. Eastward, as dirt roads developed, the little hamlets of Bushwick, Flatbush, Flatlands, New Utrecht, and Gravesend prospered, these five towns later forming the nucleus of the enlarged area that became the village of Brooklyn. The flight from crowded Manhattan continued unabated, and the town across East River kept pace with New York's growth until it became the fourth largest city in the United States. Fast and frequent ferry service helped ensure this rapid population rise.

Another section bordering on Brooklyn's Atlantic shoreline, called Coney Island, with its long sandy beaches and invigorating surf, soon attracted thousands of pleasure-seekers. One could reach there by Smith Street and Culver Road streetcars, a long tedious journey of over an hour from New York. In the beginning the resort was a rendezvous of platoons of toughs and hoodlums who threatened respectable citizens until, after much protest, the police made better protection available. The building of the Culver Railroad Line, and the inauguration of the Iron Steamboat Company sailing from lower New York, in the 1870s, assured Coney's popularity and with it neighboring Brighton Beach, Manhattan Beach, and Sheepshead Bay. Together, these formed a favorite amusement mecca for New Yorkers. Large summer hotels, restaurants, boardwalks, pavilions, and amusements in great variety were provided. Dance bands and fireworks helped make the city folks' visits more memorable.

With the ferries carrying capacity crowds between New York and Brooklyn, the age-old dream of linking the two cities by bridge became more and more a necessity. This dream was realized when an Alsatian engineer who had built the Niagara Falls bridge, John A. Roebling, was determined that Brooklyn should have its bridge. He gave his life, literally, to the project and could not live to witness its completion. His son, Washington, crippled by the "bends" inflicted in the course of underwater inspection, followed through and directed construction by watching its progress from his nearby home. David Steinman, another great bridge designer, wrote years later that Washington Roebling was like a wounded general directing battle from his hilltop command post through a devoted chief of staff. With the bridge's completion, in 1883, "Manhattan's Dormitory" enjoyed phenomenal growth as a dozen trolley lines fanned out in all directions, contributing to making the borough a place of more comfortable habitation for New York's outbound workers.

The heights of Staten Island afforded excellent views of New York harbor, and provided means of signaling about incoming vessels when first seen.

VIEW OF THE NEW YORK BAY AND HARBOR, FROM THE TELEGRAPH STATION

From *Gleason's Pictorial Drawing-Room Companion,* November 27, 1852.

THE NARROWS, FROM STATEN ISLAND, NEW YORK

Looking due south from the Battery, lower tip of Manhattan, one views the large bay, New York harbor. Due west is Jersey City, and southwesterly, Staten Island. About four miles to the south are the Narrows, formed by the lands of Staten Island and the Brooklyn shore to the east. "Staten Island, or Staaten Eylandt as the ancient Dutch settlers wrote the name, was known to the Indians . . . [as] Squehonga Manackmong . . . extending some fourteen miles in length, and about eight miles to the point of its greatest breadth. Guarding as it does the great access to the city from the sea, it is, in a military point of view, a place of high consequence. So the British General, Sir William Howe, regarded it, when he established himself there, first of all, at the period of the American Revolution, keeping possession from 1776 to the close of the conquest. The island, lying as it does within half an hour's sail of the metropolis, and possessing great and varied topographical advantages, has become a favorite resort for summer residence, and many are the stately chateaux and cozy cottages which crown its beautiful heights or nestle in its peaceful glens. . . ."

From "New York Circumnavigated," by T. Addison Richards, in *Harper's New Monthly Magazine,* July 1861.

Brooklyn's extensive dock basins supplemented Manhattan's, thus enlarging New York's overall maritime facilities . . .

The population of Brooklyn, just a short ferry ride across the East River from lower Manhattan, had increased fivefold between 1840 and 1860. The city had grown so, as Whitman wrote, it contained more than a million people. Many of the immigrants pouring into New York, in this period, found it an advantage to leave the dense districts of the East Side and live in "a city of cottages . . . and villas . . . among cultivated fields and miniature groves." The Atlantic Dock, a square basin surrounded by granite stone, was capable of holding several hundred ships at a time. It was located near South Ferry, facing Butter Milk Channel and Governor's Island.

"In consequence of the extreme cold weather, ranging from zero to ten below, the rivers and the bay became bridged with ice of about four or five inches in thickness. Ferry boats were almost useless during the freeze. The firmness of the ice, however, in some degree compensated the Long Islanders for the lack of boat service, as hundreds of the young and venturesome crossed on the ice bridge. About sunrise, long files of men were seen, like pigmies, winding carefully across, feeling carefully for 'air holes,' avoiding suspicious-looking spots. Thousands achieved a feat of which they will hereafter boast to their gaping grandchildren—they had actually walked across the East River on the ice."

From *Gleason's Pictorial Drawing-Room Companion*, February 14, 1852.

From *Gleason's Pictorial Drawing-Room Companion*, July 19, 1851.

ATLANTIC DOCK, BROOKLYN, N.Y.

From *Gleason's Pictorial Drawing-Room Companion*, February 14, 1852.

CROSSING FROM BROOKLYN TO NEW YORK ON THE ICE

... while the frequent ferry service from Fulton Street was important, as more and more residents preferred to move across the river.

From *Ballou's Pictorial Drawing-Room Companion,* June 6, 1857.

VIEW OF THE FULTON FERRY BUILDINGS, BROOKLYN, LONG ISLAND

From *Ballou's Pictorial Drawing-Room Companion,* January 3, 1857.

FULTON STREET, FROM THE FERRY, BROOKLYN, N.Y.

"To describe the city of Brooklyn, either historically, geographically, municipally, or pictorially, is a task of no ordinary character, and requiring much greater space in your paper. So indissolubly is she united to the city of New York—so intimately connected in all her interests and feelings with her neighbor, that to speak of her individually would be to write the biography of one of the 'Siamese Twins.' Growing with her growth, and strengthened with her strength, she stands side by side with the Empire City in the march of improvement and rapid development, so characteristic of the American people. The idea of her absorption by her more gigantic sister is by no means an improbable one; indeed, while I write, the subject is being debated in the legislative halls of the State. . . . Whether this result is immediate or not, such is her manifest destiny. . . . The engravings herewith give but a limited view of the extent of the water-front. The Fulton Ferry is the busiest; here, too, is a small glimpse of the busy scene with its multitude of crafts of all shapes and sizes from the packet ship of vast proportions to the scow with its load of mud to be emptied into the sea. Fulton Street near the ferry, is the principal avenue of the city, and is a steep, crooked street extending across the city. The omnibuses have now been superseded by cars propelled by horse-power which run in all directions to distant points, from Greenwood on the south to Green Point on the north."

From *Ballou's Pictorial Drawing-Room Companion,* June 6, 1857.

From the top of the bridge piers, an unsurpassed panorama of New York's harbor, with hundreds of clippers and schooners, the ferries and Boston boat in full view . . .

Look'd toward the lower bay to notice the vessels arriving,
Saw their approach, saw aboard those that were near me,
Saw the white sails of schooners and sloops, saw the ships at anchor,
The sailors at work in the rigging or outside the spars,
The round masts, the swinging motion of the hulls, the slender serpentine pennants,
The large and small steamers in motion, the pilots in their pilot-houses,
The white wake left by the passage, the quick tremulous whirl of the wheels,
The flags of all nations, the falling of them at sunset . . .

From "Crossing Brooklyn Ferry," by Walt Whitman.

Engraved from a drawing by C. E. H. Bonwill, *Harper's Weekly*, November 1, 187

NEW YORK HARBOR, AS SEEN FROM THE BROOKLYN TOWER OF THE SUSPENSION-BRIDGE

... as workers slowly spun the spidery cables and catwalks, risking perils from the dizzy height some several hundred feet above the East River.

From *Harper's Weekly,* April 14, 1877.

FROM TOWER TO TOWER—THE SUSPENSION-BRIDGE OVER THE EAST RIVER—VIEW FROM THE BROOKLYN TOWER

"At the end of the Civil War, a German-born engineer named John August Roebling, who had grown up in a walled town amid the Gothic churches where Bach had worked a century before, designed a suspension bridge to connect the cities of New York and Brooklyn. It was to be the most ambitious bridge in the world—sixteen hundred feet across, three hundred feet and more from the center of the bridge to the river below. The cablework was to be strung across two stone towers and anchored at both sides by a unique system of supports embedded in stone. It was to have five lanes, with a central passageway for walkers as well as roadways for carriages and electric railways. 'This elevated promenade,' Roebling wrote in his prospectus, 'will allow people of leisure and old and young to stroll over the bridge on fine days. I need not state that in a crowded commercial city such a promenade will be of incalculable value.'

... 'The Great East River Bridge,' as it was called then, was to be his masterpiece. Suddenly, in 1869, while making a preliminary survey for the Brooklyn tower, he had an accident and died soon after from lockjaw. He never saw his bridge. But when it was finally completed in 1883 by his son, Washington, it was faithful to the original design and to John Roebling's prophecy. When the design was made, he had said, 'The Bridge will be beautiful.' "

From "Brooklyn Bridge," by Alfred Kazin,
in *Harper's Bazaar,* 1946.

As new engineering techniques had to be developed in mastering the bridge spanning, little day-to-day progress seemed evident...

"Brooklyn Bridge is beautiful—as a complex piece of machinery, as a work of architecture, and as the symbol and connecting tissue of the human history around it. It is a perfect reflection of the mind of its designer and of the world in which he planned it. John Roebling's childhood saturation in Gothic is forever recalled in the port of New York, where two open-stone towers stand in the river like cathedral doors, opening the way to the bay on one side and to the river on the other. It also reflects John Roebling's extraordinary ability to adapt his massive suspension bridge to the esthetic and religious images of his childhood. As a bridge-builder his mind was all on the problems of stresses and strains, masonry and cables. He had to devise that intricate union of materials, from wire and steel ropes to wood and rock, that would give support and provide the tension necessary to a bridge in the railroad age. As an architect he worked on the memory of walled towns, early and massive stone. But architect and bridge-builder could never be separated in the same mind. The problems of support became the problems of form."

From "Brooklyn Bridge," by Alfred Kazin, in *Harper's Bazaar*, 1946.

Engraved from a drawing by Schell and Hogan, *Harper's Weekly*, March 31, 187

A PROMENADE IN MID-AIR— THE BROOKLYN ASCENT TO THE BRIDGE TOWER

... but finally, after thirteen long years under construction, the bridge opening thrilled New Yorkers as thousands crossed afoot, in carriages, or in trolleys.

From *Harper's Weekly,* May 26, 1883.

THE NEW YORK AND BROOKLYN SUSPENSION-BRIDGE—THE APPROACH ON THE NEW YORK SIDE

"A bridge connects New York and Brooklyn, overhanging an arm of the sea. Seen even from afar, this bridge astounds you like one of those architectural nightmares given by Piranesi in his weird etchings. You see great ships passing beneath it, and this indisputable evidence of its height confuses the mind. But walk over it. Feel the quivering of the monstrous trellis of iron and steel interwoven for a length of sixteen hundred feet at a height of one hundred and thirty-five feet above the water; see the trains that pass over it in both directions, and the steamboats passing beneath your very body, while carriages come and go, and foot passengers hasten along, an eager crowd, and you feel that the engineer is the great artist of our epoch, and you will own that these people have a right to plume themselves on their audacity, on the *go-ahead* which has never flinched.

"At the same time you ask yourself what right they have to call themselves, as a people, young. They are recent, their advent is so astonishingly new that one can hardly believe in dates in the face of these prodigies of activity. But recent as is this civilization, it is evidently *mature,* at least here. The impression upon me this evening is that I have been exploring a city which is an achievement and not a beginning. Its life is not an experiment; it is a mode of existence, with its inconveniences as well as its splendors."

From *Outre-Mer: Impressions of America,* by Paul Bourget, 1895.

It was a great day for New York when President Arthur and a host of notables celebrated the opening of Brooklyn Bridge...

Opening day, May 24, 1883, was marked by elaborate ceremonies to which the city's and nation's notables were invited. President Arthur and a large party officiated; the police were on hand to hold back the milling crowd eager for a glimpse of this "eighth wonder of the world." The police cordon was vigorous and effective as thousands were unceremoniously pushed back by the butt of nightsticks. Six days later, on Decoration Day, the bridge was jammed with holiday crowds and a bad snarl ensued. An accident occurred on the short flight of steps leading to the footpath. People panicked and were trampled upon. The panic cost twelve lives and many injuries, a tragedy that marred the festive occasion. Another unexpected by-product resulted in many people seeking a road to notoriety or suicide by jumping from the dizzy heights of the bridge spans. One who managed to survive and find his way to fame was Steve Brodie, a newsboy who became a stellar attraction at a Bowery museum, following which he opened a saloon nearby.

Engraved from a drawing by Schell and Hogan, *Harper's Weekly*, June 2, 1

THE GREAT BRIDGE—PRESIDENT ARTHUR AND HIS PARTY CROSSING THE SUSPENDED HIGHWAY

... but only six days later tragedy struck as crowds crossing the bridge panicked, and a dozen people were trampled to death.

"The Brooklyn Bridge was both a fulfillment and prophecy. In the use of steel in tension it disclosed a great range of new possibilities: for the great mission of steel as a building material is essentially to span and enclose space, and to remove the inconvenient bulkiness of bearing walls and stone columns. In its absence of ornament, its refusal to permit the steel to be other than its own unadorned reality, the Brooklyn Bridge pointed to the logic and aesthetics of the machine; and it did this far more rigorously than its later rival, the Eiffel Tower in Paris, with its early Art Nouveau treatment of the base. Finally, the bridge existed in its own right, independent of its influences and potentialities, as a work of art, a delight to the artist and the poet, but equally well appreciated by the man in the street."

"In 1883, the battle was over. The bridge was opened, and the Brooklyn Bridge took its place with the Eads Bridge in St. Louis and the Pont Garabit in France as one of the victories of modern engineering. But it was more than that. If anyone doubts that a bridge is an aesthetic object, if anyone doubts that it reveals personality, let him compare the Brooklyn Bridge with the other suspension bridges on the same river. The first bridge is in every sense classic. Like every positive creative work, the Brooklyn Bridge eludes analysis, in that its effect is disproportionate to the visible means, and it triumphs over one's objections even when it falls short of its highest possibilities."

From *The Brown Decades*, by Lewis Mumford, 1931.

From *Scientific American*, May 26, 1883.

1. CARRIAGEWAY, RAILWAY, AND PROMENADE 2. STAIRWAY AROUND TOWER
3. BROOKLYN APPROACH, LOOKING TOWARD NEW YORK
BROOKLYN ENTRANCE, RAILWAY STATION, AND BOILER HOUSE 5. NEW YORK ENTRANCE AND RAILWAY STATION

OPENING OF THE GREAT SUSPENSION BRIDGE BETWEEN NEW YORK AND BROOKLYN

The bridge spanning water that had separated the two neighboring cities not only accelerated population growth outward from crowded New York...

"The bridge itself was a testimony to the swift progress of physical science. The strong lines of the bridge, and the beautiful curve described by its suspended cables, were derived from an elegant formula in mathematical physics—the elastic curve. If the architectural elements of the massive piers have perhaps too much the bare quality of engineering, if the pointed arches meet esthetic betrayal in the flat solidity of the cornices, if, in short, the masonry does not sing as Richardson alone perhaps could have made it sing, the steel work itself makes up for this, by the architectural beauty of its pattern; so that beyond any other aspect of New York, I think, the Brooklyn Bridge has been a source of joy and inspiration to the artist. In the later bridges the spanning members are sturdier and the supporting piers and cables are lighter and less essential; and they suffer esthetically by the very ease of their triumph over the difficulties of engineering. All that the age had just cause for pride in—its advances in science, its skill in handling iron, its personal heroism in the face of dangerous industrial processes, its willingness to attempt the untried and the impossible—came to a head in the Brooklyn Bridge. What was grotesque and barbarous in industrialism was sloughed off in the great bridges. These avenues of communication are, paradoxically, the only enduring monuments that witness a period of uneasy industrial transition; and to this day they communicate a feeling of dignity, stability, and unwavering poise."

From *Sticks and Stones,* by Lewis Mumford, 1924.

THE NEW YORK AND BROOKLYN SUSPENSION BRIDGE, FROM THE BROOKLYN SIDE

... its majesty became a living symbol of technical achievement and an inspiration to all, a triumphant mark of pride in progress.

93

Engraved by Charles Graham from original sketches and from a photograph by Gubelman, *Harper's Weekly Supplement*, May 26, 1883.

O harp and altar of the fury
    fused,
(How could mere toil align thy
    choiring strings!)
Terrific threshold of the
    prophet's pledge,
Prayer of pariah, and the
    lover's cry . . .

                Hart Crane

The nuptial knot at last is
    firmly tied;
A hundred bells ring out a
    merry chime,
A hundred wires proclaim to
    every clime—
Manhattan takes fair Brooklyn
    as its bride.

                Wallace Bruce

The bridge whose wing-like
    sweep
Like space and joy and ecstacy
Was mixed like music in his
    blood,
Would beat like flight and joy
    and triumph,
Through the conduits of his life
    forever.

                Thomas Wolfe

Painted, photographed, etched, and drawn from every angle,
the bridge was adopted by all in the arts,
poet and painter alike...

It is not surprising that the bridge, so monumental in scope with its breathtaking spans and spidery cables, massive Gothic-arched piers and overall grandeur, should inspire artists and photographers to record its beauty. Every phase of its construction was reported in the illustrated weeklies and well documented by contemporary artists. Countless lithographs and prints were issued and bought by a hungry public. Currier and Ives, experts in promoting events of the day, anticipated the bridge's completion with a view showing the finished structure in 1876, seven years before opening day. The engraving herewith, made in 1882 by Horace Baker, Jr., from an original watercolor by F. Hopkinson Smith, antedated the bridge's completion by over a year. "Hop" Smith was a noted artist and author, in addition to being an engineer by training. He was well known for the design of lighthouses and was responsible for the masonry plan and pedestal of Bartholdi's Statue of Liberty.

Engraved from a painting by F. Hopkinson Smith, *Harper's Weekly*, February 18, 1882

"UNDER THE TOWERS"—FROM THE WATER-COLOR PAINTING BY F. HOPKINSON SMITH "for in New York . . . there is always felt that deep inner longing to integrate, to complete the process sundered by the waters," as Alfred Kazin has noted.

Engraved by J. Clement from a painting by J. H. Twachtman

BELOW THE BROOKLYN BRIDGE—FROM A PAINTING BY J. H. TWACHTMAN

"All bridges, if they are well built, have their own beauty. They recall the passageway that is perhaps the most enduring symbol of life. They speak of the journey across, and they mark the limits within which we must live. At the same time they are something given to us by others, on which we cross. For we never cross entirely naked and alone, and we always rest on some base of human ingenuity provided by others. There is this in Brooklyn Bridge, and something more: the many tangible lives of New York which it projects and unites. For in New York, a series of islands pressing against the mainland, there is always felt that deep inner longing to integrate, to complete the process sundered by the waters and islands that nowhere else does the whole of New York seem so near and full."

From "Brooklyn Bridge," by Alfred Kazin, in *Harper's Bazaar*, 1946.

The northern extremities of Manhattan bordering on the
Harlem River presented a peaceful and bucolic scene as
if in a distant countryside setting . . .

The High Bridge over the Harlem River, completed in 1851, was erected to carry water from the Croton Aqueduct across to Harlem and then down to the city proper. It was a magnificent arcaded structure, built at a cost of one million dollars. Its height above high water mark was 114 feet, and it was 1,450 feet from the Harlem side into the neighboring West Farms area.

"The view along the Harlem River near the bridge, is one of the most pleasing in the State of New York, where Nature has been most generous in spreading its rich profusion. This spot, shown in the accompanying engraving, is enhanced by the romantic scenery in the vicinity. Nowhere else in the close proximity of New York is there comparable quiet serenity and bucolic beauty. The calm aspect of this river valley makes it an ideal resort for the lover of retired meditation—for one who seeks a pleasing retreat for the while from the stirring strife, the toilsome occupations and corroding cares of the city."

From *Gleason's Pictorial Drawing-Room Companion*, September 23, 1854.

From *Gleason's Pictorial Drawing-Room Companion*, September 23, 1854

VIEW ON HARLEM RIVER, NEAR HIGH BRIDGE, NEW YORK

... while across the waters in West Farms and Westchester New Yorkers vacationed when they wished to avoid the turmoil of New York.

97

Engraved from sketches by Schell and Hogan, *Harper's Weekly,* November 22, 1873.

ANNEXED TO NEW YORK—SCENES IN WESTCHESTER COUNTY

"In 1856 the suburbs of the city still retained many of their rare attractions. Harlem was a quiet country town, shut off by a long ride or sail from its ruling center; there was yet no city beyond the Harlem River— only country-seats, and scenery of rare beauty."

From *The Memorial History of the City of New York,* 1892.

". . . Commodious steamers now convey passengers every hour of the summer days through the whole length of the Harlem River, from Harlem via the High Bridge to the immediate vicinity of King's Bridge, taking them at once from the cars of the Third Avenue Railway or the Peck Slip steamers, by which they arrive from the lower parts of the town; the whole trip by both boats, or car and boat, costing them but ten or twelve cents each way. Thousands daily avail themselves of these precious facilities for escape from the hot and dusty city to the pure air and sunshine of the country, filling the cool and shady woods all around with happy groups of ruralizers, and the waters with merry voyagers. The elevated grounds of this part of the island are called Washington Heights, and upon the crown, just above the Dam, lies the village of Carmansville. . . . The Spuyten Duyvil is a little stream: the prettily-wooded points here, the rocky shores there, and the vistas ending in villa or castle-crowned heights, revealed at every unexpected turn. The origin of the eccentric name of this capricious little river, meaning 'in spite of the devil,' is authentically determined by the veracious Diedrick Knickerbocker in his story."

From *New York Circumnavigated,* by T. Addison Richards, 1861.

98

The many bridges spanning a short distance along the banks of the Harlem gave evidence of the population thrust into the Bronx and nearby Westchester...

The relentless northward thrust of the city's growth can best be told as newer bridges were needed to span the Harlem River from New York's upper regions across into the Bronx. The bridges are a mixture of vehicular traffic crossings and the High Bridge to accommodate the Croton water supply. Looking north, we see in the far reaches the Jersey shore of the distant Hudson and the cliffs of the Palisades. Uppermost in our picture, where the Harlem runs into the Spuyten Duyvil, numbered 1, is the railroad bridge of the Hudson River R.R. King's Bridge is numbered 2, and 3 is called the Farmers' Bridge. The High Bridge, with stone masonry arches, is numbered 4. Number 5 is called the Sixth Avenue Railroad Bridge. McComb's Dam Bridge is number 6. The stone piers in the river, numbered 7, shows the Madison Avenue Bridge, under construction. Number 8 is the Harlem River Railroad Bridge, and number 9 is the Harlem Bridge. In the immediate foreground, number 10, is the Suburban Rapid Transit and Foot Bridge as it will appear when it is completed, in 1883.

From *Harper's Weekly*, November 18, 1882

BRIDGES OVER HARLEM RIVER

1. HUDSON RIVER RAILROAD BRIDGE 2. KING'S BRIDGE 3. FARMERS' BRIDGE 4. HIGH BRIDGE 5. SIXTH AVENU[E] RAILROAD BRIDGE 6. McCOMB'S DAM BRIDGE 7. MADISON AVENUE BRIDGE 8. HARLEM RIVER RAILROA[D] BRIDGE 9. HARLEM BRIDGE 10. SUBURBAN RAPID TRANSIT AND FOOT BRIDGE AS IT WILL APPEAR WHEN CO[M]PLETED

... while the joys of boating and sailing on the river's tranquil waters delighted week-enders from the city's rapidly filling streets and boulevards.

Engraved from a drawing by C. A. Keetels, *Harper's Weekly*, June 28, 1879.

SATURDAY AFTERNOON ON THE HARLEM RIVER

The Harlem River, of the many waters surrounding Manhattan Island, was the only body narrow and tranquil enough to permit rowers and small sailboats as enjoyable weekend pastimes. For a stretch of several miles, extending from the stormy Hell Gate waters northward to Spuyten Duyvil, the waters of the Harlem offered New Yorkers the advantages of an inland lake. Several boathouses dotted the shores, and in the summertime skullers and crew races were much in evidence. Small yachts and sailboats could be seen, especially at race time. Because the large Sound steamers turned off at Hell Gate for entrance to the Long Island Sound, and tugs and barges were few, the Harlem River became a rendezvous for boating enthusiasts because it was so pleasant, so convenient, and so easy to reach. On land, one could travel to Harlem points on the Third Avenue Railway. Or, coming by boat, one could take the speedy Harlem boats from Peck Slip to the pier at 130th Street, a general debarkation point for the Harlem valley.

Excursion trips of an hour or so were a popular means of getting to places, rather than by slow surface horsecars the entire length of Manhattan . . .

"No city in the world is more favorably situated than New York for holiday excursions by land and water. Coney Island, Rockaway, Long Branch, dozens of places up the river, on both shores of the sound, and down the bay, tempt people into the open air with their varied attractions. Some of these excursions require the greater part of the day, or an afternoon and evening, for their complete enjoyment; others but two or three hours. Nothing can be pleasanter, for those who have only a short time at their disposal, than an afternoon trip to High Bridge, where the scenery is delightful, and where one can enjoy the sight of the great structure over which rushes the supply of water for New York. Take a walk over the high banks, or sit on shaded benches to watch the rowers on Harlem River. The end comes all too soon. The cry of All Aboard! startles the most lazily inclined, and then comes a rush like the one depicted by our artist. But the day has been pleasant, and the excursionists return to their city homes refreshed and invigorated by their healthful outing."

From *Harper's Weekly*, July 24, 1880.

Engraved from a drawing by William A. Rogers, *Harper's Weekly*, July 24, 1880

AT HIGH BRIDGE, HARLEM RIVER—"ALL ABOARD!"

... and the ride up to High Bridge, on the Harlem River, proved a delightful destination for a day's ride or a weekend outing.

High above the Harlem River was a popular promenade built over the conduits carrying the Croton waters across to Manhattan. Completed in 1842, and celebrated by massive parades and displays, the aqueduct system, for the first time, provided New Yorkers with an adequate supply of fresh water. High Bridge was a part of this overall system, and the bridge designers, with good forethought, utilized the broad avenue of space as a boon for residents and visitors to the neighborhood. Below, on the river, may be seen one of the Harlem steamers which brought Gothamites from lower Manhattan. This line of handsome white boats carried the names *Sylvan Stream, Sylvan Glen, Sylvan Dell,* and *Sylvan Grove.* They made the trip from Peck Slip in the East River to 130th Street, a most delightful journey of about an hour up along Manhattan's Jones' Wood, past Blackwell's Island, Ravenswood, and Astoria on the Long Island side, through the boiling waters of Hell Gate to the dock at 130th Street. There one could transfer for points along the Harlem River by the smaller steamers, the *Emily* and the *Tiger Lily.* From a nearby dock below the bridge, many passengers left the boat and took the pleasant path through the woods, climbing almost 150 feet to reach the promenade, and then across High Bridge to the Washington Heights area.

Engraved from a drawing by Charles Graham, *Harper's Weekly,* August 22, 1885.

HIGH BRIDGE ON SUNDAY

More than ten years before its completion, the advance publicity and press releases about the Statue of Liberty appeared in the newspapers...

On October 26, 1886, more than a decade after the Centennial it was supposed to celebrate, the Statue of Liberty was officially dedicated as a symbol of Franco-American relations. Before an assemblage of distinguished citizens of both nations headed by President Grover Cleveland, elaborate ceremonies marked the opening day. The original idea for the statue was credited to M. Laboulaye, a friend of the sculptor F. A. Bartholdi, a native of Colmar, in Alsace. Within a close circle of friends the plan was privately formulated in 1870, with funds to be raised by popular subscription as a gesture of goodwill. Various fund-raising festivals were held, and moneys slowly dribbled in. The arduous process of building models was commenced; Bartholdi was obsessed with creating for himself this crowning achievement. By 1876, the first portion of the statue was shipped to the United States. The huge hand holding the torch of Liberty was displayed at the Centennial in Philadelphia, where crowds climbed the inner stairway to reach the rim above. This was a most popular observation point from which to view the entire fairgrounds. Later, the torch was removed and erected in Madison Square where it remained for many years awaiting the arrival of the main statue, in 1885. The dimensions of the . . .

From *Harper's Weekly*, November 27, 1875.

PROJECTED STATUE OF LIBERTY FOR NEW YORK HARBOR

... as graphic illustrators and print makers pictured the goddess in New York harbor, beckoning to all a proud welcome to these shores.

103

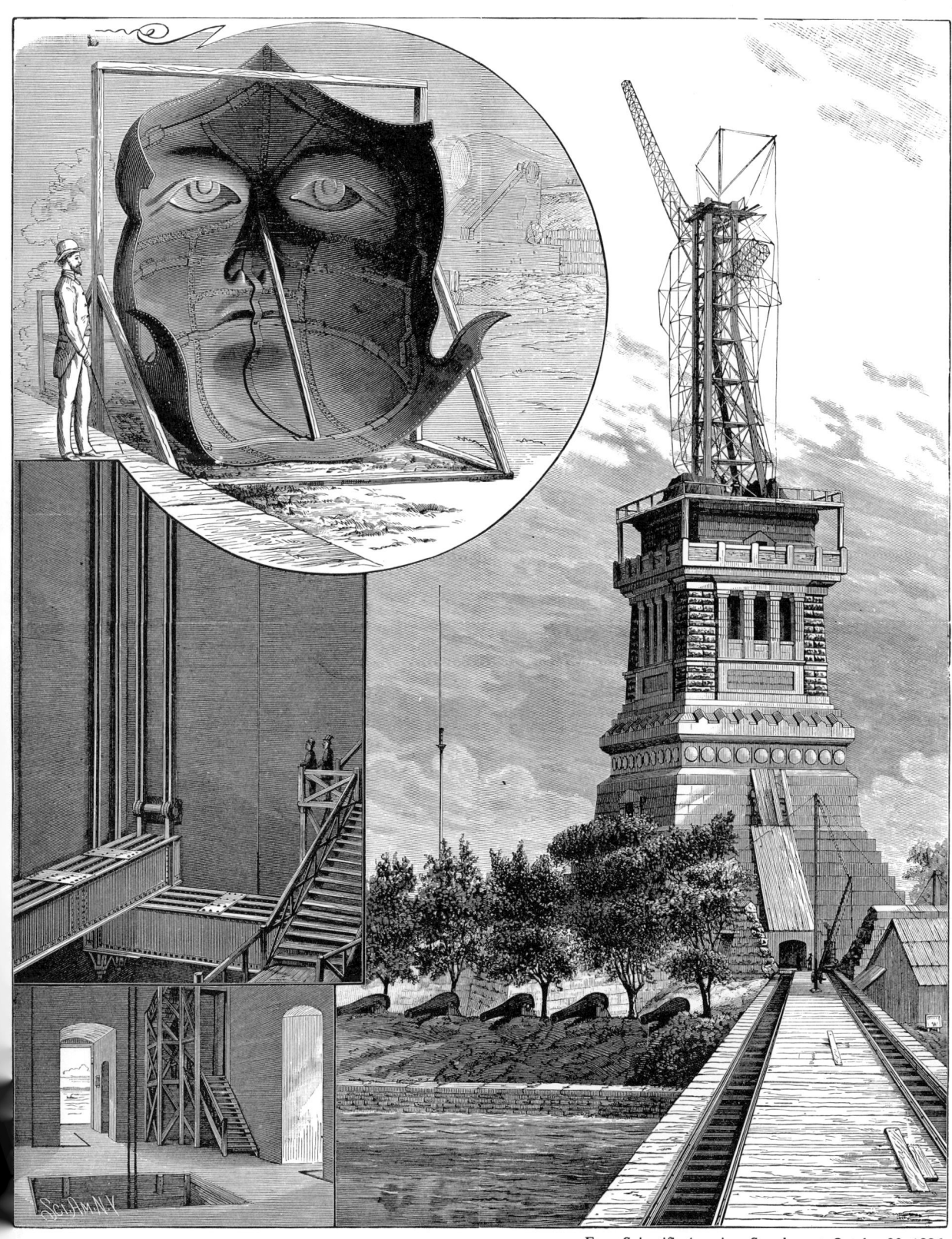

... monument were staggering at that time: height of the figure alone, 151 feet, much taller than the fabled Colossus of Rhodes or that of Nero by Zenodore. Including the masonry base, the uppermost tip of the torch rose 301 feet above sea level. Now, with the statue's completion just three years before the opening of the Brooklyn Bridge, New York could boast of its twin glories, marvels of modern engineering.

In the early projection (opposite) the proposed statue and its relation to distant Manhattan Island, the artist has taken the liberty of positioning his subject out into mid-harbor and facing it due south for the best pictorial composition. Actually, Bedloe's Island and its giant lie somewhat to the west. Note, also, that the design for the pedestal, as finally built, is quite different from earlier plans. Funds for its completion resulted from active solicitation to raise the sum of $100,000. Through the energetic campaign conducted by the *New York World,* spurred on by the personal efforts of its publisher, Joseph Pulitzer, the money was raised from contributions averaging under one dollar each. The engraving herewith appeared almost eleven years before opening festivities, and was part of the long-sustained interest that focused on this event.

From *Scientific American Supplement,* October 23, 1886.

THE STATUE OF LIBERTY—VIEWS SHOWING THE METHOD OF ERECTION

The arm and torch of Miss Liberty "enlightening the world," sent on well in advance to be seen at the Centennial, was displayed in Madison Square for many years.

At the entrance to the statue's pedestal, for all visitors to read, is the tablet on which are carved those immortal lines written by Emma Lazarus (1849–87):

Not like the brazen giant of Greek fame
With conquering limbs astride from land to land
Here at our sea-washed, sunset gates shall stand
A mighty woman with a torch, whose flame
Is the imprisoned lightning, and her name
Mother of Exiles. From her beacon hand
Glows world-wide welcome; her mild eyes command
The air-bridged harbor that twin cities frame.
"Keep, ancient lands, your storied pomp!" cries she
With silent lips. "Give me your tired, your poor,
Your huddled masses yearning to breathe free,
The wretched refuse of your teeming shore.
Send these, the homeless, tempest-tossed to me.
I lift my lamp beside the golden door."

Emma Lazarus

From *Frank Leslie's Illustrated Newspaper*, June 20, 1885.

NEW YORK—THE TORCH OF THE STATUE OF "LIBERTY,"
AS IT WILL APPEAR WHEN COMPLETED, ON BEDLOE'S ISLAND

Finally, on October 28, 1886, the statue was unveiled.
A decade after the Centennial of our Independence,
tumultuous crowds hailed the event from land and sea.

From *Frank Leslie's Illustrated Newspaper*, November 6, 1886.

NEW YORK—THE UNVEILING OF THE BARTHOLDI STATUE OF LIBERTY, OCTOBER 28th—PRESIDENT CLEVELAND
SSING THROUGH THE FLEET OF ASSEMBLED VESSELS IN THE LAUNCH "VIXEN" ON HIS WAY TO BEDLOE'S ISLAND.

"Last Thursday was a great day for New York, and a proud and happy one for M. Auguste Bartholdi. The artist-enthusiast's dream of twenty years was at last fulfilled, and he saw his statue of 'liberty Enlightening the World,' the mightiest of colossi, standing for the grandest idea ever symbolized by the sculptor's art, dedicated amidst the rejoicings of the two great Republics. M. Bartholdi, since his arrival on Monday morning, had been made lion of the day. He bore his honors with grace and modesty. As he said in response to Mayor Grace, when the latter presented him with the freedom of the city, 'I know just enough of your language to express to you the feelings of gratitude that I entertain.' The sculptor's wife accompanies him. Among the distinguished Frenchmen who came with him to assist at the unveiling ceremonies is Count Ferdinand de Lesseps, builder of the Suez Canal, and many others of note in his party."

From *Frank Leslie's Illustrated Newspaper*, November 6, 1886.

President Cleveland, on board the U.S.S. *Despatch,* headed the American delegation. Many ships of the navy thundered a twenty-one-gun salute. But heavy fog hung over the water's surface. An armada of almost three hundred yachts and steamers groped their way toward Bedloe's Island where 2,500 elite guests were seated about the base of the new statue, as a light rain fell.

Coney Island, once discovered as a watering place by the masses, became a favorite resort, though to reach it one had to make the long trolley trip through Brooklyn.

Coney Island's fame as a watering place "for the masses" really dates from the 1860s, although not until a decade later did concessions and amusements appear on the scene. Earliest mention of Coney Island may be traced back more than two full centuries before. A land-sale deal was made between the Canarsie Indians and the Dutch West India Company, the same charter group who had negotiated for the original purchase of Manhattan Island in 1626, for a mere twenty-four dollars in trade goods. The Coney Island deal, dated May 7, 1654, conveyed a certain "Neck of Land" and an "island called Conyne," both located at Gravesend, for "15 fathoms of sewan [wampum], two guns and three pounds of powder." In comparison with the price paid for Manhattan, and the relative area involved, this makes Coney Island a much more expensive land transaction. The Indians called the neck of land Manahamung (it was all marsh and meadow at the time) and the other plot of land to the west Narriohk, meaning "the island." An early visitor to these shores was Walt Whitman, who rhapsodized about "the long, bare, unfrequented shore, which I had all to myself, and where I loved, after bathing, to race up and down the hard sand, and declaim Homer or Shakespeare to the surf and seagulls by the hour."

Engraved from a drawing by Ben Day, Jr., *Harper's Weekly*, August 17, 1867.

THE BEACH AT CONEY ISLAND

Later on, when regular sailings by steamboat brought all beaches within easier reach, Brighton and Manhattan beaches developed, as hotels and amusements were added.

From *Frank Leslie's Illustrated Newspaper,* August 12, 1882.

NEW YORK—A SCENE AT BRIGHTON BEACH, THE NEW AND POPULAR SEASIDE RESORT

"Coney Island, the American Brighton, grew in popularity as the city increased in size and congestion in the seventies. On a hot Sunday, half a million people (making a 'carpet of heads') might crowd its wide stretch of sand in a few hours, a traveler of 1887 reported in the London *Times*. 'They spread over the four miles of sand strip, with . . . bands of music . . . in full blast; countless vehicles moving; all the miniature theatres, minstrel shows, merry-go-rounds, Punch and Judy enterprises, fat women, big snakes, giant, dwarf, and midget exhibits, circuses and menageries, swings, flying horses, and fortune telling shops open; and everywhere a dense but good-humored crowd, sightseeing, drinking beer, and swallowing "clam chowder."' Fireworks enlivened the scene at night until time to go home, when 'the swelling torrents of humanity,' flowing out upon station and pier, emphasized the 'vast magnitude of a Coney Island Sunday.' While the 'masses' frequented Coney Island, the 'classes,' in this city of increasing contrast, spent a more extended 'season' at such resorts for the wealthy as Long Branch, New Jersey, and Newport, Rhode Island."

From *Mirror for Gotham,* by Bayrd Still, 1956.

The new iron pier at West Brighton now enabled the steamboats to dock, as thousands came ashore to enjoy the delights of bathing and the amusement areas...

Such was the growing popularity of Coney Island that it became necessary to schedule regular sailings from downtown Manhattan to reach the beaches of Coney and West Brighton. The new Iron Pier extended out into deep water, and was several hundred feet long. Now, the Iron Steamboat Line could disgorge its weekend crowds as they poured in by the thousands. "For one end of Coney Island had been transformed into the most pretentious of Atlantic watering places, and the other end had been made into a popular amusement park. You could go down to Coney by railroad, from Brooklyn, or take a steamboat at the Battery and sail down the harbor. Prosperous New Yorkers who formerly sent their families, for the summer, to Long Branch and joined them only over week-ends, were now able to have their nights at the shore and return to the city, every day, refreshed for business. The splendid new resort had been brought within an hour's journey of New York. Manhattan Beach, at the far eastern end of the Island, was the most exclusive and expensive section of the resort. Two enormous, ornate wooden hotels—the Manhattan Beach and the Oriental—had broad piazzas that looked, over lawns and flowerbeds, to the beach and the sea. . . ."

From *Incredible New York*, by Lloyd Morris, 1951.

Engraved from a drawing by Charles Graham, *Harper's Weekly,* August 9, 1879.

THE NEW IRON PIER AT WEST BRIGHTON BEACH, CONEY ISLAND

... until midnight, when whistles shrieked announcing the departure of the last boat for Manhattan as many rushed to get aboard.

"West of Manhattan Beach lay Brighton Beach, another resort with a great hotel and bathing pavilion. Brighton Beach attracted the sporting crowd drawn to the races at the Sheepshead Bay track, sponsored by the Coney Island Jockey Club, organized by a group of millionaires that included August Belmont and James R. Keene, the California plunger. Beyond Brighton Beach to the west, Coney Island proper offered its very different enticements to a plebian public. Sea-food restaurants and saloons, variety shows, shooting galleries, bathing pavilions, an iron pier and band concerts delighted thousands who left the heat of New York for a day or evening at the shore. Day and night the sands were crowded with bathers, and the noise of the great amusement park seemed never to cease. . . . The amusement park at Coney Island was, in its breezy way, a summer equivalent of the urban Tenderloin."

From *Incredible New York,* by Lloyd Morris, 1951.

It was difficult to break away from the entertainment that Coney had to offer. The last boat for New York left about midnight, and it was always jam-packed with last-minute revelers who tried to squeeze in every ounce of the divertisements offered before sailing back to the hot city.

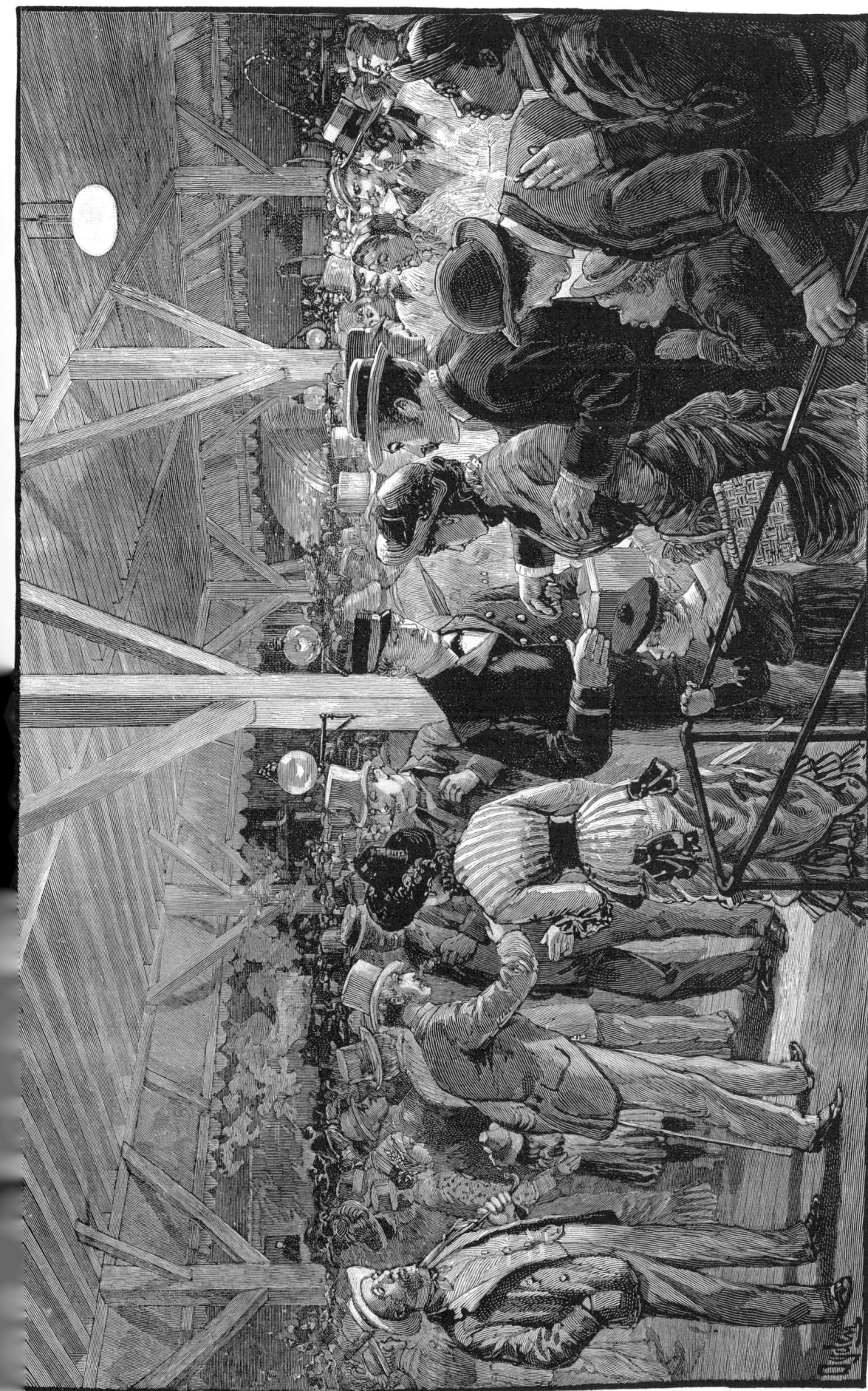

Engraved from a drawing by H. A. Ogden, *Harper's Weekly,* July 29, 1882.

ON THE IRON PIER, CONEY ISLAND—THE RUSH FOR THE LAST BOAT

The popular beaches soon became the summertime mecca of New York's vacationers eager to get away from the city's hot streets if only for a few hours . . .

"Despite its advance in the scale of grandeur, the early Coney Island was a far more fascinating resort than it has ever been since. It had been a real beach for most of its length, only partly obscured by 'concessions.' The principal ways of approaching the island were by the Iron Steamboat Company and by steam-cars from Bay Ridge. Tickets to Coney Island were sold on the Manhattan 'L' stations for the Bay Ridge Lines. The terminal of one of these, the 'Sea Beach,' at Coney Island, was an exhibition building from the Philadelphia Centennial, which continued as a kind of miniature fair, containing glass blowers, crayon artists, astrologers, quack doctors etc. besides a bewildering variety of catch-penny machines, from model locomotives to the recently introduced phonograph.

The island itself was a picturesque congeries of shanties, pavilions, clapboard hotels, fishing huts, bath-houses, etc. mostly assembled in what was known as the West End. The outstanding features were the old and new Iron Piers; the Observatory, a tall iron tower near the piers; and the great wooden elephant hotel, a caravansary built to resemble that eccentric beast. This was . . .

SCENES AND INCIDENTS ON CONEY ISLAND

... where every American quick-lunch snack from hot dogs to hamburgers and popcorn and saltwater taffy first saw the light of day.

111

Engraved from drawings by William A. Rogers, *Harper's Weekly,* August 10, 1878.

... the most noted feature of the place, and 'seeing the elephant' passed into popular slang. Coney Island then abounded with fake sideshows, fortune tellers, soap-game swindlers, monte men, crooked roulette wheels, tin plate games, and every conceivable fraud ever invented. These games were pursued with brazen effrontery upon the open highways, and even boys in their teens were fleeced without mercy.... One of the delights of Coney Island bathing was the probability that one's clothes or valuables would be missing from one's bath-house on emerging from the water. They were extracted by hooks passed over the tops of partitions. In later times this was circumvented by a wire screen laid over the top of the rude compartment dignified by the name of bathroom.... The predecessor of the 'hot dog' at Coney Island was clam chowder. The qualities of this sustaining comestible varied from a mysterious compound sold for five cents and served on rude counters, to the very excellent article on the bill of fare of the Manhattan Beach Hotel.''

From *Valentine's Manual of Old New York,* edited by Henry Collins Brown, 1926.

Harper's noted illustrator Thure de Thulstrup pictured a well-dressed, sedate group of excursionists enjoying the sail, as a musical trio provided a pleasant concerto.

The iron steamboats that plied the pleasant course from Pier One at Battery Place, New York, to the Iron Pier at Coney Island was, in its heyday, one of the most memorable short sea journeys to be taken anywhere in the United States. Regular sailings started about 1880, just after the long iron landing pier had been completed. The popular hour's run continued well into the twenties, when the subways and the automobile brought Coney Island within easy reach of any section of Manhattan and Brooklyn. On Saturday and especially Sunday, during the height of the summer rush, the boats were so packed that safety measures had to be tightened and people held back for fear of overcrowding. But during weekdays, in the 1880s, a scene depicted here by Thure de Thulstrup, one of *Harper's Weekly*'s most capable illustrators, there is none of the rowdy, boisterous elements that occasioned the remark "Coney Island was an extension of the Bowery." The very sedate and proper gathering is being entertained by the three-piece group, including a harpist, while en route for the day's outing. Often passengers did not leave the boat, but preferred the enjoyment of a round-trip excursion of fresh air and the sea breezes.

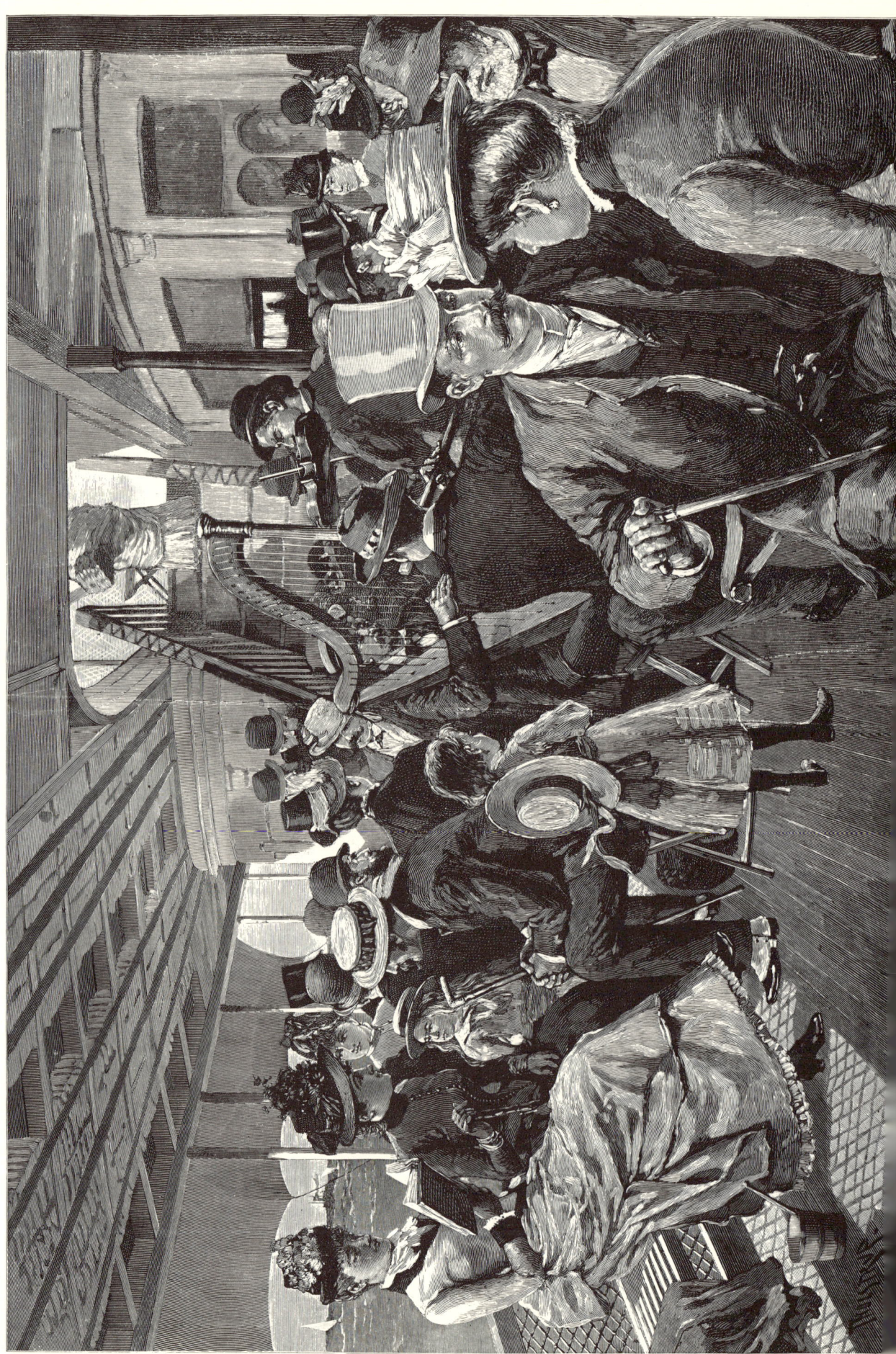

Engraved from a drawing by Thure de Thulstrup, *Harper's Weekly*, August 28, 1886.

ON THE WAY TO CONEY ISLAND

PART FIVE
Manhattan on the Move

From *Harper's Weekly*, December 5, 1885.

THE OLD BROADWAY STAGE IN 1831

"A 'continuous chain' of omnibuses crowded Broadway, creating such a 'crush of traffic' that a visitor of 1850 reported that 'you often have to wait ten minutes before you are able to cross the street.' Gone was the condescension with which British travelers had viewed Broadway a generation earlier. By the fifties they were willing to admit that London could not provide its equal. Not even the cluttered and dirty condition of many of the city's streets and pavements, which most of the foreign visitors continued to criticize, or the obstructing festoons of telegraph wires overhead checked their admiration for a city whose 'monster hotels,' handsome shops, and 'stately mansions' equaled, if not surpassed, Old World standards."

From *The Diary of George T. Strong*, 1851.

Manhattan on the Move

BECAUSE OF ITS peculiar geographical limitation—a long, narrow island with numerous north-south thoroughfares to bear the burden of traffic flowing from crowded downtown to outlying districts—Manhattan has always been faced with a chronic condition of congestion. As early as 1829, an English visitor talked about lower Broadway, "the boast of the city, an overcrowded, bustling street lined with shops and crammed with street traffic." By the 1850s, the dense traffic had reached a point of paralysis, or so it seemed at the time. Special police were dispatched to assist pedestrians trying to navigate the street crossing. Another attempt to solve the impossible problem resulted in the construction of Genin's footbridge near St. Paul's, but this, too, had its objectionable features and was demolished after only two years. There seemed no way for New Yorkers to enjoy that special bustle that became its trademark; they were resigned to it as Manhattan's way of life, a nightmare to many.

Since New York had become a city of inconvenient distances, its manifest destiny was to continue its northward growth. The problem of "rapid transit" was now a civic obsession. Complaints about horsecars and omnibuses were commonplace. Surface transportation had reached its limits when it took an average worker an hour or an hour and a half for a one-way trip to his place of business. Everyone acknowledged the city's outstanding need was for "some sure means of rapid transport between the upper and lower parts of the city." Planners, dreamers, inventors, and engineers were busy at their drawing boards. Plans poured in, some bordering on the fantastic. The Beach Pneumatic Tunnel, less than 350 feet long, was built under Broadway from Warren to Murray streets. Its capitalist backers claimed that with the strong blast of air from its giant blowing machines, some twenty thousand New Yorkers per hour could be blown, like a sailboat before the wind, on their way uptown. Many other rival schemes were proposed, but the strongly entrenched railroad interests fought every scheme that might rob them of their profitable franchises.

Since burrowing underground met objections from landowners who claimed that underpinning might result in the collapse of their buildings, there remained no other alternative but the elevated railway. But the elevated systems met with another set of arguments as each new proposal advanced furious protests from irate property owners. Shopkeepers and residents along the routes argued that the long "bridge," as it was called, would shut off the sunlight and plunge the streets into darkened canyons. People would be afraid to shop on the street below as the steam locomotives would spew hot cinders on them (which turned out to be true). They argued for horse-drawn trains, as these would be most sanitary!

But the transportation interests forged ahead and the "els" were built, radiating from the Battery northward along Sixth and Ninth avenues on the west, and Second and Third avenues on the east. The elevated traveled into the barren sections of Yorkville, Harlem, and Manhattanville. The trains drawn by steam locomotives rattled along at the astounding rate of thirty miles per hour, as engines belched sparks and black smoke, dropping ashes and cinders along the way. The explosive noise of trains caused horses to become frightened, and accounts of runaways and accidents were daily reported in the newspapers.

Dickering among the various promoters of the early elevated systems was sparked by charges of graft and corruption at every stage, from the granting of franchises, rights of way, construction contracts, and maintenance. The original, experimental track built by Charles Harvey up Greenwich Street was extended into the New York Elevated Railroad. Then came the Gilbert Elevated, followed by the Metropolitan line, organized by Cyrus Field, of Atlantic cable fame. As one franchise after another was given to powerful interests, the hue and cry against private controls became vociferous. It was claimed that the city was being exploited by political factions. As defeated rivals went to court to sustain their positions, it was finally declared that the city had no right to award franchises privately. Momentarily, the "big interests" were halted and the railroad lobby moved to Albany. Agitation for public ownership continued, resulting in a huge mass meeting at Cooper Union in support of the Opdyke Bill to permit the city to build and operate its own rapid transit system. Out of this protest meeting, there emerged real leadership in the person of Abram S. Hewitt, who was elected mayor in 1887, and thus became the real father of the city's modern transit.

The system of els running longitudinally was supplemented by the many horsecar lines, some below the els and others on the transverse streets and the more important crosstown avenues. The important railroad connection with northern areas had its depot at Fourth Avenue and Twenty-sixth Street. A new main station called Grand Central Depot had been built by Commodore Vanderbilt to replace the old one.

The pedestrian bridge over Broadway took fourteen years of controversy before it was finally erected, and then only two years before demolition.

Engraved by J. W. Orr, *Gleason's Pictorial Drawing-Room Companion,* December 25, 1852.

GENIN'S NEW AND NOVEL BRIDGE, EXTENDING ACROSS BROADWAY, NEW YORK

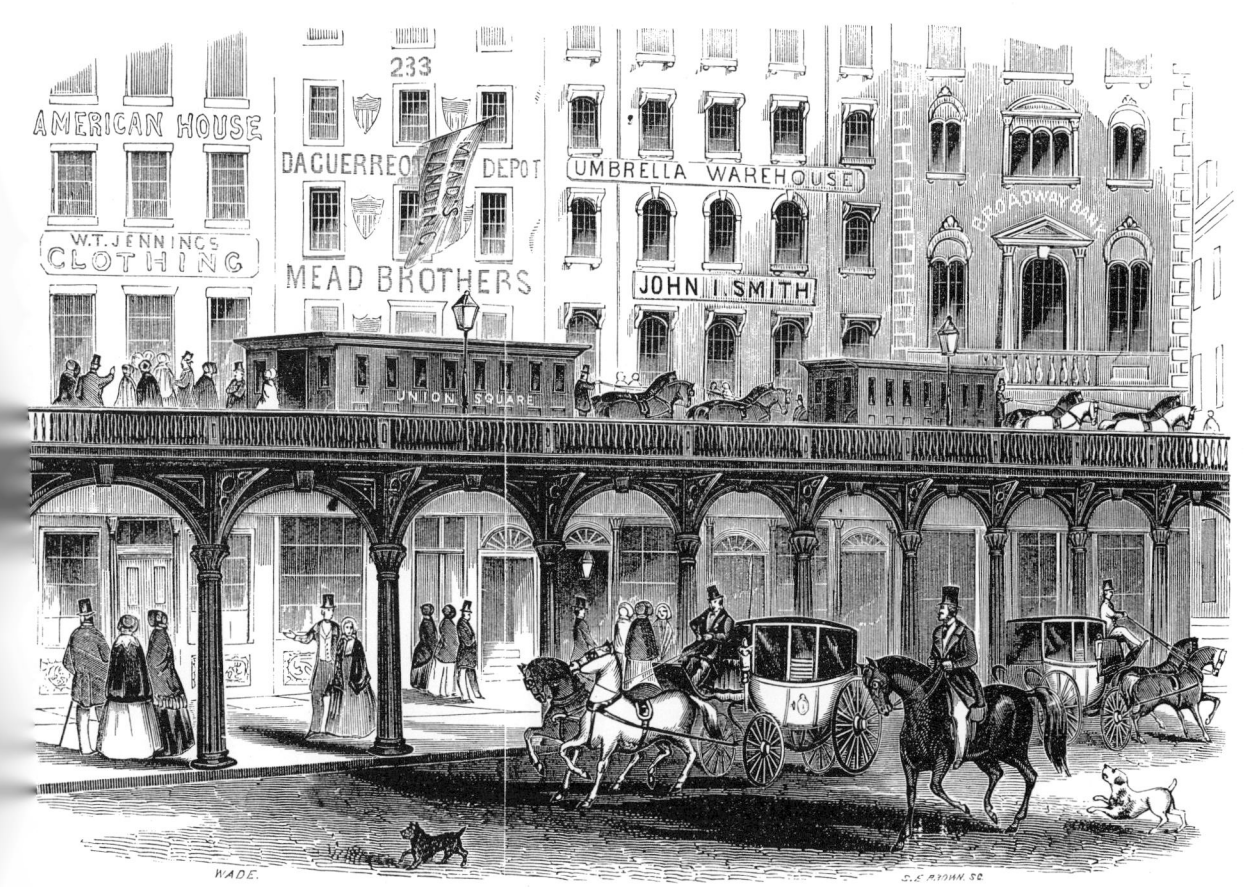

From an engraving in *Gleason's Pictorial Drawing-Room Companion,* April 1, 1854.

PROPOSED ELEVATED RAILROAD TERRACE FOR BROADWAY, NEW YORK

Lower Broadway, in Manhattan, was so congested with traffic reaching impossible limits that each day brought new proposals from inventors and promoters for transit relief. ''Plans for constructing an 'Elevated Railroad,' heretofore presented, have all possessed some grossly objectionable features that rendered them impractical in benefitting this world-renowned thoroughfare. In the present plan it is proposed to build a railroad, and an additional sidewalk over the present one, elevated to the level of the second story, and projecting in the form of a balcony, supported by columns planted on a line with the curb. This road and sidewalk are intended to occupy both sides of Broadway, connected at both termini by a continuous track, forming an endless railroad. The cars will be drawn by horses, until some of the new plans are more fully developed for propulsion by atmospheric pressure. The stairways or landings would soon become known by the names of the occupants of the premises, as 'Genin's Landing,' etc. The overall plan is considered entirely feasible, and finds many ardent supporters among the people of the metropolis.''

From *Gleason's Pictorial Drawing-Room Companion,* April 1, 1854.

Endless overhead bridges, among the many far-fetched plans, never reached construction stage as debate between promoters and shopkeepers raged on . . .

From early accounts and contemporary photographs traffic conditions in downtown New York in the 1850s and '60s had reached an impossible stage. Countless plans, some in the realm of the fantastic, were proposed to bring transit relief as the streets could no longer stand any extra congestion. Surface transportation had reached an impasse, so it became necessary to devise lines to run either underground or on an elevated level. A committee in the State Senate, appointed in 1866, declared that "the traction of freight and passenger trains by ordinary locomotives on the surface of the streets is an evil which has already been endured too long and must be speedily abated."

The committee approved Charles T. Harvey's experiments with his patented elevated railroad. Harvey proposed a route from the Battery up along Greenwich Street, to be extended to Kingsbridge and Yonkers. Among the new proposals one patented by William Hemstreet received . . .

BROADWAY RAILROAD—THE GRAND ELEVATION OF THE OVERGROUND RAILROAD—
DESIGNED AND PATENTED BY WILLIAM HEMSTREET, BROOKLYN

... for years, little thought being given to methods of practical locomotion. Cable traction, fire-belching engines, and horses were considered and none actually approved.

From *Frank Leslie's Illustrated Newspaper*, March 3, 1866.

... serious consideration though it was never constructed. Hemstreet's plan was called the Broadway Overground Railroad. It promised that "there would be no more going into a filthy, dangerous street for a bounding thundering omnibus . . . it would cost nothing for extra lighting, warming or police—like the underground plan." Approached by balconies from shops and museums along its route, the proposed overground was to span and roof the street, saving many thousands of dollars in street cleaning "by catching the rain and snow which would run off through the iron pillars." The decorated cable cars, with curtained windows, retained a coachlike elegance. "There is no more a necessity of consuming a quarter of a business day, going to and from residence and place of business. This lowers rents in town, and builds up the suburbs." The opposition of many rival traction interests aided by vigorous protests from shopkeepers who saw only their darkened windows doomed the plan, as it did many others.

Among the many proponents of transit systems was Rufus Gilbert, arguing for his atmospheric-powered tube trains, and Charles Harvey, whose cable-drawn "el" was built on Greenwich Street.

A continuous clamor of the disgruntled public, enraged at the slow pace of transit improvements, resulted in hundreds of letters to the daily press. Typical, in 1866, is this from an irate reader: "We cannot live here . . . and it is inconvenient to live across the arms of the sea on either hand. We want to live uptown, or in the adjacent county of Westchester; and we want facilities for getting quickly, cheaply, comfortably from our homes to our work and back again. . . . Gentlemen of the Legislature! Give us both the Underground and the Aerial Railways!" A first effort to solve the matter of overhead transit was Charles T. Harvey's experimental track, a quarter-mile stretch on Greenwich Street. The cars were drawn by cable, but the operation was not too successful. By 1871, the line was taken over and steam locomotives were substituted, while the system was extended northward to reach the growing uptown districts. Another of the audacious elevated plans was invented by R. H. Gilbert, who envisioned a "continuous overhead bridge, with compound Gothic iron arches spaced every 50 to 100 feet, which shall span the street from curb to curb. Through the tubes, cars carrying passengers are to be propelled by atmospheric power. The stations are to be about a mile apart, and will be provided with pneumatic elevators to raise passengers from the place of transit with perfect safety, thus obviating the necessity of climbing up and down stairs."

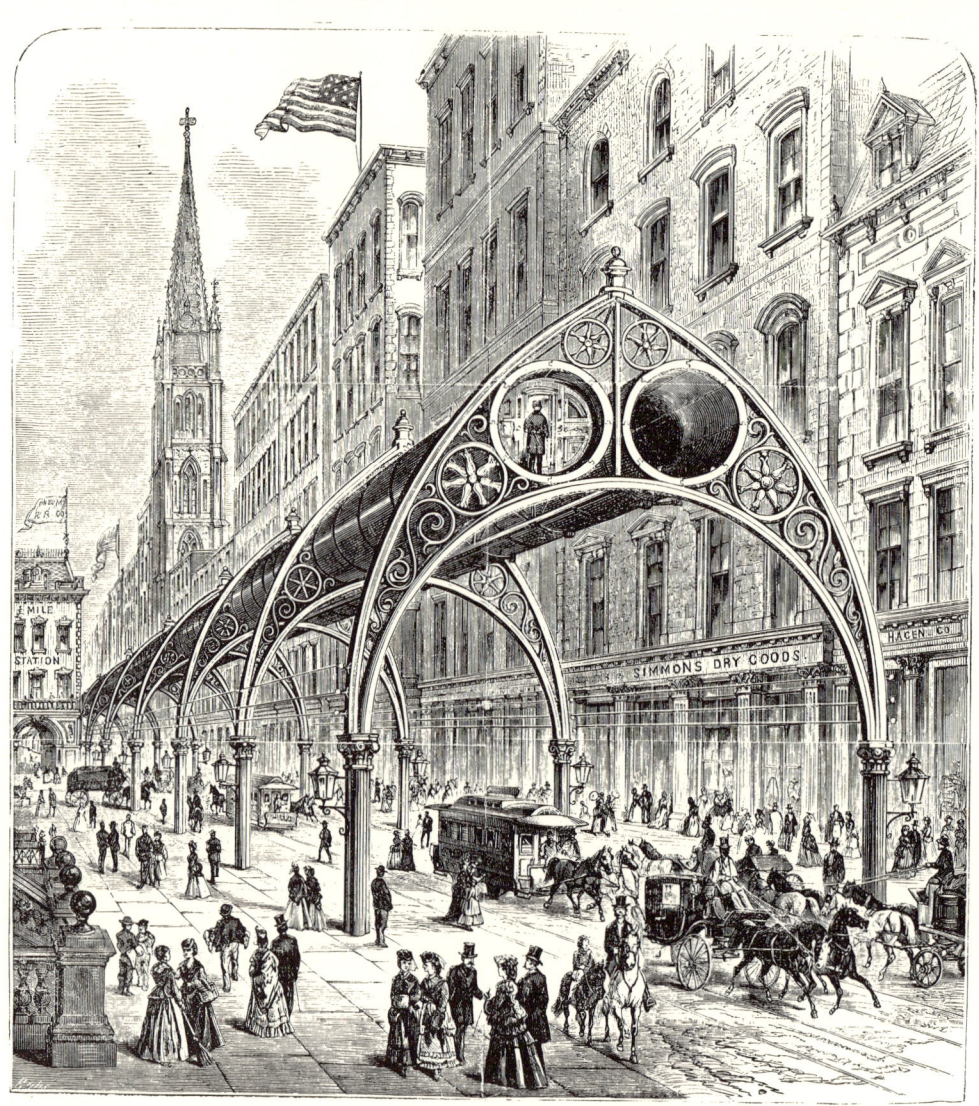

From *Scientific American,* April 13, 1872.

GILBERT'S PROPOSED CITY ELEVATED RAILWAY

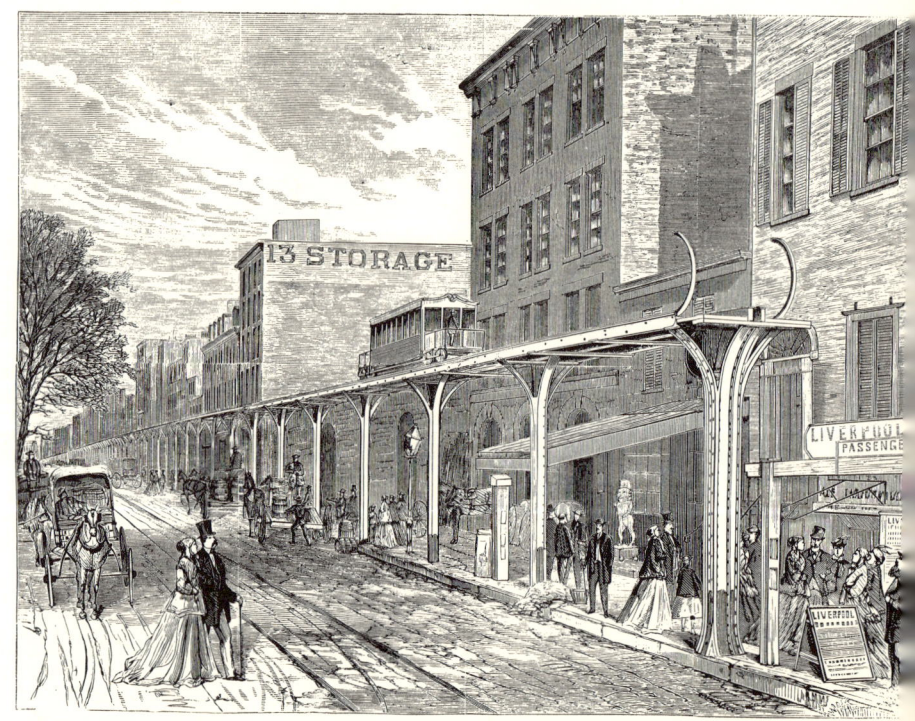

Engraved from a drawing by Stanley Fox, *Harper's Weekly,* July 25, 186

ELEVATED RAILWAY IN GREENWICH STREET, NEW YORK CITY

Each day saw a new scheme proposed for consideration by the city's council, as public and promoters voiced their opinions in heated debate and traffic congestion worsened.

HANNAH'S PATENT METROPOLITAN RAILWAY
Engraved by Ten Eyck, *Scientific American*, May 13, 1871.

At the time when Harvey's short stretch of track on Greenwich Street was in operation, still other ambitious promoters' plans were being published. J. M. Hannah of Chicago offered his "Patent Metropolitan Railway" to New York. The double overhead track was to be constructed of "girders of iron or steel of proper thickness, on a row of single columns or double, depending upon the width of the street below." The "Pen and Ink Sketches" give quick thumbnail renditions of a variety of elevated plans under consideration. "Gilbert's Elevated Road, lately begun on Sixth Avenue, temporarily suspended," is shown on the left. The saddle railway of General Le Roy Stone, on the right, "claimed by the ingenious inventor and his friends to be the cheapest, best and least objectionable form of the elevated street railway that has ever been devised. A highly successful trial on a section was tested at Phoenixville, Pa. recently." Whatever the relative merits of the individual plans offered, they met with universal disapproval from the merchants on the streets below. Their darkened windows and showrooms and the extra light for illumination were the basis of vigorous protests, until they were overwhelmingly defeated by the need for drastic action. A baffled citizenry only knew that transit conditions were getting worse; the city's future desperately cried out for some form of relief, and the elevated seemed to provide the only immediate answer.

From *Scientific American*, April 1, 1876.

NO. 1, GILBERT PLAN NOS. 2, 3, HANNAH PLAN NOS. 4, 5, GENERAL LE ROY STONE'S PLAN

While rapid-transit controversy raged, pedestrian tempers flared. Broadway was a sea of tangled traffic endangering life and limb...

Attempting to cross Broadway at one of the city's worst crossings, near St. Paul's Church, presented almost insurmountable obstacles. Traffic policemen—"Large, fine looking men, in blue uniforms, well studded with brass buttons . . . jack boots, and . . . batons worn like a dagger" according to Mark Twain—gave them "an imposing military aspect." As "New York's finest" charged through this sea of traffic, trying to disentangle carts, omnibuses, and pedestrians, timid females were being escorted across by these special messengers. "The women like it," reported Twain. "I stood by for two hours and watched one of them cross seven or eight times on various pretences, and always on the same handsome policeman's arm." Charles Dickens, on his second lecture tour in 1867, remarked that "nowhere, at home or abroad, is there such a fine police as the police in New York." "The 'torrent of traffic' was no new phenomenon for the 'million-footed' city; but observers were now more likely to be exasperated by it than impressed. Visitors complained that the horse-drawn streetcars were always packed. A double row of riders jammed the central aisles; the drivers' platforms were occupied to overflowing; and passengers even clung, like bees on a bough, to the platform behind," reported Bayrd Still, in *Mirror for Gotham*.

From *Harper's Weekly*, August 27, 1859.

AUGUST IN TOWN—BROADWAY, OPPOSITE ST. PAUL'S CHURCH, NEW YORK

... matched only by the daily jam at ferry gates where trucks, carts, and carriages had to join long lines in the hope of boarding the next ferry.

Manhattan was not always the "island paradise" someone had once called it. Trying to cross on the crowded ferries offered another point of view. Bounded on all sides by waterways—the North River to the west, the East River to the east, the Harlem up north, and vast New York Bay to the south—the city dweller needed little to remind him of the city's insularity; at no point was he more than a mile from water. Long before Roebling first planned his bridge across to Brooklyn, the numerous ferry lines were his only connection to either Long Island or the mainland. Traffic converged at the ferry entrances. Invariably the jam at the gates caused lost time and lost tempers. As unscrupulous drivers edged for a better position in line, foul language and often fisticuffs followed, not to mention broken wheels and bloody noses. The rush-hour delays often meant as much as a two-hour wait.

Engraved from a sketch by Thomas Worth, *Harper's Weekly,* December 11, 1869.

JAM AT THE FERRY GATE

As Mark Twain observed, the overcrowding of New York's streetcars is like a step backward toward original barbarism . . .

"Authority winks at the overloading of the cars—and permits one car to do the work of at least two, instead of compelling the companies to double the number of their cars, and permits them, also, to cruelly over-work their horses, too, of course, in the face of the Society for the Prevention of Cruelty to Animals. The result of this over-crowding is to set the people back a long stride toward semi-civilization. What I mean by that dreadful assertion is that the over-crowding of the cars has impelled men to adopt the rule of hanging on to a seat when they get it, though twenty beautiful women came in and stood in their midst. That is going back toward original barbarism, I take it. A car's proper cargo should be twenty-two inside and three upon each platform—twenty-eight—no crowding. I have seen fifty-six persons on a car here, but a large portion of them hanging on by teeth. Some of the men inside had to go four or five miles, and naturally enough did not like to give up their seats and stand in a packed mass of humanity all that distance. So, when a lady got in, no man offered her a seat—no man dreamt of doing such a thing."

From *Mark Twain's Travels with Mr. Brown*, 1867.

NEW YORK STREET RAILROAD CARS—A REAR VIEW

NEW YORK STREET RAILROAD CARS—AN INTERIOR

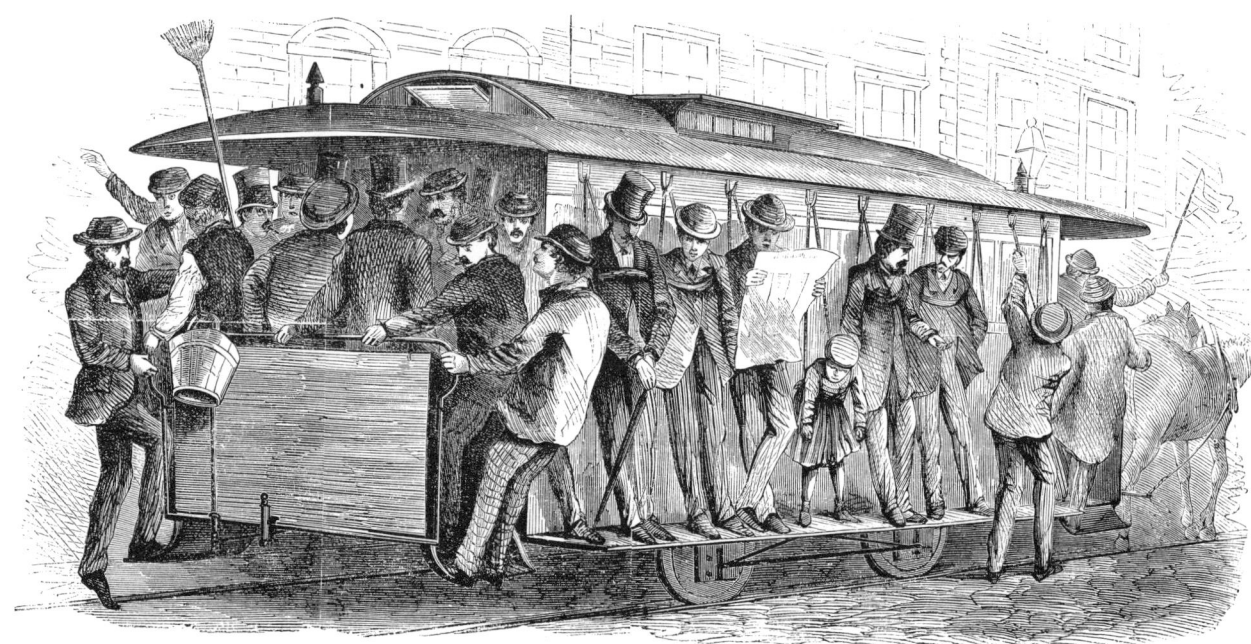

From *Harper's Weekly,* March 23, 1867.

NEW YORK STREET RAILROAD CARS—WHAT ARE WE COMING TO

. . . and the inhumane treatment of the horses prompted the founding of the Society for the Prevention of Cruelty to Animals.

Engraved from a drawing by Max F. Klepper, *Harper's Weekly*, July 19, 1890.

NINETY IN THE SHADE

Engraved from a drawing by Sol Eltinge, Jr., *Harper's Weekly*, September 21, 1872.

THE CROWDED CAR

For over three-quarters of a century public conveyances drawn by horses were a common sight on the streets of New York. John Stephenson, master coach and car builder, in his plant on East Twenty-seventh Street, built his first two horsecars for the Fourth Avenue Line in 1832. The omnibuses, as they were first called, came in closed and open models, for summertime use. The firm grew with the popularity of stage lines in the city. Its success became worldwide, shipping to many countries abroad, beating out established British and German makers in its competition for markets around the globe. When car rails were laid down on principal thoroughfares, the cars grew much larger, resulting in overcrowding and excessive strain on the overworked animals. Henry Bergh's pioneering efforts were in part directed to bettering conditions for the poor car horses. *Harper's Weekly,* on September 21, 1872, reported: "Mr. Bergh is doing a good thing for humanity as well as horseflesh by his efforts to stop the scandalous overcrowding of the street cars. On some of the lines leading to the upper part of the city scenes like the one depicted on this page are of too frequent occurrence. The car is packed and jammed with passengers until there is scarcely room to breathe, and the jaded team can hardly pull the load." Horsecars continued in use well into the twentieth century. The last of the cars, running along West Street, disappeared in 1918.

The Beach Pneumatic Tunnel, with a huge blower fan to propel cars along an underground track, operated under Broadway in 1870, but its life was a short one...

From *Scientific American,* March 5, 1870.

Clearly, there were only three choices for relief of the traffic congestion that plagued New York over a century ago: surface transportation, the elevated, and the underground. There were endless arguments for and against each method, and as various groups debated, the congestion continued. There were at least a dozen different elevated systems being proposed, and one already in operation. Finally, in 1870, the first underground railway, known as the Beach Pneumatic Tunnel, was opened. It was only several hundred yards long, extending from Warren Street to Murray Street under Broadway. The station was equipped with fancy fixtures, frescoed walls, gas lighting, and a goldfish tank. To entertain waiting passengers, and help them forget the din of the huge blower fans, there was a pianist playing a grand piano.

The tunnels, eight feet in diameter, were dry and clean, and painted white. The strong blast of air was forced against the rear car sending it "along the track like a sail-boat before the wind." The company claimed that "it would be able, when the road was completed, to transport more than 20,000 passengers per hour, each way." The fare was twenty-five cents for a very uncertain ride, and it was not long before the Beach system closed for lack of patrons and funds to extend the system.

From *Scientific American,* March 5, 1

From *Scientific American,* April 1, 1876.

GENERAL DESIGN FOR STATIONS—BROADWAY UNDERGROUND RAILWAY

. . . yet this hardly put an end to fantastic schemes such as the monorail streamliner straddling a single track, many years ahead of its time.

The Meigs Elevated Railway System, another of the proposed transportation plans that never did get off the ground, might well have been promoted as the "World's first streamliner . . . a train of the future." Its cylindrical cars reduced wind resistance, and straddled a monorail, unique in its day. Its promoters claimed "the locomotive has some minor novelties of construction besides the track arrangement; but its main features are the horizontal driving wheels which pull the train by side pressure on the rails of the upper boom of the girder. . . . The motor draws itself and the attached train with apparent ease and at great speed around sharper curves and up heavier grades than the ordinary locomotive can pass. With so radical a departure from the ordinary mode of applying power, it is only to be expected that perfection will develop slowly, but it will succeed. The experimental section of the Meigs railway now in use at East Cambridge, Mass., is abundantly strong and safe for the passage of its equipment." Thus did the *Scientific American* report on the newest of many elevated systems, but nothing did materialize when the proponents of the Meigs Railway argued before the city's aldermanic chamber, in 1886.

From *Scientific American*, February 5, 1887.

THE MEIGS ELEVATED RAILWAY SYSTEM

In the beginning, the elevated system designed to accommodate Manhattan as a long, narrow island, consisted of several lines running north and south . . .

After many setbacks including that caused by the Panic of 1873, the plan to have an elevated system extending all the way from the Battery, Manhattan's southernmost tip, to the northern extremities of the island was slowly making headway. The "new aerial line" was said to be little more than an iron bridge, built as lightly as possible for its purpose, and entirely lacking in any ornamental charm. Though the builders had hoped to make the el unobtrusive, it still darkened the lower stories of dwellings in narrow streets and people were saying that a gracefully arched structure would have been preferable and much more pleasing to the eye. Declaring the new el looked more like an endless bridge, *Harper's Weekly* of February 9, 1878, continued: "It cannot be pleasant to have trains of cars whizzing by one's second story windows every five minutes, even though the rate of speed precludes a too-close scrutiny of private apartments; and it must be confessed that the tracks . . . do not improve the appearance of the streets. But private objection must always yield to the greatest good for the greatest number." The grievances of the few would be as nothing compared to the benefits that countless thousands would enjoy on completion of the elevated roads. The vast tenement population in lower New York would be the first to profit, as rapid transit, it was thought, would lead many to move to the suburbs, allowing more space for those who chose to remain. The partial disfigurement of a few streets by the el would be . . .

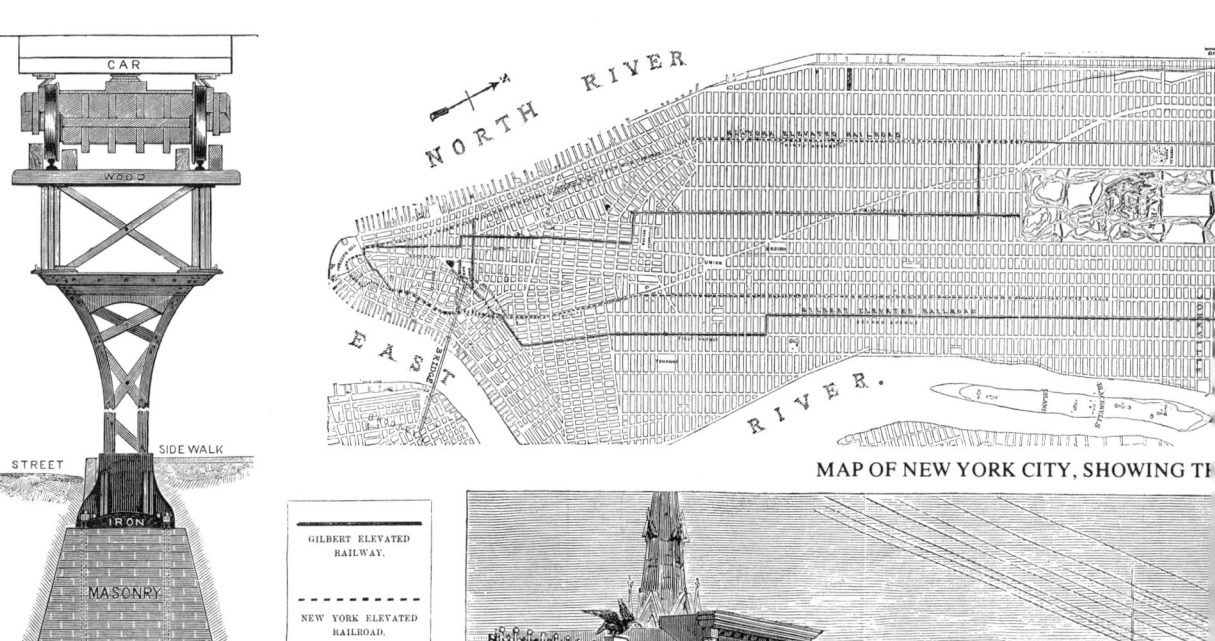

MAP OF NEW YORK CITY, SHOWING T[HE]

GREENWICH STREET FOUNDATION, COLUMN, AND TRACK, NEW YORK ELEVATED RAILROAD.

STATION IN SIXTH AVENUE, AT THE JUNCTION OF BROADW[AY]

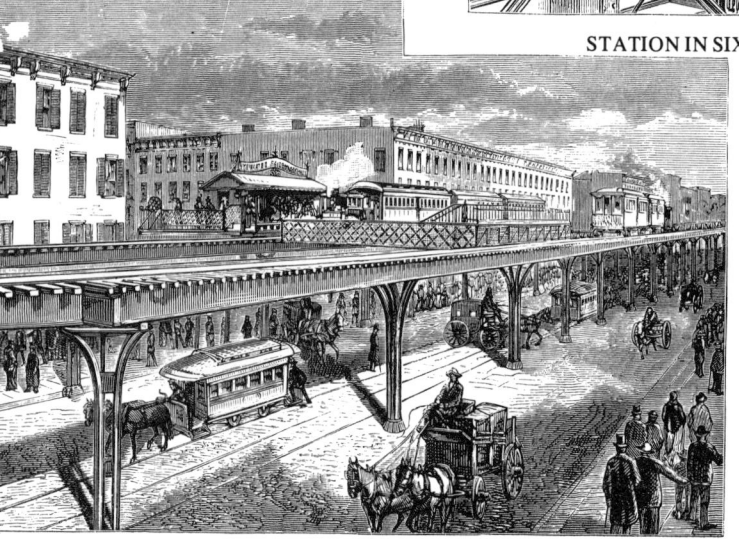

STATION IN NINTH AVENUE, NEAR FORTY-SECOND STREET, NEW YORK ELEVATED RAILROAD

RAPID TRANSIT IN NEW YOR[K]

. . . the Sixth and Ninth avenue lines on the West Side, and the Second and Third avenue lines on the East Side, terminating near the Battery at South Ferry.

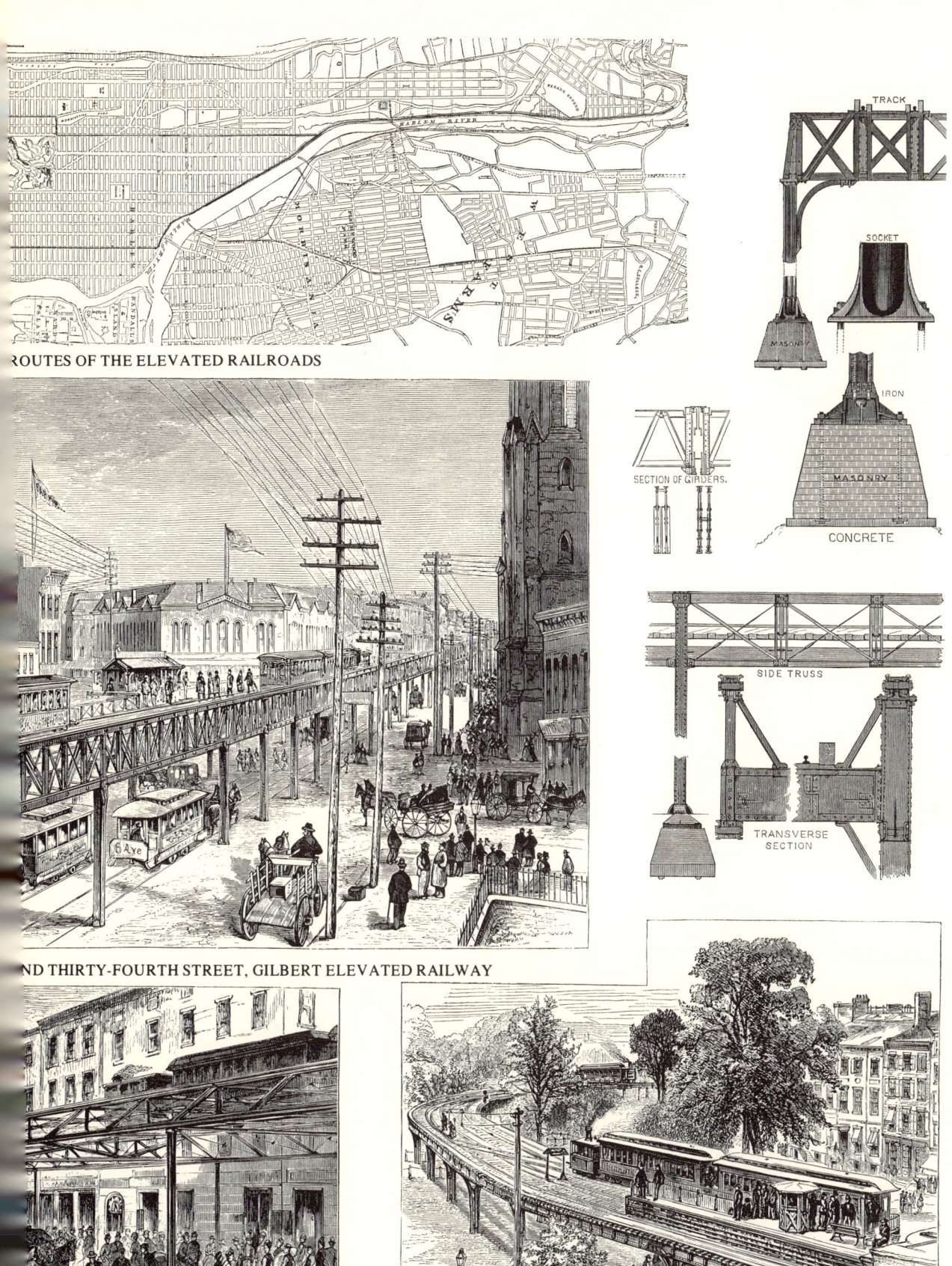

ROUTES OF THE ELEVATED RAILROADS

...ND THIRTY-FOURTH STREET, GILBERT ELEVATED RAILWAY

Engraved from photographs by Pach, and sketches by Theo. R. Davis, *Harper's Weekly*, February 9, 1878.

JOINT TRACK FOR BOTH ROADS, PEARL STREET AND MAIDEN LANE
STATION ON THE BATTERY, NEW YORK ELEVATED RAILROAD

. . . compensated by the great improvements in living it would bring to many "now abandoned to misery and squalor." New York's citizens were clamoring for more speedy and convenient means of getting to and from their business than the horsecars and stages afforded, and more cheaply than the cheapest lines of hacks could offer. The els held the promise that the working classes would not have to leave their homes so early, and the *weary ride when worn out with the day's toil* would be shortened. No longer would people have to shiver in a crowded, cold, ill-smelling horsecar in winter; they would ride in a comfortable conveyance, without jolt or jar. In *Scientific American*, June 15, 1878, it said: "When the elevated railways, now in progress of construction in this city, are completed, four great iron bridges will run lengthwise over Manhattan island. When finished, they will aggregate in length between 60 and 70 miles and there will be two on each side of the city." The ills inflicted by the els were already being deplored. Trains thundered overhead; thoroughfares were blocked by great iron columns; ash, oil, and sparks were distributed impartially over pedestrians and awnings (several awnings had been set on fire); dirt floated into upper windows; life was endangered from runaway horses; carriage wheels were broken against the el columns; streets were so shaded they remained damp, long after wet weather had cleared. The annoyances cited were many, though the els were only in their infancy.

To reach the elevated, one had to climb three flights
of stairs, making the lines dangerous for invalids
and cardiacs...

"In the 'seventies, elevated railroads were built; and for miles and miles, on each side of these ill-designed iron ways, which contrasted so unfavorably with those Berlin built only slightly later, tenement houses were planted. Thousands of people lived under the shadow of the elevated, with the smoke of the old-fashioned locomotives puffing into their windows, with the clank and rattle causing them to shout in daily conversation to overcome the roar outside. The obliviousness to low sounds, the indifference to cacophony which makes the ideal radio listener of present-day America, was part of the original acquisition of Manhattan in the Brown Decades. This torment of noise-troubled sleep, lowered the waking efficiency, depleted vitality; but it was endured as if it were an irremediable fact of nature. In the lull of the elevated's thunder, the occasional tinkle of the cowbells of the ragman on a side street, or the solemn *I—l—l—l cas' clo's* of the second-hand clothing buyer, would have an almost pastoral touch; while *Carmen,* on an Italian's clanking hand organ, could splash the sky with color."

From *The Metropolitan Milieu,* by Lewis Mumford, 1934.

Engraved from a drawing by W. P. Snyder, *Harper's Weekly,* July 20, 1878.

THE FORTY-SECOND STREET AND SIXTH AVENUE STATION, METROPOLITAN (GILBERT) ELEVATED RAILWAY

Engraved from a drawing by C. J. Taylor, *Harper's Weekly,* February 20, 1886.

THE PROPOSED EXTENSION OF THE EAST RIVER BRIDGE

... the records tell of many who made a headlong dash upstairs to catch an incoming train, only to suffer a heart attack from overexertion.

On the morning of September 16, 1878, a steam locomotive chugged along the newly built Third Avenue El structure, pulling a few plushseated railroad cars behind. For the upper East Side of Manhattan this was a momentous event, exposing the amorphous region that at best was a spotty no man's land punctuated here and there with squatter's shacks, sprawling breweries, stables, and wretched three- or four-story frame houses. These "flats" imparted a dismal air to the entire area whose corners were marked with the ubiquitous saloon, always within easy reach. In his excellent book, *This Was New York,* Maxwell Marcuse says: "The advent of the Third Avenue El brought on a dense concentration of clapboard buildings and tenements along Third Avenue and its purlieus to the east of it. These 'cold water' dwellings featured the 'railroad flats' of the day. With more and more people constantly moving into this area the upper East Side soon took on a slumlike aspect, what with its proliferation of saloons, cheap bistros, dives and pool 'parlors.' Eventually, many of the saloons were displaced by antique shops for which Third Avenue became famous."

From *Scientific American,* June 15, 1878.

ELEVATED RAILROAD STATION, 23d STREET, NEW YORK

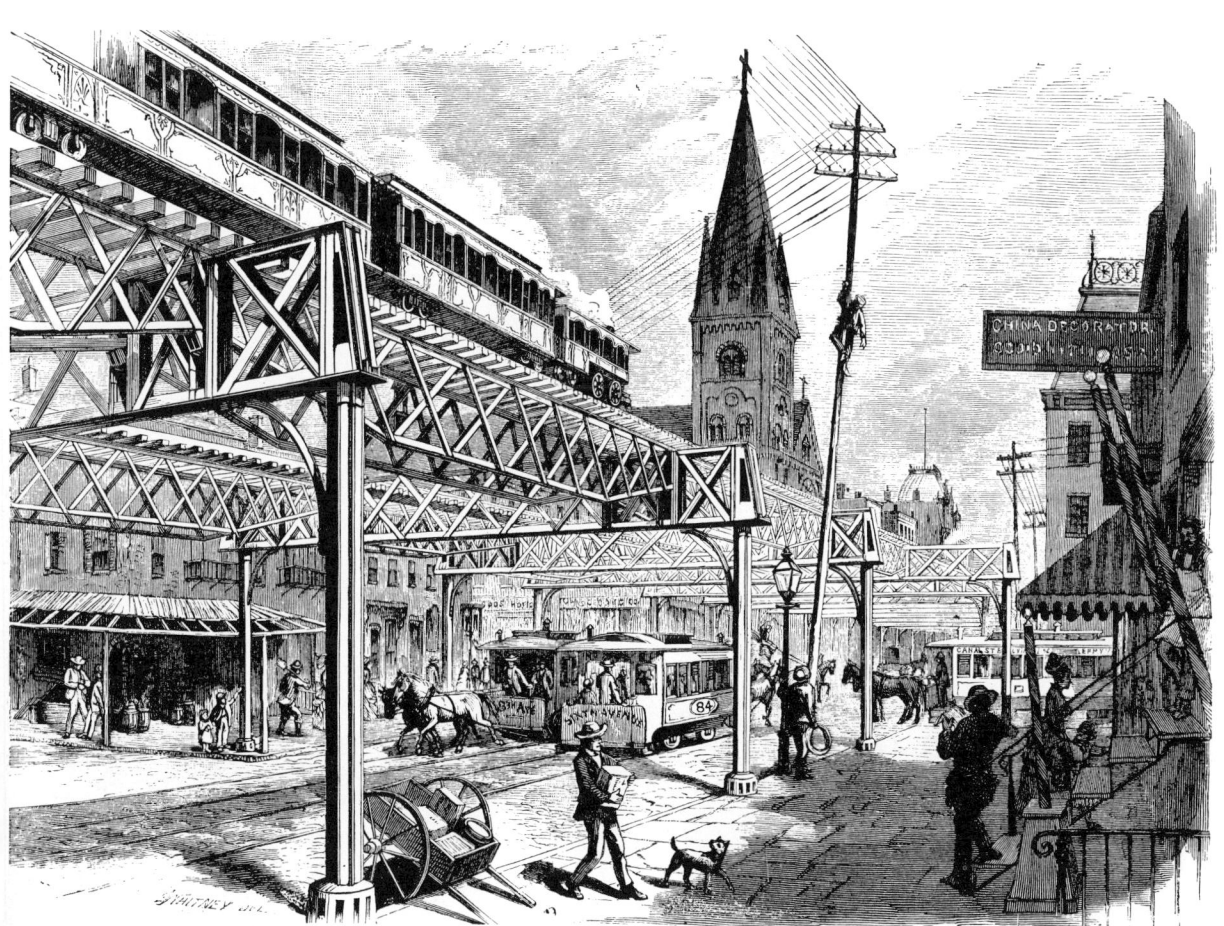

From *Scientific American,* June 15, 1878.

ELEVATED RAILROAD, WEST BROADWAY AND CANAL STREET

People who road the elevated trains were always well dressed and well mannered, as depicted by the artist-reporters for the popular newspapers . . .

Brooklyn's residents, complaining for years about being subjected to a subservient treatment, finally celebrated opening day ceremonies of its elevated railroad on May 13, 1885. From adjacent rooftops people waved as the thundering, flag-bearing, first-run train went by, carrying hundreds of the borough's notables in plush cars. "The Brooklyn Elevated Railroad Company was organized in 1874, to provide 'silent safety' transit from the Bridge to Woodhaven. A Fulton Street Elevated was proposed by O. Kirkup, an Englishman who had worked with John Stephenson. A unique feature of this scheme was that meetings to raise money for the railroad were opened with prayer. . . . General Roy Stone, who had displayed his single-rail invention at Fairmont Park, Philadelphia, tried to put his hanging cars in operation in Brooklyn, in 1877 and 1878, but his project never advanced far. The Brooklyn Elevated Company's route was changed to Myrtle Avenue. The Fulton Street Elevated to Brooklyn Bridge and the ferry was not opened until 1888, five years after the bridge was opened. While the bridge was under construction the plans were changed so that trains could be operated over it."

From *New York: The World's Capital City,*
by Cleveland Rodgers and Rebecca B. Rankin, 1948.

Engraved from a drawing by W. P. Snyder, *Harper's Weekly,* May 23, 1885.

OPENING OF THE BROOKLYN ELEVATED RAILWAY, MAY 13

... but in inclement weather, there was the usual rush to board trains and uncomfortable packing that resulted.

Engraved from a drawing by Thure de Thulstrup, *Harper's Weekly,* February 8, 1890.

A STATION SCENE IN THE "RUSH" HOURS ON THE MANHATTAN ELEVATED RAILROAD

The success of the elevated system was such that its growth in popularity kept pace with New York's constant surge into uptown areas. In fact, the extension of the system northward pointed the way for development of districts that just a few years before had been open farmlands with little sign of habitation. Now the el brought new lands within easy reach. Blocks upon blocks of newly built "French Flats," rows and rows of apartments stretched from avenue to avenue. "These afforded undreamed of conveniences to former dwellers of old-fashioned houses, in the way of door openers, dumbwaiters, electric bells, and in some of the better class, steam heat and hot water," as reported in *Valentine's Manual,* edited by Henry Collins Brown in 1926. But the congestion on the elevated trains continued in almost inhuman fashion. In bad weather, when rain or snow only added to the confusion, the pushing and shoving left the more timid souls waiting on el stations, hoping, somehow, to avoid being jostled by the unruly mobs. At a much later date, when the subway crowds proliferated, the fine art of "sardine-packing" a few more into each car was accomplished by a corps of "pushers," either former heavyweight contenders or barroom "bouncers" who had some professional experience in handling crowds.

Uptown, near Morningside Park, it was necessary to build the el tracks at such a height that a lift was later installed at the 110th Street station.

"And now how to get about in New York. There is first the elevated railway. Answering to our 'underground' in London, in affording rapid conveyance through the city without interfering with the traffic, it is raised high above the streets instead of being tunnelled under them. The effect of the 'elevated', the 'L,' as New Yorkers generally call it, is, to my mind, anything but beautiful; but this, perhaps, is only a matter of taste. The tracks are lifted to a height of thirty feet (in some places higher) upon iron pillars, the up line on one side of the street and the down on the other. . . . Beneath the raised lines is the roadway for horses and carriages, and the lines of rail for the tramway cars, with the pavements beyond. As you sit in a car on the 'L' and are whirled along, you can put your head out of [the] window and salute a friend who is walking on the street pavement below. In some places, where the streets are narrow, the railway is built right over the 'sidewalks' . . . close up against the walls of the houses. . . ."

From *Through America; or Nine Months in the United States*, by Walter G. Marshall, 1882.

THE ELEVATED RAILWAY AT 110th STREET AND EIGHTH AVENUE, NEW YORK CITY

From *Scientific American*, October 25, 1879

PORTION OF THE ROAD BEYOND CENTRAL PARK ON POSTS FIFTY-SEVEN FEET HIGH

The terminus at South Ferry was an important transfer point and connection with ferries for Staten Island.

NEW YORK ELEVATED RAILROAD AT THE BATTERY

MODE OF CONSTRUCTION ON THIRD AVENUE

From *Scientific American*, June 15, 1878.

NEW YORK ELEVATED RAILROAD STATION AT SOUTH FERRY

"For a quarter of a century after Harvey's first experiment in New York saw all manner of transit schemes launched, with endless bickering and conflicts over franchises. The grafters and stock promoters were engaged in a great game to get rights to the use of the public streets. . . . This included the Beach Tunnel, and the Gilbert Elevated, whose route was fixed, but the panic of 1873 intervened and stopped construction. The first Rapid Transit Commission was created in 1875 and began fixing routes for the railroads. The Gilbert idea was adapted to open-track steam locomotives, and the route was integrated with that of the New York Elevated Railway. . . . Cyrus W. Field, of Atlantic cable fame, and other able men became interested in transit. Field and his associates got control of the existing elevated roads, but there was increasing opposition to the exploitation of the public by private interests. It was found that the city was giving away its valuable rights and was being plundered by politicians and schemers."

From *New York: The World's Capital City*, by Cleveland Rodgers and Rebecca B. Rankin, 1948.

Manhattan's simple gridiron street plan, originally adopted in 1811, has been both praised and damned. In 1867, the *Evening Post* complained that "New York is the most inconveniently arranged commercial city in the world." Henry James referred to it as a curse of "petty-fogging parallelograms." But the long avenues running north and south did provide an easy arterial system of delivering residents to uptown areas, thus enabling the city to extend its population growth northward. In contrast, today's transportation chart of "criss-crossing subway and elevated lines marked in red, yellow, and blue somewhat resembles an anatomical chart showing veins and arteries," wrote Richard Gehman in *The Nether World*.

The hue and cry of angry protests succeeded, after some years, in having the railroad tracks along Park Avenue sunk below street levels and finally covered over.

With the opening of the New Grand Central Depot, attention was directed to improving the right of way leading to it from the north. A number of fatal accidents and the constant pollution of the air from dense clouds of smoke culminated in the sunken viaduct and its eventual covering over, along Park Avenue. "Few of the proposed metropolitan improvements appeal so heartily to the practical sense of the public as that now in process of construction on Fourth Avenue. The press of New York has published almost daily the complaints of pedestrians and horse-car travelers. Every few days there were accounts of the killing or wounding of persons about that frightful network of rails just beyond the depot. Occasionally, owing to the misplacement of a switch, a locomotive leaped its own pair of rails, rushed away, crashing through buildings, and fetching up in tracts of ground reserved for less destructive objects. The people clamored for immunity from the dangers of such accidents, and from one end of the city to the other a strong cry arose, 'Sink the tracks.' While committees were forming to embody the protests in an attractive form, and indignation meetings were reflecting the sentiment of a large mass of our citizens, a company was quietly formed, and as quietly inaugurated the great work of prevention. . . .

Seldom has there been so promising a field for architectural ornamentation. The open track will be repeatedly broken with cross-over bridges for pedestrians and horse-cars, but these will create an unusually picturesque *tout ensemble*."

From *Frank Leslie's Illustrated Newspaper*, February 15, 1873.

VIEW OF THE BEAM TUNNEL FROM 59th TO 76th STREET, LOOKING NORTH

THE STONE VIADUCT FROM 99th TO 115th STREET— THE STATION AT 110th STREET

ELEVATED BRIDGE FOR FOOT PASSENGERS BETWEEN 52d AND 53d STREETS

Engraved from drawings by Albert Berghaus based upon engineer's charts, *Frank Leslie's Illustrated Newspaper*, February 15, 1873.

VIEW OF THE ELEVATED BRIDGE FOR CARRIAGES AND FOOT PASSENGERS ACROSS 45th STREET NEW YORK CITY—THE IMPROVEMENTS ON FOURTH AVENUE AS THEY WILL APPEAR WHEN COMPLETE

PART SIX
Up in Central Park

From an engraving in *Scientific American,* April 26, 1873.

VIEW OF BOW BRIDGE AND LAKE, CENTRAL PARK, NEW YORK

"The planning and the planting of Central Park was the beginning of a stormy but fruitful public life.... The park was an aristocratic symbol of the Old World: it cost money and it withdrew building lots from speculation: some opponents even believed that the pleasure ground would be used only by ruffians and gangsters, who would rob decent citizens or drive them out by their bawdy antics: others thought that the park would never be reached or visited by the common people. Even those who favoured the reservation of the land distrusted any efforts to improve it. Landscape architecture was an effeminancy: what was the country coming to?"

From *The Brown Decades,*
by Lewis Mumford, 1931.

Up in Central Park

New Yorkers owed a great debt to a small handful of civic-minded men whose vision and persistent advocacy brought about the creation of a park and playground, originally designed for "family picnic parties and gregarious pleasures." Eminent men of letters, among them Washington Irving, William Cullen Bryant, and historian George Bancroft, councilman and public servant Andrew H. Green, often called "the Father of Central Park," journalists Horace Greeley and Charles A. Dana, landscape architect Andrew Jackson Downing, and a group of influential citizens fought hard, both in the city councils and in newspaper columns, to create an oasis of pastoral retreat from the civilized community that threatened to swallow them. Convinced that "That waste of land, now given over to goats could well be turned into a restful park for the delectation of our fellow citizens," the agitation of Downing and Bryant made the building of the park a political issue, in 1850. After winning the mayoralty campaign, Ambrose Kingsland urged the Common Council to take immediate action, but another five years elapsed before a Board of Commissioners was appointed to legislate, acquire land, and define limits of the park area.

Frederick Law Olmsted, as Park Superintendent, was assigned the task of clearing the region. It was interspersed with the debris of run-down shanties, hog farms and "swill-mills," swamps and creeks with open sewers, and no fewer than three hundred hovels where animals and fowl roamed the land with freedom. It was in 1858 when much land had been cleared that architect Calvert Vaux joined forces with Olmsted in submitting their "Greensward" plan that won in open competition, the best of thirty-three plans submitted. After six years of actual construction and an expenditure of nine million dollars, the park was opened to an enthusiastic public, in 1864, just before the close of the Civil War. The most sanguine dreams of its promoters were realized. The world of fashion, the middle classes, and the poor met on common ground, heaping praise on the park planners for their foresight and ingenuity. They had transformed a dreary wasteland of swamps and rude projections from the rocky backbone of Manhattan into a varied and inviting reach of countryside. Generous provision for "fields and meadows and the preservation of winding valleys among the little hills, endowed by nature and clothed by man with green, growing things."

When spring came, all New York turned out in Central Park. Its planners had judiciously provided many splendid features: the Mall, a stately esplanade, a quarter of a mile long, where afternoon concerts were given in the ornate, pagodalike music pavilion. Here were to be seen the fashionable folk who arrived in their carriages which could be parked in the nearby carriage concourse. These pleasant promenade concerts were not paid for by the municipality, but by the horsecar lines who brought New Yorkers by the thousands to the park entrance by "railroad." Just north of the Mall was the picturesque terrace from which one could view the Bethesda Fountain and the beautiful lake where boating could be enjoyed in a variety of boats from the private rowboat to "omnibus" launches or swan boats, pedaled by a guide.

The many miles of excellent carriage drives served as a vast parade ground for the fashionable turnouts that were a daily afternoon feature for the equine cult. This was considered one of the notable "sights" of the town, and took place on the East Drive, from Fifty-ninth Street to the Mall. As one watched the continuous procession of fancy equipages, the city's first families could be seen in great numbers—the Jays, Livingstons, Jeromes, Stuyvesants, and others—some concealed behind shade-drawn broughams, others in open, sporty phaetons. The more formal coaches carried their footmen and coachmen, appropriately liveried.

Many of the hundreds of spectators, less interested in the aristocratic displays, came to view another show—the steady stream of trotters en route to Harlem Lane, just north of Central Park. Here, the current passion for trotting which had infected all classes of horse-fanciers could be enjoyed by viewing the speedsters in their harness carts, curricles, and sulkies. Known rivals like Robert Bonner, the newspaper publisher, and Commodore Vanderbilt raced their favorite steeds at breakneck pace, to the delight of the sightseers who crowded the porches of inns that lined the course.

The park's many lakes and ponds provided exhilarating diversions enjoyed by all classes, from the wealthiest to the poorest. Skating on the larger lakes became the setting for some of New York's most delightful scenes, colorfully pictured by Currier and Ives, Winslow Homer, and other magazine illustrators. The thousands who thronged the skating sites—the expert figure skater and the beginner stumbling awkwardly about, often gliding to the merry tunes of Strauss—were an unforgettable scene. In nearby drives, the clang and jingle of sleigh bells heralded the huge sleighs or cutters, as sleighing parties added to winter's merriment "Up in Central Park."

To the early foreign visitor Central Park was a "vast American Bois de Boulogne, with wild terrain situated beyond the suburbs."

From *Harper's Weekly,* October 13, 1860.

"... My friends took me to Central Park, vast American 'Bois de Boulogne,' with its valleys, rocks, cascades, aqueducts, lakes, and cliffs, opening out from the end of Fifth Avenue. The vicinity of the Park, for the length of a league, and the cross streets nearby are the abode of the most fashionable society. . . . The Park, if one can believe its name, will one day be in the center of the city. Nothing is more American than this ambitious name, given at first sight to wild terrain situated beyond the suburbs. What limits can be assigned to this rapidly expanding city, which already flows into its outskirts and has perhaps doubled in size in the past fifteen years? . . . The Park is recent, hardly finished, yet it already swarms each evening with beaux and carriages, especially those remarkable American vehicles whose slender wheels resemble filigreed jewelry, and which run along like big spiders with long legs. . . ."

From *French Travellers in the United States,* by Duvergier de Hauranne, edited by Frank Monaghan, 1864.

Among the park's many noted features, New Yorkers were attracted to the Terrace overlooking Bethesda Fountain and Lake, and the Mall and Concert Stand.

"To the park, accordingly, and to the Park only, hitherto, the aesthetic appetite has had to address itself, and the place has therefore borne the brunt of many a peremptory call, acting out year after year the character of the cheerful, capable, bustling, even if overworked, hostess of the one inn, somewhere, who has to take all the travel, who is often at her wits' end to know how to deal with it, but who, none the less, has, for the honor of the home, never once failed of hospitality. That is how we see Central Park, utterly overdone by the 'run' on its resources, yet also never having had to make an excuse. . . . It has had to have something for everybody, since everybody arrives famished; it has had to multiply itself to extravagance, to pathetic little efforts of exaggeration and deception, to be, breathlessly, everywhere and everything at once, and produce on the spot the particular romantic object demanded, lake or river or cataract, wild woodland or teeming garden, boundless vista or bosky nook, noble eminence or smiling valley. . . . You are perfectly aware, as you hang about her in May and June, that you *have,* as a travelled person, beheld more scenery and communed with nature in ampler or fairer forms; but it is quite equally definite to you that none of those adventures have counted more to you for experience, for stirred sensibility—inasmuch as you can be, at the best, and in the showiest countries, only thrilled by the pastoral or the awful, and as to pass, in New York, from the discipline of the streets to this so different many-smiling presence is to be thrilled at every turn."

From *The American Scene,* by Henry James, 1907.

Engraved from a photograph by Rockwood, *Harper's Weekly,* September 14, 1867

THE TERRACE IN CENTRAL PARK, LOOKING TOWARD THE MALL

From *Harper's Weekly,* September 14, 186

RIDING THE DROMEDARY IN CENTRAL PARK

Originally the park's zoo was housed in the Armory and circus tents before special structures were built for wild animals, birds, and snakes.

139

Engraved from a photograph by Rockwood, *Harper's Weekly*, October 12, 1867.

THE TERRACE AT CENTRAL PARK, VIEWED FROM THE LAKE

Engraved from a drawing by Stanley Fox, *Harper's Weekly*, October 12, 1867.

THE ANIMALS AT CENTRAL PARK

"Central Park's southern extremity, hardly a gem's throw from Tiffany's, nestles among the towers of some of the world's finest hotels. Here the Park is visibly a fantasy in which children romp and lovers coo and old folk doze in the sun. Ladies take afternoon spins in victorias driven by coachmen with stove-pipe hats and pulled by horses that have long since learned to read traffic signals. Younger people go cantering along the bridle paths, and their juniors, balloons in hand and high in peanut content, disport themselves on bicycles, skates, in pony carts or on the Carrousel. Others address themselves to handsome meals either at the Zoo cafeteria or at the Tavern-on-the-Green. If the fleet's in, the Lake is dotted with sailors in rowboats. Artists are busily sketching away, and amateur photographers are taking dead aim and firing. The air is enlivened with kites and model planes. If it's evening, there may be dancing on the Mall, with four thousand couples waltzing by the light of the moon. Perhaps this scene approximates the vision which editor William Cullen Bryant had back in the 1840's, when he said, in the columns of the *Evening Post*, that New York's people ought to have somewhere they could go to find solitude. This made sense to the public...."

From "Look Ma—Real Grass!" by George Sessions Perry, in *Saturday Evening Post*, 1947.

The idyllic setting in the park enabled the citizens to escape from Civil War memories and the noise and dirt of city streets...

"The most expensive adornment on earth is not the Hope Diamond, which isn't even in the running, but New York City's gracious, sprightly Central Park. Anything good costs more in New York than anywhere else. This park, which is the queen of the world's finest park system, would, if put under the hammer, bring enough to repay the United States Treasury many times over what it spent for the entire territory of the Louisiana Purchase.... And yet the people of New York City, whose government, just like any other, sorely needs the money, almost never feel an urge to sell the Park. Central Park is both an altar and a refuge. It was built, like many others, in the brave hope of compensating an actual aching vacuum in human experience. In this regard, Central Park is the grandiose symbol of the front yard each New York child hasn't got. On this island where people live in the confining interstices of steel and stone columns, the Park serves as a reminder of what the earth is really like before it is paved, pressed into brick or smelted into metal. To hundreds of thousands of New Yorkers, the Park is like an old and fiercely personal love song that was being played at a beautiful and telling moment in their lives. To still other hundreds of thousands of adults, it is a beloved part of their childhood. Each year twenty million people visit, react to and on the Park. On any fine spring Sunday, one hundred thousand people will visit its altogether charming little Zoo. And, through some sort of benign alchemy, New York's elbows are somewhat blunted as they enter the Park—just as, in the old days in the West, when people entered an amiable household, they left their hats and guns at the front door."

From "Look Ma—Real Grass!" by George Sessions Perry, in *Saturday Evening Post*, 1947.

Engraved from a drawing by W. W. Waud, *Harper's Weekly*, October 14, 1865.

CENTRAL PARK, NEW YORK—MUSIC ON THE LAKE

... as the numerous playgrounds provided youngsters with slides, swings, the carousel, and the menagerie.

From *Harper's Weekly Supplement*, July 8, 1871.

OUT-DOOR SUMMER AMUSEMENTS—THE SWINGS IN CENTRAL PARK

The diversified recreational facilities offered by the park included features designed for both adults and children, concert lovers and sports enthusiasts. From its earliest inception, musical concerts were the popular attraction for people of all ages. The outdoor swings for children did not long survive, as accidents were many, and vandalism made its mark. Summertime sports have, over the years, changed to meet what was in vogue; croquet and tennis no longer are the main attractions they once were. Gone are the graceful swan boats and the sheep meadow, and with it, the sheepfold, later transformed into the Tavern-on-the-Green, presently in limbo.

In a city of violent contrasts, nothing gave greater evidence than the community of dilapidated shanties scattered throughout the park's adjacent areas.

In the upper regions of Manhattan, immediately adjacent to Central Park, an entire community of tumbledown shanties covered vast sections of the city. The appalling contrast between the mansions of New York's wealthy classes and these weather-beaten hovels revealed the lowly aspects of which residents and visitors alike were aware. The task of clearing the Central Park area was begun in 1857, when many of the unfortunate shanty dwellers dismantled their shacks, picked up their sparse belongings, and moved elsewhere. Water had to be drawn from nearby ponds; sanitation was unheard-of. Fowl, goats, pigs, and dogs ran about freely, adding to an unhealthy state of affairs. A study of unsightly conditions was made by Charlotte G. O'Brien, an Irish author and social reformer, who wrote: "What was to be seen outside? Filth indescribable, naked-limbed children, slatternly women. . . . As a sample of infant mortality resulting from these conditions, in a family which had borne eleven children, only two pale boys were the survivors. . . ." Twenty years after this scene was depicted, the same degrading conditions persisted, as seen in the engraving on the facing page. Apartment buildings were being erected in the fashionable properties bordering on Central Park West. But for the very poor, both here and in the overcrowded Lower East Side, relief was slow in coming.

Engraved from a drawing by D. E. Wyand, *Harper's Weekly*, June 26, 1869.

THE SQUATTERS OF NEW YORK—SCENE NEAR CENTRAL PARK

Along Central Park West, in the shadow of new, modern apartment buildings, lived the poor and unfortunate in a world apart from its neighbors.

From *Frank Leslie's Illustrated Newspaper*, September 7, 1889.

NEW YORK CITY—BUILDING CONTRASTS—A MODERN FLAT ON THE WEST SIDE, NEAR CENTRAL PARK, AND ITS HUMBLE NEIGHBORS

"The contrast between the buildings erected in New York in recent years—massive, costly, and rich in decoration—and the humble little cottages which formerly occupied their sites is indeed most striking. Such a contrast can be found near Central Park in many places. Our artist has availed himself of the opportunity to make a picture that well illustrates the subject. The great overshadowing mass of brick and stone rises as if it would overwhelm the humble cottage that was built upon the plot when it was all a part of a garden or a farm. We find in the one wealth, luxury, and refinement, in the other the humble home of the poor. Who shall say that there is more happiness in the former than in the latter?"

From *Frank Leslie's Illustrated Newspaper*, September 7, 1889.

Winslow Homer, in this noted engraving, has captured the delight and sheer joy experienced by New Yorkers when winter beckoned to skaters of all ages.

An annual report of the park commission, in 1858, reported: "It is certain that about 80,000 persons visited the Park on one day, and half of this number were probably together at one time on and about the twenty acres of ice, the larger part moving rapidly, in exuberant spirits, while the roads were crowded with carriages.... It is undeniable, that the concentration of such numbers of pleasure-seekers upon the little space of twenty acres, while it imposes some restraint upon the skaters, and calls for constant exercise of skill to avoid collisions, adds vastly to the general gayety, and thus causes an excitement of healthful hilarity which, if it can be enjoyed in safety, is in itself of no small value. None of the various exhibitions of crowded life of this metropolis are more interesting, or can be viewed with more unmingled satisfaction than the skating scene upon the park."

"When the Lake ice was ready to welcome skaters, horsecars coming to the park broke out flags, and from a belltower on Vista Rock, now the site of Belvedere Castle, was hoisted a red ball. Calcium reflectors provided light for night skating, and a northern portion of the Lake was reserved for ladies. For those persons too fragile or clumsy to skate, ice chairs with runners could be hired. Park attendance reached its peak on a frosty winter day when the ice sparkled and snow piled up on the drives through which sleighs could crunch...."

From *Central Park: A History and a Guide,* by Henry Hope Reed and Sophia Duckworth, 1967.

SKATING ON THE LADIES' SKATING-POND IN THE CENTRAL PARK, NEW YORK

The cry "The ball's up" brought thousands of pleasure-seekers to the park's many ponds, as every horsecar carried a white flag with red disk announcing the good news.

145

Engraved from a drawing by Winslow Homer, *Harper's Weekly*, January 28, 1860.

"Winter sports are now principally indulged in at the country clubs, but forty years ago there was no lack of skating, hockey, lacrosse and even tobogganing on Manhattan island. In fact, there was a great toboggan slide built at the Polo Grounds, on Fifth Avenue and 110th Street, in imitation of the famous Montreal slide. There was a great deal more interest in ice-skating than there is today and the park lakes were crowded on winter evenings with ruddy skaters. The comic press had no end of fun writing of ice skaters, the favorite butt being some showy performer who comes to grief by the various misadventures which only a cartoonist could invent. Besides the park, ponds were located in what are now congested retail sections. There was a sizeable pond on Fifth Avenue between Thirty-seventh and Thirty-eighth streets; Beekman's Pond, between Fifty-ninth and Sixtieth streets; Alexander McMillan's, at Forty-sixth Street, site of Windsor Hotel; the New York Skating Club, at Fifty-ninth Street, site of the Plaza, and later, corner of Fifth Avenue and Seventy-second Street."

From *Valentine's Manual of Old New York*, edited by Henry Collins Brown, 1926.

In a most glorious illustration of the New York scene, one can almost hear the sleigh bells tinkling, as cutters and sleighs glide along the park drive...

"Snow laid in our streets for a long time in these days and every vehicle took to runners. The uptown drives and Central Park were alive with sleigh riders. In the early morning and all through the forenoon happy fathers might have been seen taking an airing behind the staid family horse, harnessed to the family sleigh. The fair young lady with the 'bang-tailed' pony, russet harness and 'natty' cutter was also noticeable. The 'swell' young man with his Russian drosky drawn by three horses decorated with red plumes was the observed of all observers, while the fashionable man reclined lazily in the regulation sleigh with the English 'tiger' drawing the lines over the prancing steeds. In the afternoon and evening the butcher, the baker, and all kinds of tradesmen who possessed horses that worked through the working days helped make the holiday gathering. The proprietors of the road houses were joyous, and as they went to bed with the prospect of a continued run of sleighing, they dreamed of fortunes that the best of modern Utopias could not hope to realize."

From *Valentine's Manual of Old New York,* edited by Henry Collins Brown, 1926.

SLEIGHING IN CENTRAL PARK

... near the West Side entrance at Seventy-second Street before the Daniel Webster statue, and the Dakota Apartments in the background.

Engraved from a drawing by W. P. Snyder, *Harper's Weekly*, February 27, 1886.

"William H. Vanderbilt was out behind his famous team Early Rose and Aldine. He drove up as far as McCombs Dam Bridge, turned around and without stopping returned home. Nathan Strauss at different times took a spin behind Majolica, Majolica Maid and J. D. Ripley. As he passed Alderman Hugh J. Grant driving a chestnut pacer he shouted a challenge for a brush down the road. Shepard Knapp was one of the first to go up the road and one of the last to turn his horse's head homeward. Frank Work was out in the morning with Regina, and in the afternoon with Edward. An old man driving a black gelding harnessed to a Portland sleigh, painted yellow, made the frequenters of Seventh Avenue open their eyes as he let his horse out for all there was in him. He didn't linger long enough for anybody to ask his name and nobody could keep within hailing distance."

From *Valentine's Manual of Old New York*, edited by Henry Collins Brown, 1926.

Homer, in this close-up study, prefers to concentrate on the feminine passengers and their costumes, as background figures convey the wintry atmosphere.

When Winslow Homer sketched this scene in 1869, winter snows were heavy and lingered on the city streets and drives for long periods. Besides beautifully decorated family cutters there were long sleighs of the type drawn by four or more horses, accommodating as many as twenty persons. The drives through Central Park were like a visit to the open country. Sleighing was fashionable, a counterpart to the carriage parade that took place in the summertime.

"When there is real good sleighing, my sister hires a stage sleigh and takes me and a lot of my schoolmates for a sleighride down Broadway to the Battery and back. The sleigh is open and very long: and has long seats on each side, and straw on the floor to keep our feet warm, and the sleigh bells sound so cheerful. We see some of our friends taking their afternoon walk on the sidewalk, and I guess they wish they were in our sleigh!"

From *The Diary of a Little Girl in Old New York,* by Catherine Elizabeth Havens, aged ten, in 1849.

Engraved from a drawing by Winslow Homer, *Harper's Weekly,* January 2, 1869.

CHRISTMAS BELLES

The park drives were crowded with every type of sleigh, especially after the new-fallen snow proved most inviting.

Engraved from a drawing by P. Frenzeny, *Harper's Weekly*, February 18, 1882.

SLEIGHING IN CENTRAL PARK

In the city with the coming of the snow appeared the sleigh. The jingling of bells on a frosty morning announced its presence. Everywhere wheels gave way to runners and the snow was soon hard packed for smooth sleighing. "On one of the wide roads of the town, any clear winter afternoon, you will see hundreds of sleighs dashing hither and thither, the daintiest and jauntiest of equipages, luxuriously warm and cosy by the aid of skins and blankets, drawn by spirited horses of finest temper and occupied by the male and female fashionable world. There is racing in spite of all that policemen and legislators can do; the very air tempts it and intoxicates and makes hilarious. Sleigh after sleigh—their little bells jingling in a frenzy—whirls by you, filled with excited gentlemen half-rising from their seats, and timid ladies trying to look unconcerned; two broad lines of them, one passing down on the right, the other up on the left. Thus they rush, up hill and down dale, defiant alike of the law and the danger."

From *American Society,* by George M. Towle, London, 1870.

With ten miles of fine carriage roads and another six miles of bridle paths, Central Park catered to the equine cult, but especially to the coaching enthusiasts.

"Coaching has come to be one of the most popular sports among those who can afford it. It is not only healthful and invigorating, but a means of sociability beside which many of its rivals among sports—even yachting, with its ever possible dangers—can not be compared. There is a sense of safety while rolling over mother earth—no treachery there from winds or tides. That sense of security gives zest to the social spirit. The invigorating air, the beauties of the landscape, and the pictures of country life are never-failing themes for wit or sentiment, suggestions for poetry or story. To be sure, the coaching enthusiasts can not control the weather. Showers will come. But there are seats inside for the ladies. Your true coachman rather enjoys than regrets such an interruption. His great-coat, with prodigious buttons, always provided for such an emergency, is sufficient protection for him, and a race for a place of shelter, when thunder and lightning accompanies the storm and frightens the horses a bit, is a source of additional exhilaration for him; and a successful race under such circumstances forms a fruitful topic of conversation for many days to come."

From *Harper's Weekly*, June 2, 1883.

Engraved from a drawing by Schell and Hogan, *Harper's Weekly*, June 12, 1886

COACHING IN NEW YORK—A DRIVE THROUGH CENTRAL PARK

Broughams, landaus, rockaways, phaetons, dogcarts, curricles, and almost every type of vehicle made may be seen in the midafternoon procession at driving time.

From a pen and ink drawing by Gray-Parker, *Harper's Weekly*, May 19, 1883.

THE DRIVE—CENTRAL PARK—FOUR O'CLOCK

"The best place to see the driving is at a point not far from the Egyptian obelisk which the Khedive gave us some years ago.... As the tide of dissatisfied and weary wealth rolls by its base here, in the fantastic variety of its equipages, does the needle discern so much difference between their occupants and the occupants of the chariots that swept beneath it in the capital of the Ptolemies two thousand years ago?... They pass in all kinds of vehicles, and there are all kinds of people in them, though at times there are no people at all, as when the servants have been sent out to exercise the horses.... I have now and then seen a gentleman driving in a four-in-hand, with everything to minister to his vanity in the exact imitation of a nobleman driving a four-in-hand over English roads, and with no one to be drawn by his crop-tailed bays or blacks except himself and the solemn groom on his perch; I have wondered how much more nearly equal they were in their aspirations and instincts than either of them imagined. A gentleman driving a pair, abreast or tandem, with a groom on the rumble, for no purpose except to express his quality, is a common sight enough; and sometimes you see a lady illustrating her consequence in like manner. A lady driving, while a gentleman occupies the seat behind her, is a sight which always affects me like the sight of a man taking a woman's arm in walking, as the man of an underbred sort is apt to do.... But these stylish turn-outs form only a part of the spectacle in the Park driveways.... There are family carryalls, with friendly-looking families, old and young, getting the good of the Park together in a long, leisurely jog; and open buggies with yellow wheels and raffish men in them behind their widespread trotters...."

From *Impressions and Experiences,*
by William Dean Howells, 1896.

Guided by a special "gondolier" who pedaled the swan boat by foot power, the family outing was complete after a ride on the lake in Central Park

"We New Yorkers had made up our minds that we must have a good-sized breathing-place, and that at the rate the city was growing it would not do to wait much longer before setting aside the land for it. The public was discontented, but it had no means of giving expression to its feeling. The rich people, when they could not endure their *ennui* any longer, took ship and went and walked in the Tuileries, or drove with the other nabobs in Hyde Park, or drank coffee under the lindens in Berlin. . . ."

From "A Talk about Public Parks and Gardens," by A. J. Downing, in *Horticulturist*, 1848.

"The long-standing want in the great city of New York of suitable pleasure grounds, has, within the past two or three years, been amply supplied in the creation of that beautiful Arcadia known as Central Park; a magnificent domain containing hundreds of broad acres of hill and valley, cliff and copse, lake and lawn, and miles upon miles of winding drives and winning walks, all radiant in a magic atmosphere of art and taste. . . ."

From "The Central Park," by T. Addison Richards, in *Harper's Magazine*, 1861.

Engraved from a drawing by J. Durkin, *Frank Leslie's Illustrated Newspaper,* July 27, 188

SUMMER SCENES IN CENTRAL PARK, NEW YORK CITY—A SAIL ON A SWAN-BOAT

PART SEVEN
Times of Trouble

Engraved from a drawing by F. V. Du Mond, *Harper's Weekly,* March 10, 1888.

THE GREAT NEW YORK FIRE AT FORTY-SECOND STREET AND LEXINGTON AVENUE.

"The members of the fire companies came from all walks of life. The firemen themselves were a power in the city and wielded considerable political influence by their members and strong organization. As an individual, the volunteer fireman was expected to stop whatever he was doing, whether work or play, and hasten to a conflagration when the alarm sounded. If he failed to follow his apparatus or violated any of the innumerable rules and regulations, he was fined, sometimes heavily."

From *Enjine! Enjine!*
by Kenneth Holcombe Dunshee, 1939.

Times of Trouble

THE VISITOR TO the city stands in awed silence, frozen, in his admiration while gazing at the marvels of man's enterprise. He surveys the pointed spires of age-old places of worship hemmed in by towering citadels of commerce, proclaiming to the world, of hope, courage, and achievement. Behind the skyline of ever-changing Manhattan lies evidence of heartbreak, disaster, and violence telling volumes about the indomitable will of its people. The recovery from much turbulence, "the sweet uses of adversity," say more than mere sticks and stones left standing about fires, panics, strikes, and blizzards—the thousand and one setbacks that have staggered New Yorkers in their constant battle for renewal.

What better way to measure their sacrifices than a quick glance at the countless conflagrations that have periodically beset the city. During the British occupation, in 1776 and 1778, the town was almost wiped out. What few traces of old Dutch houses survived were destroyed by the great fire of 1835, the worst Manhattan had ever experienced. On an extremely cold December night when the blaze started, water froze in the hydrants and rendered the firemen helpless to control the flames. Seven hundred houses in a seventeen-block area were gutted, between Broadway, Wall Street, and Coenties Slip on the East River waterfront. But almost overnight, phoenixlike, the financial community that had suffered total damage was rebuilt.

In spite of frequent, fiery devastations, it took years to reorganize the volunteer fire department. Rival laddies were more concerned with their own deviltry in battling opposing companies than in fighting the consuming flames. Records tell of many houses burned to the ground as rival gangs engaged in fisticuffs to settle internecine squabbles on the scene. The stress of the Civil War was especially difficult for fire fighters, as widespread rioting accompanied incendiary fires. The turbulent Draft Riots of 1863 were a culmination of unparalleled social upheavals which, between the years 1834 and 1874, accounted for sixteen major civil disturbances and innumerable minor disorders. Economic woes were the result of widespread unemployment and sharply rising prices. Conditions were ripe in the hot summer of 1863; the city was a veritable tinderbox. It needed only the draft to ignite the explosive situation. Lincoln's call for additional troops involved conscription, long a radical departure from established American tradition of a volunteer system. Strong opposition to the draft came from the masses, realizing that the more affluent could buy their way out of service for a paltry payment to a substitute.

As mobs of rioters, estimated at thirty thousand, broke into open rebellion, the police were helpless. Four thousand federal troops were sent in, many seasoned war veterans, but the combined police force and militia were vastly outnumbered and soon retreated after many of their number were killed or wounded. The rioters had raided gun shops, food and liquor stores, and were well supplied to carry on their violent opposition to authority. After a few bloody days in which dozens of fires had been set, and over a thousand reported killed, a small semblance of order slowly came to a city stunned in disbelief.

The ills of New York, its social inequities and inequalities, were the special investigation of Jacob Riis, superbly documented in his classic book *How the Other Half Lives:* "The sea of a mighty population, held in galling fetters, heaves uneasily in the tenements. Once already our city, to which have come the duties and responsibilities of metropolitan greatness before it was able to fairly measure its task, has felt the swell of its resistless flood. If it rises once more, no human power may avail to check it. The gap between the classes in which it surges, unseen, unsuspected by the thoughtless, is widening day by day." The unrest engendered by grave injustices became manifest when overwhelming numbers decided to take matters into their own hands. Such a situation resulted in the bread riots earlier in the century when exorbitant prices of flour brought on a major revolt, and many shops were broken into.

The strengthening of union ranks and labor's organized resistance, a newly forged weapon in the fight against employers' oppressive policies, culminated in several major labor strikes, notably against the streetcar companies in 1886 and again, a few years later. Municipal authorities resorted to the unlimited use of the police force in order to restore transport service. As a police captain stated, at the time, "There is more law in the end of a policeman's nightstick than in a decision of the Supreme Court." But the union leaders had learned a valuable lesson, at the price of many bloodied noses, that the strike would serve them in the future.

With the burning of the upper story of City Hall from fireworks, stricter enforcement of fire laws followed.

From *Harper's Weekly,* August 28, 1858.

THE BURNING OF THE CITY HALL, NEW YORK, AUGUST 18, 1858

New Yorkers had justifiable pride in their City Hall, an edifice that many consider one of the finest of municipal structures in the country. This "architectural treasure without peer," completed in 1811, was the combined work of Joseph Mangin, a French architect who collaborated with John McComb, Jr., winning a competition and the coveted prize of $350 in cash. To the prevailing French Renaissance style has been added some characteristic American Federalist influence. For his supervision of the hall's construction, McComb was paid six dollars a day. He was greatly disturbed, however, when informed one day by Mayor Clinton that in the rear part of the building, instead of white marble it would be necessary to substitute red sandstone, as a measure of economy. As if to justify this abrupt change in plans, the mayor insisted that since it was in the rear and considerably "way uptown" it would not be noticed by anyone. Architectural critics have been almost unanimous in praise of City Hall. Hamlin has called "this exceptionally elegant and airy building of delicate scale and detail the 'death blow' to the English tradition." Ada Louise Huxtable declares "the building is a symbol of taste, excellence, and quality not always matched by the policies inside." But on one hot August evening, in 1858, fireworks caused a disastrous fire, with the complete destruction of the cupola and its statue, and the roof and upper story. The figure of Justice, carved in wood, replaced the original Dixey figure. In a later restoration this was followed by a figure in copper, in 1887.

Seldom has New York witnessed such scenes of mob violence and lawlessness as during those hot summer days of 1863, when the roving bands of gangsters—the Bowery Boys, the Dead Rabbits . . .

After more than two years of fighting, the war between the North and the South saw unspeakable bloody scenes and mob violence in New York. Bitter hatreds fanned by the pending conscription culminated in the Draft Riots of 1863. Wartime austerity, high prices for food and coal, and the inequities of conscription all contributed to a smoldering unrest. A draftee could buy his exemption from service for $300, or produce a substitute in his place. The populace, angered by this injustice, declared "it was a rich man's war, but a poor man's fight." The importation of great numbers of slaves who were willing to work for scab wages further incensed striking workers. The official date for starting the draft, July 11, 1863, saw an organized insurrection led by well-planned strategies to isolate the city, cut off the approaches, capture the forts, and seize the armories, thus crippling the federal war effort. G. T. Strong, noted diarist of the time, called these rebels "agents of Jefferson Davis, scoundrels who are privily engineering the outburst." When the roster of first draftees numbering 1,236 was published and further need announced, the intense anger of the mobs could no longer be constrained. They marched upon the draft offices at Forty-seventh Street and Third Avenue, and within a few hours the building was burned to the ground, followed by many others in the next few days. Of this entire episode Carl Sandburg wrote: "Never before in an American metropolis had the police, merchants, bankers, and forces of law and order had their power wrenched loose by mobs so skillfully led."

A GORILLA ON THE LOOSE

DRAGGING COLONEL O'BRIEN'S BODY THROUGH THE MUD

SACKING BROOKS CLOTHING STORE

THE DEAD SERGEANT IN TWENTY-SECOND STREET

From *Harper's Weekly,* August 1, 1863.
NEGRO QUARTERS IN SULLIVAN STREET

THE RIOTS IN NEW YORK

... the Plug Uglies and the Shirt Tails, incensed by the injustices of the draft, rallied as one giant mob in their attempt to sack and burn the city.

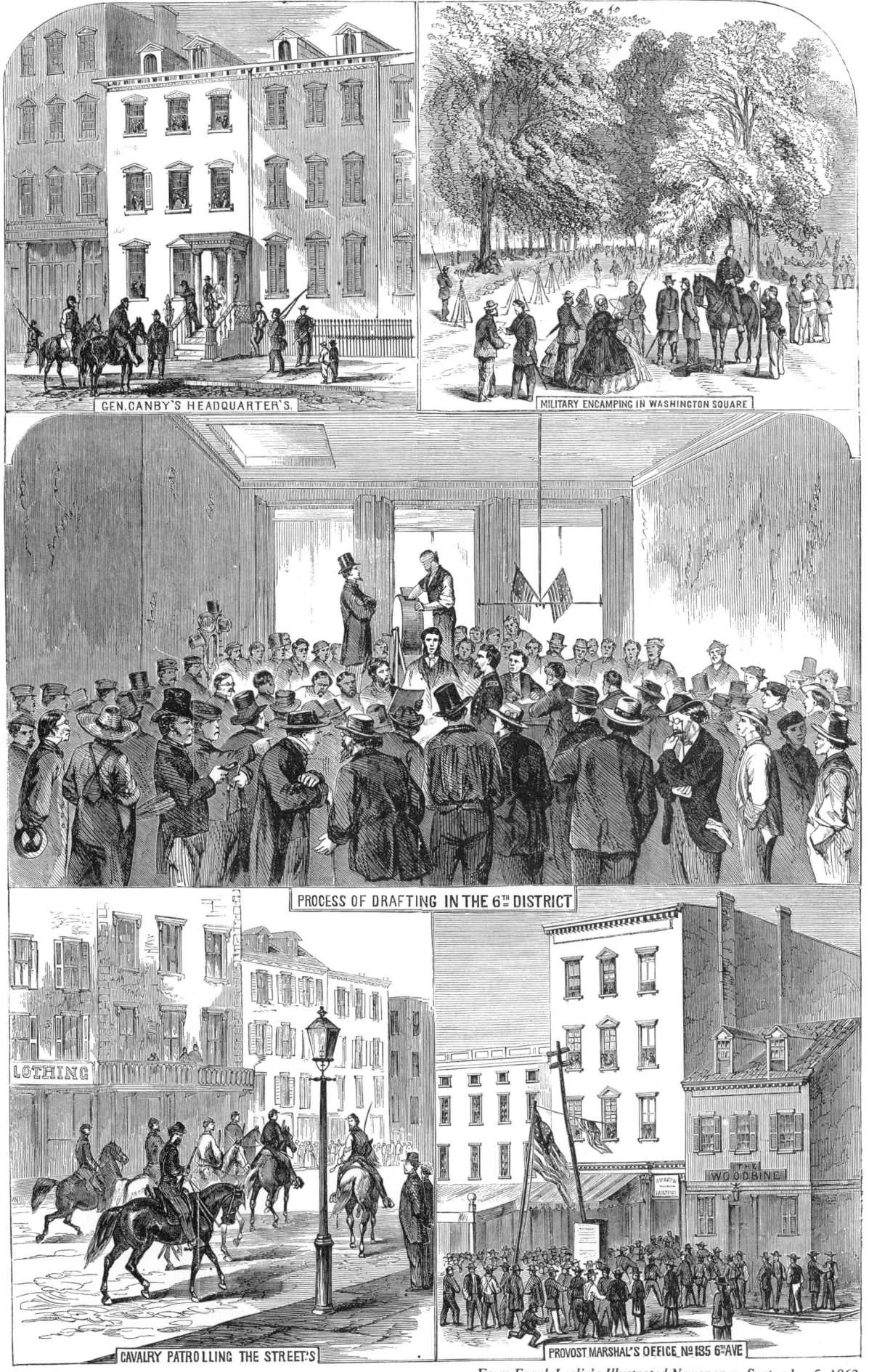

From *Frank Leslie's Illustrated Newspaper,* September 5, 1863.

THE DRAFT—SCENES IN NEW YORK, AUGUST 19, DURING THE DRAFTING IN THE SIXTH DISTRICT

"The draft was 'profoundly repugnant to the American mind,' according to the New York *World,* controlled by Fernando Wood and August Belmont. Wood's brother, Benjamin, headed the *Daily News,* which said, 'The people are notified that one out of about two and a half citizens are to be brought into Messrs. Lincoln & Company's charnelhouse. God forbid!' The proslavery *Journal of Commerce* snarled that the war itself had become the work of 'evil-minded men to accomplish their aims.' Even though his own state had already passed a draft act, Democratic Governor Horatio Seymour challenged the federal government's right to conscript citizens. By protesting the quota assigned to New York State, he postponed the first local draft lottery. On July 4, in New York City, the governor made one of the most inflammatory speeches ever uttered by a public official. Seymour shouted, 'Remember this! Remember this! The bloody, treasonable and revolutionary doctrine of public necessity can be proclaimed by a mob as well as a government!'"

From *The Epic of New York City,*
by Edward Robb Ellis, 1966.

At the firehouse the "boys" lived comfortably, prepared, at a moment's notice, to answer any alarm...

"The firemen are mostly youths engaged during the day in various handicrafts and mechanical trades, with a sprinkling of clerks and shopmen. In New York, each candidate for admission into the force must be balloted for, like a member of the London clubs. If elected, he has to serve for five years, during which he is exempt from jury and militia duty. The firemen are divided into engine companies, hook and ladder companies, and hose companies. The engine and accessories are provided by the municipality; but the firemen are seldom contented with them in the useful but unadorned state in which they receive them, but lavish upon them an amount of ornament, in the shape of painted panels, silver plating, and other finery, more than sufficient to prove their liberality, and the pride they take in their business. The service is entirely voluntary and gratuitous, having no advantages to recommend it but those of exemption from the jury and the militia, and leads those who devote themselves to it not only into great hardship and imminent danger, but into an amount of expenditure which is not the least surprising part of the 'institution.' The men—or 'boys,' as they are more commonly called—not only buy their own custume and accoutrements, and spend large sums in the ornamentation of their favourite engines, or hydrants, as already mentioned, but in the furnishing of their bunk-rooms and parlours at the fire-stations. The bunk or sleeping rooms in which the unmarried, and sometimes the married, members pass the night, to be ready for duty on the first alarm of fire, are plainly and comfortably furnished; but the parlours are fitted up with a degree of luxury equal to that of the public rooms of the most celebrated hotels."

From *Life and Liberty in America,* by Charles Mackay, 1859.

Engraved from a drawing by I. Pranishnikoff, *Harper's Weekly,* March 4, 1876.

THE NEW YORK FIRE INSURANCE PATROL

. . . but rivalry between fire companies often led to brawls and street fighting as laddies rushed to be the first to reach the fire hydrants.

While the life of a fireman was filled with danger and death-defiance, there was, nevertheless, an opportunity for fun and frolic when the fire companies marched in parades, held Fourth of July picnics with drills and demonstrations. At night fireworks made for a festive display, witnessed by hundreds of excited spectators. It was then that the old-fashioned ''masheens'' were hauled out of storage to provide nostalgic reenactment of ''olden-style fire-fighting.'' But as long as volunteers manned the pumps and hydrants, there was bound to be a battleground between companies for supremacy. Thus fire fighting developed into an internecine affair. Instead of aiming primarily to extinguish a blaze, this rivalry was bent mainly upon beating out their rivals. Reaching the fire hydrant became a first priority, in order to prevent their opponents from pumping an adequate water supply. The frustration of the losers always led to fisticuffs, as bloody noses and blackened eyes testified. This seemed the only way to settle scores in the name of fierce company loyalty. But with the invention of the steam pumper (New York's first demonstration took place in City Hall Park in 1855), and its eventual improvement, the faulty volunteer system was replaced, and its many inequities gave way to a paid fire-fighting force in which efficiency and speed replaced the street brawls of rival factions.

Engraved from drawings by Schell and Hogan, *Harper's Weekly*, October 17, 1885.

THE OLD NEW YORK FIRE DEPARTMENT CELEBRATION

Because the time element was so crucial, when fire struck in New York, complete devastation often followed...

Devastation by fire was such a common occurrence during the nineteenth century that often the fire company's main task was to contain the conflagration and prevent its spreading to other buildings, all of them of highly inflammable materials. Rarely did the fire company arrive on the scene in time to prevent a building's complete loss. All that remained, generally, were bare, blackened walls of stone or brick. Barnum's Hippodrome, located on Fourteenth Street (not the original American Museum), took fire at four o'clock on a bitter cold January morning. Within minutes the building was a veritable bonfire, and Grace Chapel, alongside, and four other buildings were soon a total loss. Of Barnum's collection of rare animals and birds, only two elephants were successfully evacuated. Lions and tigers, bears and sea lions, and exotic birds were all lost in the blaze.

Among the many mercantile houses on lower Broadway were a number of book publishers. The Appleton Building, a five-story structure, housed a large inventory of books and papers, highly inflammable. When a fire broke out on a cold March morning, the combined efforts of many hose companies failed to stop the blaze before the entire building was lost. Engines could not pump the water fast enough to quell the flames, and the resultant loss was complete. Within a year, the company had recovered its loss, though the many precious manuscripts lost in the blaze were irreplaceable.

GREAT FIRE IN NEW YORK—RUINS OF THE APPLETON BUILDING, BROADWAY From *Harper's Weekly,* March 2, 1867.

THE BURNING OF BARNUM'S HIPPODROME Engraved from a photograph by Rockwood, *Harper's Weekly,* February 11, 1873.

... as the engines rarely reached the scene in time. On the waterfront pumping operations of the fireboats could often cope better than on land.

The hazards of fire were particularly great along the waterfront, where hundreds of wooden sailing ships were berthed. Cargoes carried much that was highly inflammable, and loading operations created added danger of fire that increased with the booming shipping trade. To reach these piers at either the North or East River often took fire companies a half hour after the alarm was sounded. Ship merchants and insurance companies organized to combat this menace by commissioning the launching of several fireboats, in 1882, to be docked at Pier One off the Battery. New York's first fireboat was named the *Zophar Mills*, in honor of one of the city's ablest and most daring firemen. Of Mills it has been said: "Where the smoke was thickest, and the fire was the hottest, there he was. He is like an old warhorse—as soon as he smells battle, he is off to it. He is the fire-king . . . he is the capsheaf. As the boys say, he 'takes the rag off the bush.' He is a wonderful man, and the truest man that ever breathed a breath of life." The matter of getting to a burning vessel involved precious minutes, so steam in the boilers was kept on at all times when the boat was docked, awaiting an alarm. Its powerful pumps could shoot a dozen jets at a time, and never experience low water pressure as so often plagued the fire companies on land.

From *Harper's Weekly*, November 11, 1882.

A FIRE AT A NEW YORK DOCK—THE RIVER FIRE-BRIGADE AT WORK

The hook and ladder companies have always been able to boast about their most colorful equipment, drawn by a span of three well-matched fire steeds...

"The fire department in New York... is a most wonderful thing. As the point of honor is to be first at a fire, the director of the first engine that arrives, becomes director-general for the evening. He is, as it were, the commander-in-chief of an allied army during a battle. The company attached to each engine amounts to from 20 to 100 men, and it starts from the station-house as soon as three or four have arrived to direct its movements. The people in the streets assist in dragging it with ropes, as no horses are employed. The competition to be first is so ardent, that ambitious young men sleep as if a part of the brain were left awake to watch for the word 'fire,' or the sound of the... alarm-bell. They will sometimes put on their boots and great-coats, carry their clothes in their hands, and dress at the fire. In rushing along the streets, sometimes blowing horns, and ringing the large bells attached to the engines all the time, they often run down and severely injure passengers who are in their way; or if one of themselves falls, the rest drag on the engine, regardless of his fate, and occasionally break his legs or arms with the wheels. When two engines arrive at a fire at the same time, the companies frequently fight for the first place, and then a desperate and bloody battle will rage for a considerable time, while the flames are making an unchecked progress. They are often called out on very trivial alarms, and being...

THE MODEL NEW YORK FIRE DEPARTMENT—A HOOK AND LADDER COMPANY ON THE RUN

... especially trained to carefully, though speedily, negotiate street corners while not overturning the long ladders drawn behind them.

Engraved from a drawing by Thure de Thulstrup, *Harper's Weekly*.

... once abroad at midnight hours, they adjourn to taverns, and pass the night in nocturnal recreations. ... On inquiring one day of a bystander, if all this hubbub were necessary, he politely replied, 'I guess the youth here need excitement.' "

From *Travels in South and North America,* by Alexander Marjoribanks, in 1853.

As the metropolis grew in density, taller buildings in the downtown area required larger equipment for improved fire protection. More fire houses dotted the denser sections, and speedier horses were trained to reach the fire scene with split-second timing. The need for man and beast to work in perfect harmony resulted in a wonderful feeling of camaraderie, as the men cleaned, combed, and curried their horses with genuine affection, knowing that often life depended upon the animals in their charge. "Great is the fire-horse and mighty is his master's love and respect for him . . . No horses in the world are better treated than the fire-horses," reported a New York Fire Company official. Careful matching of horses as to size, color and appearance required meticulous spanning. Dappled grays, chestnuts, pure whites and blacks were rarely mixed so that at all times teams just seemed to belong with certain fire apparatus.

During the worst snowstorms, the battle to keep streetcar lines open tested the mettle of both men and animals, as horse teams struggled to get through.

The urgent task of the streetcar companies was to keep the tracks open, as the city's economic life depended entirely upon the surface lines before the elevated's construction. A number of traction sweepers were put in service, each pulled by a powerful team of ten horses who were whipped unmercifully by a team master. When the storms were at their worst and drifts were more than three feet deep, all was to no avail, and many bystanders pitched in, to pull and tug with the straining horsepower. A *New York Herald* reporter described one of the city's bad storms this way: "A horror of darkness deepened on the crowded city, and the terror-stricken population cowered at the awful sounds which came from the throat of the wind. . . . Sign boards were stripped from the fronts of stores and hurled through the storm clouds. Hats were picked up and carried out of sight. As the afternoon wore away, men and women were blown flat on the ground or picked up into the air and thrown against buildings. Many were run over. The very mail wagons had to be abandoned. They were left in all sections of the city."

Engraved from a drawing by I. Pranishnikoff, *Harper's Weekly,* January 20, 1877.

IN THE SNOW—CLEARING THE STREET RAILWAY TRACKS IN NEW YORK

The city's wintry disasters also provided illustrators and cartoonists a chance to dwell upon the lighter side.

Pen and ink sketches by L. Hopkins combined with center engraving, *Harper's Weekly*, January 29, 1881.

It was customary, in January, for New Yorkers to brace themselves for the midwinter rigors that struck, so frequently, without special warning. The weather forecasters were dependent upon telegraphic advices from Washington, and these broke down when the worst storms were in progress. Julian Ralph, star reporter for the *New York Sun*, described the current storm thus: "The wind howled, whistled, banged, roared and moaned as it rushed along. It fell upon the house sides in fearful gusts, it strained great plate glass windows, rocked the frame houses, pressed against the doors so that it was almost too dangerous to open them. It was a visible, substantial wind, so freighted was it with snow. It came in whirls, it descended in layers, it shot along in great blocks, it rose and fell and corkscrewed and zigzagged and played merry havoc with everything it could swing or batter or bang or carry away. At half past ten o'clock, not a dozen stores on Fulton Street had opened for business. Men were making wild efforts to clean the walks, only to see each shovelful of snow blown back upon them and piled against the doors again."

With street transport solely dependent upon the horse, ice and snow drifts made travel impossible at times.

The hazards of travel and transport in the city where everything was horse-drawn were especially difficult during the winter storms. Snows to a depth of two and three feet were quite common in the 1870s and '80s. Streets were cleared very slowly, being limited to main thoroughfares; in the side streets the snow remained for the entire winter, making travel almost impossible in spots. "It may be difficult to realize how important was the horse in the domestic economy of our everyday lives in the Seventies. Everything was horse-drawn. You could transport no goods, or go anywhere without the aid of this indispensable animal. So utterly dependent were we on the horse that when a mysterious epidemic called the 'epizootic' afflicted these animals, so that temporarily we were without the services of our dumb friends, the business of the entire city was paralyzed. Instead of streetcars we walked. Such goods as had to be delivered were moved by handcarts and wheelbarrows, often by the merchants themselves. Foremost in the fight to protect our horses was Henry Bergh, the organizer of the Society for the Prevention of Cruelty to Animals. When he found evidence of any inhumane treatment such as the over-crowding of streetcars, he was in the forefront, arresting the drivers responsible. Much grumbling ensued as passengers had to get out and walk in the snow after these stoppages."

From *Valentine's Manual of Old New York*, edited by Henry Collins Brown, 1926.

Engraved from a drawing by George Inness, Jr., *Harper's Weekly*, January 12, 1884.

THE STREETS OF NEW YORK AFTER A SNOW-STORM

The city suffered severely from fires that could not be arrested, as engine companies failed to break through the giant snowdrifts.

Engraved from a drawing by Thure de Thulstrup, *Harper's Weekly,* March 24, 1888.

A STRUGGLE TO ANSWER A FIRE-ALARM DURING THE NEW YORK BLIZZARD

The terrors of the Great Blizzard were nowhere more strenuous than in the efforts of the city's fire companies to keep up with the many alarms turned in. Answering a call proved an almost impossible task from the moment the engine entered the street. The high drifts, the icy blasts, and terrific wind all combined to making the going tough, as man power had to add its strength to horse power in helping to drag the engines through the clogged streets. Henry Collins Brown told of the chaos after the storm: "In the morning an ice bridge formed over the East River and several thousand persons crossed on foot between New York and Brooklyn. The floe broke with the turn of the tide and a tugboat was essential to the rescue of five men who were drifting to sea on small cakes. Wednesday was bonfire day. All over town fire was brought into play to assist the sun. Soon there was fire leaping up from snow heaps everywhere and the gutters and sewers were flooded with the melted snow. On Thursday the bonfires continued and the sun came out strong. The horse cars broke into Park Row and the gutters sang merrily. On Friday the crosstown cars were running and the town returned to 'normalcy'."

Every aspect of the Great Blizzard was grist for the news reporter's mill, as New Yorkers had seldom been put to such a devastating experience...

"Walls of snow blocked all the streets west of Seventh Avenue. Traffic halted. Horse-drawn streetcars bogged down, and although first four horses, then six horses, and finally eight horses were hitched to one car, the cars couldn't be budged. Steam trains were immobilized in the suburbs, some plowing to a stop in a deep railroad cut at Spuyten Duyvil just north of the city limits. A New York Central locomotive tried to butt through snow packed in the Fourth Avenue tunnel, only to topple off its rails. Some idiot asked Chauncey M. Depew, president of the New York Central, if the line could maintain its train service. Depew snorted, 'Trains! Why, we don't even know whether we've got a railroad left!' Vehicular traffic on the Brooklyn Bridge was halted, and police warned pedestrians not to walk across in the shrieking storm. Now Brooklyn was entirely cut off from Manhattan. After various adventures, ferryboats gave up trying to reach Manhattan; thus, Staten Island and New Jersey almost became inaccessible. A few brave and greedy cabdrivers still slogged through the streets. Some poured whiskey into their horses to keep them from freezing to death, and the price of a cab ride rose to thirty dollars, then forty dollars, and ultimately to more than fifty dollars.''

From *The Epic of New York City,*
by Edward Robb Ellis, 1966.

Engraved from drawings by Charles Graham, *Harper's Weekly Supplement,* March 24, 1888.

DOWN-TOWN SKETCHES IN NEW YORK DURING MONDAY'S BLIZZARD

... Illustrators and sketch artists limned their impressions on the scene, giving a vivid pictorial record of the terrors of that momentous event.

"There have been a good many tempestuous snow storms in New York since then, and certain statistics have been referred to by wiseacres, in the way of inches of snowfall and velocity of wind in subsequent storms to at least rival if not surpass that classic hurricane, but nothing that New York has experienced since has been a marker to it in spectacular devastation. Some of its details are worth recalling. The Staten Island ferryboats had their flagstaffs snapped off the instant they put out their noses in the morning. A Sixth Avenue elevated train loaded with passengers consumed six hours and twenty minutes in covering a distance of two blocks. Many of the passengers effected their escape after hours of waiting by means of a ladder reared against the 'L' structure by private enterprise. It cost fifty cents a head to go down the ladder into the comparative freedom of the blizzard and the drifts. The electric lights had failed and the great thoroughfare was in total darkness. Mr. Barremore, a merchant, was found dead of cold and exhaustion the next morning, within four blocks of his home."

From *Valentine's Manual of Old New York*, edited by Henry Collins Brown, 1926.

From *Scientific American*, March 24, 1888.

NEW YORK CITY—THE GREAT SNOW AND WIND STORM OF MARCH 12 & 13

The streetcar workers' rebellion resulting from oppressive
work hours and niggardly pay erupted in a serious strike . . .

"The strike of New York horse-car drivers, conductors, and stable-men, which began with a single line on Tuesday, March 2, and culminated on Friday in a universal tie-up on every road, was the most extensive ever known in the city. The strikers numbered 800. Several days before the strike the men had presented their petition to the president of the company. He advertised in Sunday's paper for new employees, but those who were engaged were gathered in by the strikers, so that the strike on Tuesday was complete. An attempt was made to run blue car No. 155 through Grand Street. A big brewery wagon was overturned at one point; goat-carts became stalled, and relieved themselves by leaving their contents on the tracks; lumber, cobble-stones, hogsheads, bricks, and barrels rapidly accumulated, and at East Broadway junction the switch-plate was taken up. The hard job was then abandoned, and the car retreated. The municipal authorities now found themselves face to face with a formidable riot. Accordingly, Supt. Murray of the police force was prepared to discharge his duties to maintain order. He collected 750 policemen, and at half past 2 P.M. essayed the task of taking blue car 155, which had been blocked in the morning, on the round trip from river to river and back. He had already distributed 500 of his men along Grand Street, and now . . .

THE STREET RAILROAD STRIKE IN NEW YORK—THE POLICE OPENING THE WAY FOR A HORSE-CAR

... as the eyes of the nation turned to New York, caught in a battleground of labor strife that was to affect labor relations of the future.

Engraved from a drawing by Thure de Thulstrup, *Harper's Weekly,* March 12, 1886.

"... placed the remaining available forces around the car, strong platoons being in front, on both sides and in the rear. Thus it proceeded like a military procession, and two officials of the company acting the unenviable role of passengers. The streets were thronged with a mob that groaned, hissed, and jeered from the sidewalks, while from every window there were angry jabbering and shaking fists. Before long a pile of lumber was encountered, which the police escort removed. Soon the obstructions multiplied—cobble-stones, heaps of ashes, loads of sand, bales of rags, barrels and boxes, and even big baggage trucks, wheels uppermost. It was near one of these, at Eldridge Street, which had brought the cortege to a full stop, that the first serious trouble occurred. Scarcely had Murray called to his men, 'Lift off that truck,' when from the crowd which surged and eddied in closer at every pause in the progress, a stone whizzed past his head. The cry 'Charge' rang out, and instantly the heavy clubs went aloft, and descended on the heads and shoulders nearest. With wild cries of alarm the crowd scattered in all directions, a few badly clubbed, some injured by being trampled on, while show windows were smashed, and hats and bonnets were strewn on the street as the result of the fray.''

From *Harper's Weekly,* March 12, 1886.

As the city's transit came to a standstill, conflicting theories of labor's rights and purposes were hotly debated by leaders of opposing factions.

"The year 1886 was blotched by depression, mass unemployment, strikes, and lockouts. Among other labor disorders, New York's streetcar employees struck for shorter hours. While city aldermen took bribes in exchange for franchises paying enormous profits to rapid transit owners, the workers themselves were paid a pittance for slaving up to 16 hours a day. Most aldermen were indicted for bribery, New Yorkers turned in anger on their public servants, and labor leaders decided to channel the mood to their own ends. The Central Labor Union (C.L.U.), organized in 1882, now banded together 207 separate unions, representing 50,000 workers in New York, Brooklyn and Jersey City. Then, deciding to plunge into politics, the C.L.U. pledged support to Henry George in the forthcoming mayoralty race. The Democrats nominated Abram S. Hewitt. The Republicans picked Theodore Roosevelt."

From *The Epic of New York City,* by Edward Robb Ellis, 1966.

Less than three years had elapsed since the serious car strike of 1886. Labor's grievances again threatened disruption of New York's streetcar service. After the failure to settle the workers' differences, a general tie-up was ordered. Trouble broke out on the most prominent thoroughfares and important crosstown lines. Many heads were clubbed and faces bruised. Cars were overturned and horses injured. The Society for the Prevention of Cruelty to Animals, caught in the midst of the labor dispute, tried to exercise special vigilance, with a few veterinarians in constant attendance. The strike lasted more than a week before it was called off by the strikers' representatives, who agreed to the slight raise in wages that the company was forced to accept.

A RIOT ON FORTY-SECOND STREET, NEAR BROADWAY — Engraved from a drawing by Charles Graham and J. Durkin

STARTING A CAR ON THE SIXTH AVENUE LINE — Engraved from a drawing by W. P. Snyder, *Harper's Weekly,* February 9, 1889

THE STREET-CAR STRIKE IN NEW YORK

PART EIGHT

In Pursuit of Pleasure

Engraved from a drawing by A. B. Frost, *Harper's Weekly*, February 26, 1881.

AN OLD-TIME SLEIGH-RIDE IN NEW YORK
WINTER AMUSEMENTS

The heavy snows that marked New York's winters over a century ago necessitated a complete change-over in transportation on the crowded thoroughfares of the city. A two or three foot snowfall rendered the streets impassable, as teams of horses struggled to make headway against great odds. The stage people on these occasions ran large sleighs drawn by four or more horses. Eyre Crowe, writing in his *With Thackeray in America* speaks of the sleighs as "long affairs with huge curved and decorated fronts, filled with a lot of men and children standing, shouting, and enjoying much merriment." The largest, called man-of-war sleighs, appeared on principal avenues, especially downtown Broadway. As they raced up and down there was a genial air of excitement and good humor brought on by snowballing from the street Arabs who ran alongside.

In Pursuit of Pleasure

WITH THE CLOSING YEARS of Civil War strife came a slow relaxation of tensions, pointing the way for New Yorkers once again to enjoy lighter moments of diversion. There followed the swift development of outdoor pastimes, both in competitive games and in the area of spectator sports. On the athletic fields of the nation, the great social inequalities of the new age of industrialism mattered little; the prize went to those most proficient and fleetest. Actual players were few in number, but those who watched hailed the winner regardless of his station in life or background. Democracy, however warped by wealth or the lack of it, was willing to reward those triumphant on the field of athletic endeavor. The young of the republic learned to play the game vigorously, yet the emphasis was on the winning, rather than mere playing.

As a prelude to the rise in sportsmanship and outdoor activity, many of the nation's sages had openly decried the lack of participation. Oliver Wendell Holmes, writing in *Atlantic Monthly*—while referring to Boston society, his remarks applied equally to any urban community—commented: "I am satisfied that such a set of black-coated, stiff-jointed, soft-muscled, paste-complexioned youth as we can boast in our Atlantic cities never before sprang from loins of Anglo-Saxon lineage. . . . We have a few good boatmen, no good horsemen that I hear of, nothing remarkable in cricketing, and as for any great athletic feat performed by a gentleman in these latitudes, society would drop a man who should run around the Commons in five minutes." In similar vein Edward Everett deplored the failure of Americans in "the manly outdoor exercises which strengthen the mind by strengthening the body."

City dwellers, whether in New York, Boston, or Philadelphia, needed a substitute for that robust life in the open that had, in earlier days, characterized its conquest over rugged nature. Our native genius for organization formed local athletic clubs and founded national associations whose committees developed governing rules of the game. Several minor diversions swept the country. Croquet, lawn tennis, and archery gained universal appeal with the more affluent. Bicycling, a popular activity for the masses, took on a fervor that reached into every community. In New York, where streets and park drives afforded cyclists proper ground for their sport, there developed a whole mania that created wheel clubs, "schools of the velocipede," outings into the neighboring countryside, and competitive races for both male and female. Particularly significant with milady's newfound freedom brought on by the wheel's popularity was a release from the fetters that had restricted feminine participation in strenuous sports. When the "safety" supplanted the "ordinary," or high-wheeler, the impetus swept through the ranks of women, signalizing an important step in their emancipation.

Horse racing, and the age-old romance of the turf, had long held Americans enthralled as a primary source of entertainment. At the very start of this native interest, before the Revolution, Americans had imported their thoroughbreds; stables were established; racecourses developed; jockey clubs formed. The opening of Jerome Park in New York marked the era of thoroughbred racing. The more affluential who could afford expensive racehorses took to the road as informal contests between trotters and pacers whetted the equine appetites of the wealthy. Harlem Lane and the Bloomingdale Road were the scenes of spirited racing duels between leading rivals in the "horsey set." To this was added the coaching spectacles that afforded display of ostentatious equipages up Fifth Avenue and into Central Park drives where, during the driving season, crowds gathered to enjoy these daily events.

The birth of baseball as "the New York game," long before it was nicknamed our "national pastime," is said to have started in the vicinity of the present Madison Square, about 1850. Much later, as the game developed, it was played at a polo field just north of Central Park, from which it moved up to 155th Street and the Harlem River. In its newer location the field retained its name "Polo Grounds." The first game between New York and Boston was played here, in 1886. As larger crowds attended, and inter-city rivalries were promoted, the future of the game was assured. The structure of a seasonal schedule and eventual settlement by "World's Series" play took years of development.

The stage, concert hall, and opera house had long held a fascination for New Yorkers, for here was a concentration of playhouses and amusement halls unequaled in any other part of the land. This was especially true of the theater, where intense rivalry existed between theater owners, producersn and stage celebrities, many of them from overseasm The mile-long stretch of Broadway starting at Madison Square and extending northward was known as the American "Rialto," where every night, before brightly illuminated lobbies, thousands poured into the many current performances to attend their favorite plays and cheer or hiss at their favorite villain. Broadw
y las a street of legend; its famous names and plays became household words across the nation.

A century ago, winter was an occasion for fun and outdoor recreation as all New York turned out to enjoy the best of sleighing.

175

The long, hard winters of a century ago presented New Yorkers with one of their most enjoyable forms of recreation, made possible because there were so many wide, open boulevards upon which sleighing could be continued for long stretches. St. Nicholas Avenue, up in Harlem, was like a trip to the open country; Bloomingdale Road, now Broadway, ran the length of the Upper West Side, and was largely uninhabited. And, of course, the various drives through Central Park, readily accessible, were most popular. The city's carriage-makers turned out a great variety of sleighing types. An ad, in 1884, offered: "Sleighs of the best class/Immense stock of elegant sleighs/ Vis-a-vis sleighs/ Victoria family sleighs/ Cabriolet family sleighs/ Canadian rumble sleighs/ French style rumble sleighs/ Russian four passenger sleighs/ Portland and Albany sleighs/ Portland road cutters/Chimes, bells, plumes, fur robes etc./ Lowest prices for all cash."

From pen and ink sketches by Schell and Hogan, *Harper's Weekly*, January 13, 1877.

SLEIGHING SKETCHES IN NEW YORK

176

Trotter and pacers, sulkies and curricles, horseflesh and hoofbeats—these made up the scene on Harlem Lane any Sunday afternoon...

"Cornelius Vanderbilt, commonly known as the Commodore, used to jog his pair of trotting horses, Plow Boy and Mate, from his house in Washington Place, east of Washington Square, through Central Park to One Hundred and Tenth Street, and whip them into a race up Harlem Lane, competing with all comers, or merely speeding them for the exhilaration of the fast movement, the joy of rushing through the air holding two spirited animals in control. He was a striking sight, with his white hair and whiskers blown back by the wind. His horses were always harnessed to a high-wheeled, leather-top buggy, with steel tires. He always had the curtains of the top on, as if fearing rain. When asked why he always drove with the top up, a thing which retarded the speed of his horses somewhat, he replied: 'A good horse, as well as a good man, should be able to overcome small obstacles—and anyhow, it is more comfortable!' His son, William, a very heavily built man, also loved fine horses, and had some of the best. He built his private house on the southeast corner of Fortieth Street and Fifth Avenue. It was a large, roomy, comfortable house, built of brownstone, and so arranged that there were only three steps up to the front door, rather than the high-stoop construction of most brownstones of those days."

From *Recollections of an Old New Yorker,* by Frederick Van Wyck, 1932.

Engraved from a drawing by Stanley Fox, *Harper's Weekly,* November 21, 1868

HARLEM LANE, SUNDAY AFTERNOON

... where horse fanciers and horse traders gathered in the city's favorite horse market to buy, sell, or merely talk about horses.

"The Bull's Head Hotel was built about forty-two years ago, when the neighboring region consisted of open fields, with here and there a country villa or a farmhouse. Lots on the Bowery at that time could be bought for $300 or $400 each. The old tavern at the corner of Twenty-third Street is almost the only relic of that time. In those days the drove-yards were here; now they are up town, and horse-dealers and stables monopolize the neighborhood. The trade in horses is always dull at this time of the year. The open winter, with very little sleighing, lessens the demand for the finest horses. The chief call right now is for railroad horses, which bring from $150 to $200 each, and for work horses which fetch from $250 to $400. The weather has been favorable for opening streets, grading parks etc., and there is a fair demand for strong, serviceable horses for this kind of labor. The stock of horses in this country has been very much reduced since the war. The call for fine park and other driving horses has been such as to lead to the conversion of many splendid stallions into geldings, leaving a scarcity of good breeders."

From *Harper's Weekly*, February 13, 1869.

Engraved from a drawing by A. R. Waud, *Harper's Weekly*, February 13, 1869.

THE HORSE MARKET, BULL'S HEAD, NEW YORK CITY

With the dawn of the Gilded Age a growing number of New Yorkers lived elegantly, drove fancy carriages, and loved fine horses...

"The uses to which the Madison Square Garden is put are various, but it is mostly enjoyed for the exhibition of animals. Barnum's show of beasts is there regularly every year. So is the dog show of the Westminster Kennel Club. At various other times those illustrious human brutes, the prize-fighters, and six-day walkers are on exhibition. And, now, in addition to these, the National Horse Show Association of America proposed to occupy the Garden annually. Horse shows are no novelty in England, but in this country they were not instituted on any extensive scale until last Fall, when this Association held its first public exhibition at the Madison Square Garden. For several years the interest in trotting, horseback riding on the road and across country after the hounds, and the breeding of horses, have been on the increase here.... The first show last fall was so admirably managed, the prizes so liberal, the awards so just, and the public interest so quickly awakened, that the directors at once decided to have another exhibition this spring. In the fall the owners of fine racehorses, both trotters and runners, have already made arrangements for stabling the animals during the winter, and are loath to send them from their quarters in the country to New York to place them on exhibition for a few days. Last fall the value of the regular prizes offered was $10,470. For this show the amount has been increased to $17,450. Among the prizes, as last fall, are those for fire-engine horses, best and trained; for the best and trained police horses, to be ridden by officers, appointments and uniforms also to be considered; and new . . .

STUDIES IN HORSES—APROPOS OF THE SECOND NATIONAL HORSE SHOW AT MADISON SQUARE GARDEN

... so that the Annual Horse Show at Madison Square Garden became a social event of prime importance.

From drawings by Gray-Parker, *Harper's Weekly*, May 31, 1884.

... prizes for cavalry horses, viz., for the best mounted and equipped staff officer, and the best mounted and equipped private. The prizes carry with them something of greater worth than the monetary value, namely, the ribbons and certificates of award granted by the Association. They are 'evidences of merit won in open competition,' and will no doubt often win over a doubtful buyer, and clinch a sale. The interior arrangements of the Garden for the purposes of the show are perfect. It is in part a stable, in part a steeple-chase course, and in part a race track. The hunters have a fine expanse of loam and tan, as springy and buoyant as the meadows to which they are accustomed. There are stalls and loose boxes for the animals, for which the charge is moderate, and the horses may be taken away overnight on a deposit of twenty-five dollars by the owner, which will be forfeited if the animals are not brought back for exhibition the next morning. The managers also furnish veterinary surgeons who examine the horses free of charge. This precaution is necessary, because an infection once started would spread rapidly where so many horses are under one roof, and infection among this array of noble horses would be a serious disaster to breeding interests the country over. ... You can tell the successful competitor by noting the color of the rosette with which a horse is decorated. If it be blue, it is the emblem of a first prize; if red, of a second prize; if yellow, of a very high commendation; and if white, of a high commendation.''

From *Harper's Weekly*, May 31, 1884.

From fashionable Madison Square the procession of elegant coaches heading up Fifth Avenue was an eye-opening spectacle...

"To the average man or woman the annual Coaching Club parade is an event of the season. And well it may be. Sleek, high-spirited horses, mated or cross-mated, carefully groomed, handsomely harnessed; clean, bulky-bodied coaches in white, cream, yellow, claret, or red, with running gear usually of some strongly contrasting color; guards well dressed, conscious of their importance, lusty of lung, and more or less noisy as to post-horn; gallants, each with *boutonnière* in his coat lapel, dressed and kidded in accord with fashion's latest dictates; ladies resplendent in costumes of the gayest and umbrellas of the very brightest colors, vying with those of the flowers in their corsage bouquets, yet always in harmony—that is the picture, and some of its characteristics shown herewith. A dozen coaches—a dozen pictures of life and beauty—whirling through the Park when spring has given life to the brown and barren lawn and trees of winter. Rushing horses, merry laughter, smiling faces, happy hearts. Such was the parade of the Coaching Club, and each participant in the day's sport felt under personal obligation to Colonel Delancey Kane for introducing the sport to Manhattan Islanders."

From *Harper's Weekly*, June 2, 1883.

Engraved from a drawing by H. A. Ogden, *Harper's Weekly*, June 2, 1883

OPENING OF THE COACHING SEASON

... destined for a picnic outing at Westchester or Jerome Park when race day attracted thousands of equine devotees.

Engraved from photographs by Bidwell, *Harper's Weekly,* June 19, 1886.

COACHES AT JEROME PARK ON A RACE DAY

" 'The opening of the Central Park saved horseflesh in New York,' said an old jockey. Few who know the truth will gainsay this assertion. The opening of Jerome Park did as much for 'horseflesh' by rescuing the sport of horse racing from the blackguards and thieves, into whose hands it had fallen, and placing it on a respectful footing. The Jerome Park Race Course owes its existence to Mr. Leonard W. Jerome, after whom it was named. He secured an immense amount of real estate, in order to effect a different route by which the New Haven could bring its trains into the city, by-passing the Harlem tracks. This was a nine-mile strip known as the Saw-Mill River Valley, with no immediate prospect of sale of the property. Then came the idea for the racecourse. This is the property of the American Jockey Club, and the Spring and Fall Meetings of that association are held there, attended by large and fashionable crowds. The Club Stand occupies the most retired and elevated portions of the grounds, but the best point of view is the Grand Stand, in front of which is the usual starting point and winning post. The price of admission is high, but the grounds are thronged with vehicles and persons on foot. The crowd, as many as ten or fifteen thousand, is orderly and good-humored, and the occasion is rarely marred by any act of rowdyism or lawlessness.''

From *Lights and Shadows of New York Life,* by James D. McCabe, 1872.

182

In contrast with the sidewalk crowds that gaped and
gawked as the parade of liveried coaches passed by . . .

"The Brunswick Hotel on Fifth Avenue and Twenty-sixth Street was the headquarters of the aristocratic 'horsey set.' The annual spring and autumn parades of the Coaching Club—major events in the lives of the elect that brought crowds to Fifth Avenue—assembled at the Brunswick and returned there to enjoy the bird and game dinners and rare vintages for which the hotel was celebrated among gourmets. New Yorkers asserted that any epicure could starve in perpetual indecision on Fifth Avenue and Twenty-sixth Street. For directly across the avenue from the Brunswick, Delmonico's opened a large and magnificent new restaurant, and the choice between their rival cuisines was, for a true gourmet, a problem of anguishing difficulty."

From *Incredible New York*, by Lloyd Morris, 1951.

Engraved from a drawing by Thure de Thulstrup, *Harper's Weekly*, May 30, 1

PARADE OF THE NEW YORK COACHING CLUB, MAY 23

... there was the splendor and full panoply of ostentation—women in gay finery and men in impeccable coaching attire.

Engraved from a drawing by Thure de Thulstrup, *Harper's Weekly*, June 4, 1892.

THE NEW YORK COACHING-CLUB MEET—LEAVING CLAREMONT AFTER LUNCHEON

Within a narrow circle of the wealthiest, exclusive coaching parties in the 1880s and '90s were *de rigueur*. "Society's amusements of the present day are exceedingly varied," reported Zeisloft, in his *The New Metropolis*, published 1899. "At the private entertainments great ingenuity is displayed in providing new and startling diversions. Magnificence of display has almost reached the limit, and other realms are invaded to gratify the satiated tastes of the seekers for amusement." For the coaching party, an outing could head for Westchester and any number of exclusive inns in the vicinity. But a much shorter excursion took them to the Claremont Inn, in upper Manhattanville. Here, situated on the newly opened Riverside Drive, with an unsurpassed view of the Hudson and the Palisades, stood the inn, a beautifully furnished and stately hostelry which formerly had been the country seat of George Pollock, a wealthy merchant. Since before the Civil War it functioned as a restaurant, and now it was taken over by society as the logical rendezvous for the day's recreation. To reach it, the party would proceed from lower Fifth Avenue, enter Central Park, and drive up its length to 110th Street. There, the coaches would turn westward to the Drive and then up to the vicinity of Grant's Tomb and the Claremont Inn.

With grandstands to seat eight thousand and fine clubhouses, the opening races at Jerome Park attracted a large following...

"The flourishing equine cult led to the revival of an old sport in circumstances of unprecedented splendor. Racing—formerly carried on at Union Course and Fashion Park, on Long Island—had lost all social prestige by attracting professional gamblers and a rowdy 'sporting' crowd. But should not New York have its Goodwood? Should not society redeem the sport of kings? To Leonard Jerome, the answers were obvious. He bought a large tract of land in Westchester County near the town of Fordham and, with the cooperation of August Belmont and William R. Travers, founded the American Jockey Club on the British pattern, enlisting the entire smart set in this new association. On Jerome's two hundred and thirty acres in Westchester, the Club laid out the most elaborate of racetracks, with a grandstand seating eight thousand people, and a luxurious clubhouse and club stand. Largely at Jerome's expense a great boulevard, later to be named Jerome Avenue, was cut through from Macomb's Dam to the racetrack. The opening races at Jerome Park were held in 1866, with General Grant in attendance, and all fashionable New York turned out for them. Thereafter, the spring and autumn meetings of the American Jockey Club became important events on the social calendar, highly favored by even the most conservative, and drawing a large popular following out from the city. Even before inaugurating his splendid racetrack, Jerome lifted the cult of the horse to a place of elegance and distinction far superior to that of noisy, competitive...

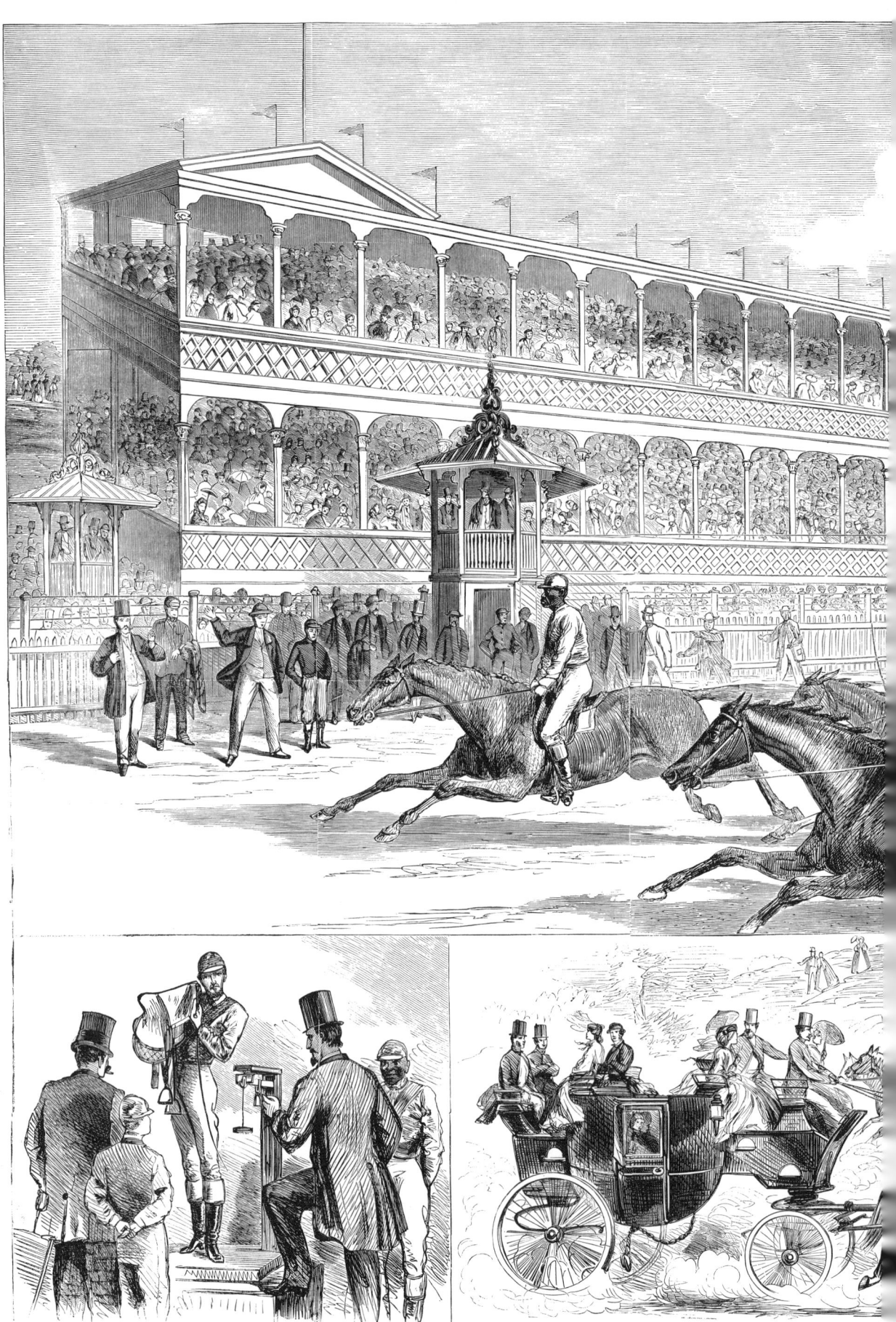

WEIGHING JOCKEYS

SCENE ON THE ROAD—

INAUGURATION OF THE RACE-COURSE OF THE JOCKEY CLUB, JEROME PARK—START FOR THE FOUR MILE HEAT

... including President Grant, in 1866, and thereafter spring and autumn meetings ranked high on New York's social calendar.

JEROME'S AND BELMONT'S CARRIAGES

Engraved from sketches by A. R. Waud, *Harper's Weekly,* October 13, 1866.

THE WINNING HORSE

... Harlem Lane. He was a connoisseur of horseflesh, an enthusiastic sportsman and no misogynist. To indulge his predilections simultaneously, he found an appropriately costly form of activity. In England, the Duke of Beaufort had recently attempted to revive the picturesqueness of stagecoach days by driving a drag, or coach, and four horses. Fired by this example, Jerome perfected himself in the art of four-in-hand driving and ordered a vehicle built. 'He turned out daily with his drag or coach loaded with beautiful women,' Ward Mc Allister recalled thirty years later, 'and drove to every desirable little country inn in and about the city, where one could dine at all well, crossing ferries, and driving up Broadway with the ease and skill of a veteran whip, which he was.' But less worldly observers were shocked by Jerome's custom of driving his coach up Fifth Avenue on Sunday mornings at the hour when the fashionable church parade was at full tide. 'His horses were trained to caper and rear as they turned into a street,' a censorious contemporary recorded. 'Gay and laughing ladies in gorgeous costume filled the carriage. Lackeys, carefully gotten up, occupied the coupe behind. Jerome sat on the box and handled the reins. With a huge bouquet of flowers attached to his buttonhole, with white gloves, cracking his whip, and with shouts of the party, the four horses would rush up Fifth Avenue, on toward the Park, while the populace said, one to the other, 'That is Jerome.' "

From *Incredible New York,* by Lloyd Morris, 1951.

At holiday time, shopping in the more exclusive retail sections of the city was one of milady's greatest pleasures.

The fashionable shopping districts of Manhattan presented a constantly changing pattern, as the trend of population growth, every few decades, moved northward. In the mid-1850s such leading mercantile establishments as Lord & Taylor and Arnold, Constable & Company were located in downtown Grand and Canal streets. Many specialty shops dotted both sides of lower Broadway below City Hall during this era. A. T. Stewart, later to become Wanamaker's, occupied two square blocks near Astor Place. By the 1870s and '80s, Madison Square became the center of metropolitan public life, attracting not only hotels, theaters, and restaurants but the better stores and shops. West Twenty-third Street from Fifth Avenue to Eighth Avenue was known as the "Ladies Mile," and here were to be found dozens of specialty shops of all kinds. The larger department stores were a few blocks distant but the smaller ones of high repute and equal costliness made this a mecca, especially at holiday time. During "shopping hours" the streets were blocked with liveried broughams, victorias, and coupes, while on the sidewalks the envious mingled with a procession of elegantly attired women.

Engraved from a drawing by W. H. Shelton, *Harper's Weekly*, December 23, 1882.

CHRISTMAS SHOPPING

The promenade on Fifth Avenue witnessed a special blend of broughams, sightseeing buses, and equestrians headed for the park.

Engraved from a drawing by Hughson Hawley, *Harper's Weekly,* May 17, 1890.

A MAY-DAY AT THE CENTRAL PARK PLAZA

Among the simpler diversions of New Yorkers was the pleasure of promenading on ever-popular Fifth Avenue. At the Plaza, just below the entrance to Central Park, a variety of coaches and double-decker buses mingle in the company of equestrians and strollers in their May Day finery. Looking south, the tall spires of a half-dozen churches tower above the residences of brownstone or marble. At the left is the steeple of St. Patrick's, James Renwick's Gothic cathedral whose cornerstone was laid in 1858, completed in 1879. On the opposite side are St. Thomas's, the Fifth Avenue Presbyterian Church, and others. "Leaving other parts neglected, these churches crowd on to one another. Two or three of them are on one block. The singing and preaching in one church is heard in another. Costly and elegant, most of them are thinly attended. Looking on their rich adornments, and inquiring the price of pews, one is at a loss to conceive where people of moderate means go to church in this city," wrote Matthew Hale Smith, in *Sunshine and Shadow in New York,* in 1869. Already the broad treelined boulevard had grown into "America's most fashionable street, with residences the like of which could be afforded only by the wealthiest." By the 1880s and '90s almost every other block boasted a magnificent chateau built for some member of the Vanderbilt family, intent upon leaving its mark upon the social horizon. None of these marble palaces have survived New York's changing scene.

> While controversy raged as to whether cricket or
> baseball should be declared our national sport . . .

There was a great deal of controversy to declare which of two popular sports might become "the Great American National Game": either cricket or baseball. A large section of the sporting world favored the former because of "its greater gentility." The conflicting views were aired by *Harper's* thus: "Whether baseball is a better or a worse game than cricket we do not now propose to answer. . . . In New York, it is well known, there are several baseball clubs which play periodically. The same thing is true of Boston, Philadelphia, and perhaps one or two other cities. But is baseball so popular that it is a regular and well-understood diversion in most of the States of the Union? Do young men naturally learn baseball in Massachusetts, Pennsylvania, Wisconsin and Louisiana? Could a baseball match be got up in every town of ten thousand inhabitants throughout the country? We leave it to those who are better acquainted with the sporting fraternity than ourselves to answer these queries. For our part we regret to say that we doubt very much whether baseball be a popular game at all in the interior, or in any part of the country except in a few large cities. We see no evidence that either baseball or any other athletic game is so generally practiced by our people as to be fairly called a popular American game."

Engraved from a drawing by W. P. Snyder, *Harper's Weekly*, May 16, 1886.

A DOUBLE PLAY—FIRST LEAGUE GAME, NEW YORK AGAINST BOSTON, APRIL 29

... thousands of spectators paid fifty cents for admission to watch at the Polo Ground, while many more crowded the outfields where coaches were permitted.

BASEBALL IN NEW YORK CITY—A GENERAL VIEW OF THE POLO GROUND, WITH A MATCH GAME IN PROGRESS

"The non-sporting reader—if there be any such in these palmy days of 'the diamond,' the turf and the American racing-yacht—may obtain an idea of the importance of the national game of baseball by attending a game at the Polo Grounds during the great League or Association season. This extensive and picturesque enclosure can, and frequently does, accommodate a multitude of from 12,000 to 15,000 spectators. For two hours and a half—the average duration of a game—this vast assemblage is kept at a high pitch of excitement resembling that of the unfolding of a stage drama of masterly construction. Every point scored, every fine hit or other bit of masterly play by the stalwart, uniformed professionals, brings a mighty storm of demonstrative applause. The spectators who crowd in to see these splendid ball-games pay an admission fee of fifty cents a head, and a large portion of them disburse another half dollar for the privilege of the grandstand. It is, therefore, easy to account for the salaries of from $3,000 to $5,000 per annum paid the average players. A bonus of $5,000, $10,000 or even more is paid to secure some pitcher or other valuable player deemed essential to the make-up of an invincible club."

From *Frank Leslie's Illustrated Newspaper*, June 23, 1888.

From *Frank Leslie's Illustrated Newspaper*, June 23, 1888.

Recently imported from England, lawn tennis appealed to a small but growing number because it could be played by both men and women and thus...

The newly imported game of "lawn tennis" made its debut in New York in 1878. American tourists traveling in England in 1874 became acquainted with this new sport at Wimbledon where a Major Walter C. Wingfield taught and introduced the game as being superior to croquet, and much more exciting. The Marylebone Cricket Club christened "lawn tennis" in March 1875, and there followed a period of activity that swept the sporting centers of England. The visiting Americans brought back the necessary paraphernalia: racquets, nets, and balls. The cricket clubs in this country soon recognized the new game's possibilities. Demonstrations and tournaments were arranged, especially at the Staten Island Cricket Club. Two of Boston's leading exponents of tennis, Dr. James Dwight and Richard Sear, defeated the best New York and Philadelphia players in some of the earliest doubles matches ever held in the United States.

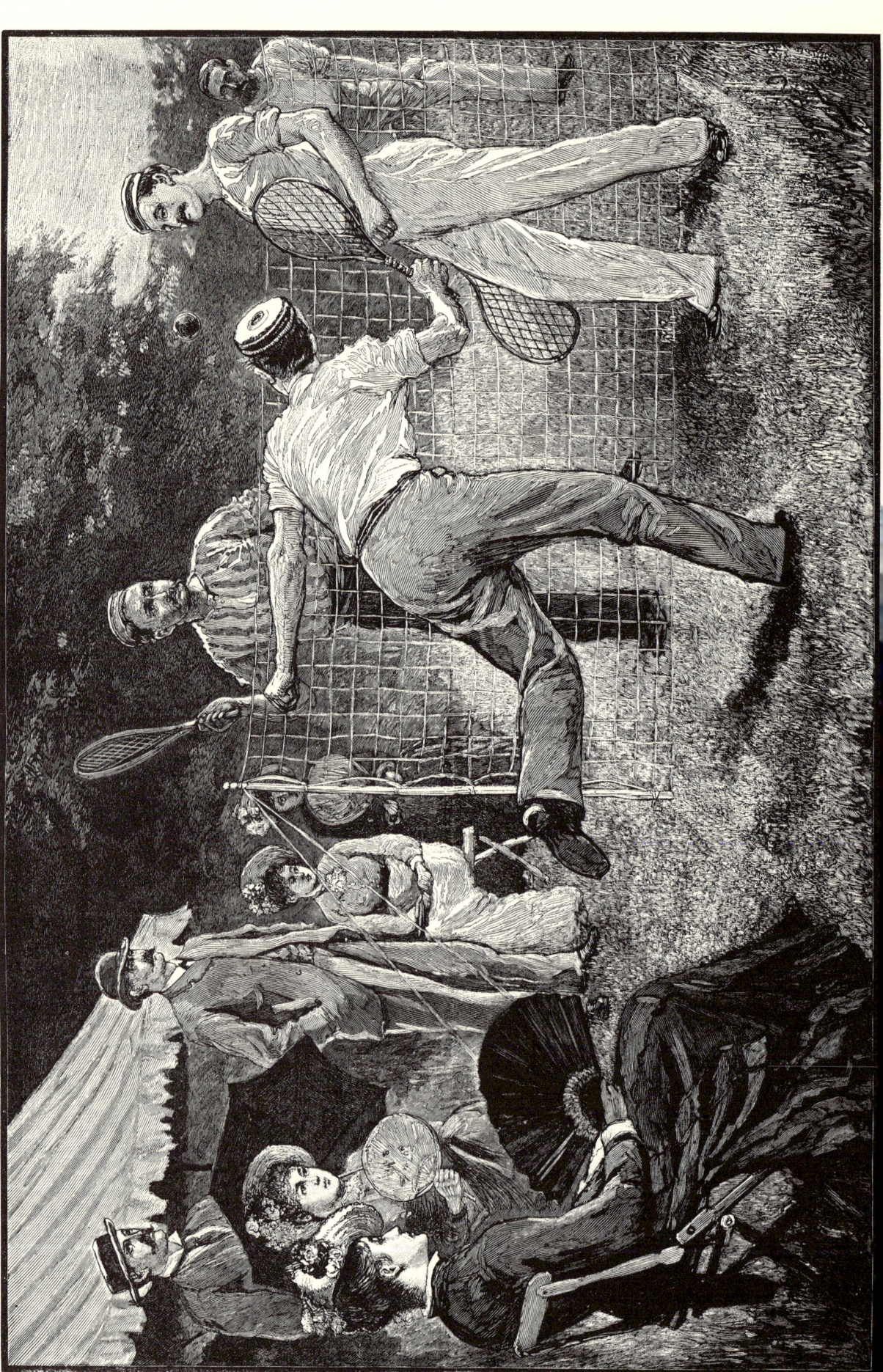

Engraved from a drawing by Charles Stanley Reinhart, *Harper's Weekly*, September 14, 1878

LAWN TENNIS

... there were social contacts, as well as athletics involved, as couples could share the court in friendly contests.

Engraved from a drawing by Thure de Thulstrup, *Harper's Weekly,* July 11, 1885.

LAWN TENNIS IN PROSPECT PARK

The popularity of the newly imported game of tennis, in which both men and women could share as equal partners, did more than any other pastime to mark the emergence of women into the world of sports. Just before the arrival of tennis, croquet had few superiors as a "courting game." Croquet had brought women out of stuffy living rooms and parlors to participate in out-of-door exercise, on a par with men. "It afforded, within the bounds of the prim proprieties of the period, just enough opportunity for innocent flirtation to add zest to the pastime. Between plays there was time for whispered asides, and acquaintance ripened quickly as partners strove to attain the common goal. As balls clicked, joyous laughter over blunders and accidents was mingled with amiable arguments concerning rules and styles of play. On many a shady lawn, where iron statuary bespoke the financial status of the household, croquet and tennis offered to bright-eyed girls and demure young women a mild transition between the restrictions that had hemmed in their mothers and the greater freedom which their daughters were destined to enjoy," as reported in the *Annals of American Sport.*

New Yorkers enthusiastically adopted the latest fad of "riding the velocipede"; schools where one could gain a few pointers were scattered throughout the city . . .

"The wheelman may use the Riverside Drive, but only by a strict observance of the following rules: Riders must keep to the extreme right of the roadway; Bicyclers must not ride more than two abreast; Tricyclers single file; No coasting, racing, or speeding will be allowed; Whistles or bells, if used at all, must be used in moderation, and lighted lamps must be carried after sunset. Riverside Drive is the favorite course of the wheelmen. So extensive has night riding become that an establishment near the Park, specializing in the renting and storing of vehicles, is kept open continuously throughout the day and night. A hundred or more bicycles of all sizes stand in little iron frames along each side of the stable, if stable it may be called, like horses in their stalls, and in the centre of the big room are tricycles of all descriptions. The rider who enters the stable for his afternoon or evening ride approaches his steed as it stands in its iron stall, pats it affectionately upon its rubber neck, then smooths its shapely hind-quarter with a caressing hand, mounts the silver beast, and is off and away as though his legs bestrode the best of horseflesh. Like the bicycle, the tricycle calls for much experience, and is more full of danger than is generally suspected."

From *Harper's Weekly*, July 17, 1886

WHEELING ON RIVERSIDE DRIVE

... but for young cyclists there was nothing to compare with the tricycle where, on moonlit nights, one rode the road to romance on the new Riverside drives.

Engraved from a drawing by Thure de Thulstrup, *Harper's Weekly*, July 17, 1886.

"The bicycle craze struck New York, and the whole city began pursuing happiness on wheels. Genteel conversatives deplored this new fad and were gratified when the Reverend Asa D. Blackburn denounced it from his pulpit. The press commended his sermon: 'You cannot serve God and skylark on a bicycle.' Yet in spite of his dire warning the smart young set took to the sport enthusiastically. They organized the Michaux Club, on Broadway near Fifty-third Street, where professional racers gave them lessons in riding single and tandem wheels. Less exclusive bicycle schools soon opened throughout the city. On fine weekday mornings feminine cyclists thronged the drives of Central Park. Lillian Russell and her friend Marie Dressler took up cycling in order to 'slenderize' their figures, and on their wheels, Miss Dressler surmised, they gave 'an imitation of two plump girls going somewhere in a hurry.' Miss Russell became the talk of the town. In a white serge cycling costume with stylish leg-of-mutton sleeves, you saw her pedaling up through the Park, making two circuits of the Reservoir before stopping to rest. Her bicycle was a national sensation. Entirely gold plated, its mother-of-pearl handlebars bore her monogram in diamonds and emeralds; the hub and spokes of its wheels were set with many jewels that sparkled in the sun. Knowing New Yorkers asserted that it was a gift of her friend 'Diamond Jim' Brady."

From *Incredible New York*, by Lloyd Morris, 1951.

Impressive vistas afforded by the beautiful new Riverside Drive along the Hudson were among the most majestic scenes in the city . . .

The natural beauty of New York's superb environmental setting is nowhere more visibly evident than along its outer fringes where land and water meet in an ever-changing series of spectacular vistas. Once the city's inner land area had been converted into unsurpassed recreational opportunities, at the hands of Frederick Olmsted and Calvert Vaux, the clamor for establishing parks and drives along the western border of the Hudson went on. The rapid development of the upper west side of the city was given a special boost with the construction, in 1875, of the Ninth Avenue El, running along Columbus Avenue as far as 110th Street. Upper Broadway and the West End areas were subjected to vast speculation and development. Finally, in 1880, after decades of planning and wrangling in the city's councils, the vast stretches between Seventy-second Street and Spuyten Duyvil were transformed into Riverside Drive. In a series of magnificently winding drives and terraces, the full splendor of the Hudson River in all its majesty was exposed for the enjoyment of strollers, cyclists, and carriage driving. The wide boulevards and paved walks were, here and there, interrupted with breaks and vantage points from which the spectator could absorb the eye-filling spectacle of nature at its best. Full advantage was taken of the hilly terrain, the rocky outcroppings, and a fine growth of aged trees. Provisions were made along the route of the esplanade for monuments to further enhance the parkside setting. Over the next three decades, many fine sculptural pieces were introduced to give the park the varied aspects of fuller cultural enrichment. These included two major monumental buildings, the Soldiers' and Sailors' Monument at Eighty-ninth Street and Grant's Tomb at 122nd Street.

Engraved from a drawing by Granville Perkins, from a sketch by A. L. Jackson, *Harper's Weekly,* April 24, 1880.

VIEW IN RIVERSIDE PARK, NEW YORK

. . . combining both a natural setting among rich groves of old trees and watery views across the river toward the Jersey Palisades.

From *Frank Leslie's Illustrated Newspaper Supplement,* June 19, 1880.

NEW YORK CITY—THE NEW RIVERSIDE DRIVE ALONG THE HUDSON, AT ONE HUNDRED AND EIGHTEENTH STREET, LOOKING SOUTH

"The city's burghers simply could not forget that on the Boulevard, as on Riverside Drive, they could go out for a spin on their bicycles and tandems in vast, undulating hordes on a Saturday afternoon or Sunday. When the craze was at its height, literally thousands of men and women would be pedalling on their wheels in a never-ending procession, and at night, the colorful lights on the bicycles added a most scintillating sparkle to the scene of gayety, and just as many thousands, it would seem, would stand on the sidewalks along the route, gazing in fascination at the vast parade of their fellow Gothamites on bicycles of every possible description. After the turn of the century, the bicycle craze began to wane, but The Boulevard remained popular as a cycle route for some years afterward."

From *This Was New York,* by Maxwell F. Marcuse, 1965.

Barnum's Museum was the most widely acclaimed mecca of entertainment in the nation where circus freaks and curiosities from the world over could be seen.

Unquestionably, Barnum's American Museum at Broadway and Ann Street was America's Number One place of amusement, the mecca of all rural visitors to New York. Its full story has been told by Barnum himself: "And now that I was proprietor and manager of the American Museum I had reached a new epoch in my career which I felt was the beginning of better days. . . . The nucleus of this establishment, Scudder's Museum, was formed in 1810, the year in which I was born. In 1842, I bought and added to my collection the entire contents of Peale's Museum, in Philadelphia; and year after year, I bought genuine curiosities, regardless of cost, wherever I could find them, in Europe or America. In 1865, the space occupied for my Museum purposes was more than double what it was in 1842. The Lecture Room, originally narrow, ill-contrived and inconvenient, was so enlarged and improved that it became one of the most commodious and beautiful amusement halls in the City of New York. At first, my attractions and inducements were merely the collection of curiosities by day, and an evening entertainment, consisting of such variety performances as were current in ordinary shows. By degrees, the character of entertainment was changed. The transient attractions of the Museum were constantly diversified, and educated dogs, industrious fleas, automatons, jugglers, ventriloquists, living statuary, tableaux, gypsies, Albinoes, fat boys, giants, dwarfs, rope-dancers, live 'Yankees,' pantomine, instrumental music, singing and dancing in great variety, dioramas, panoramas, models of Niagara, Dublin, Paris and Jerusalem . . . mechanical figures, fancy glass-blowing, knitting machines and other triumphs in the mechanical arts, all were exceedingly successful."

From *The Life of Barnum,* by Himself, 1892.

VIEW OF THE AMERICAN MUSEUM, BROADWAY, NEW YORK

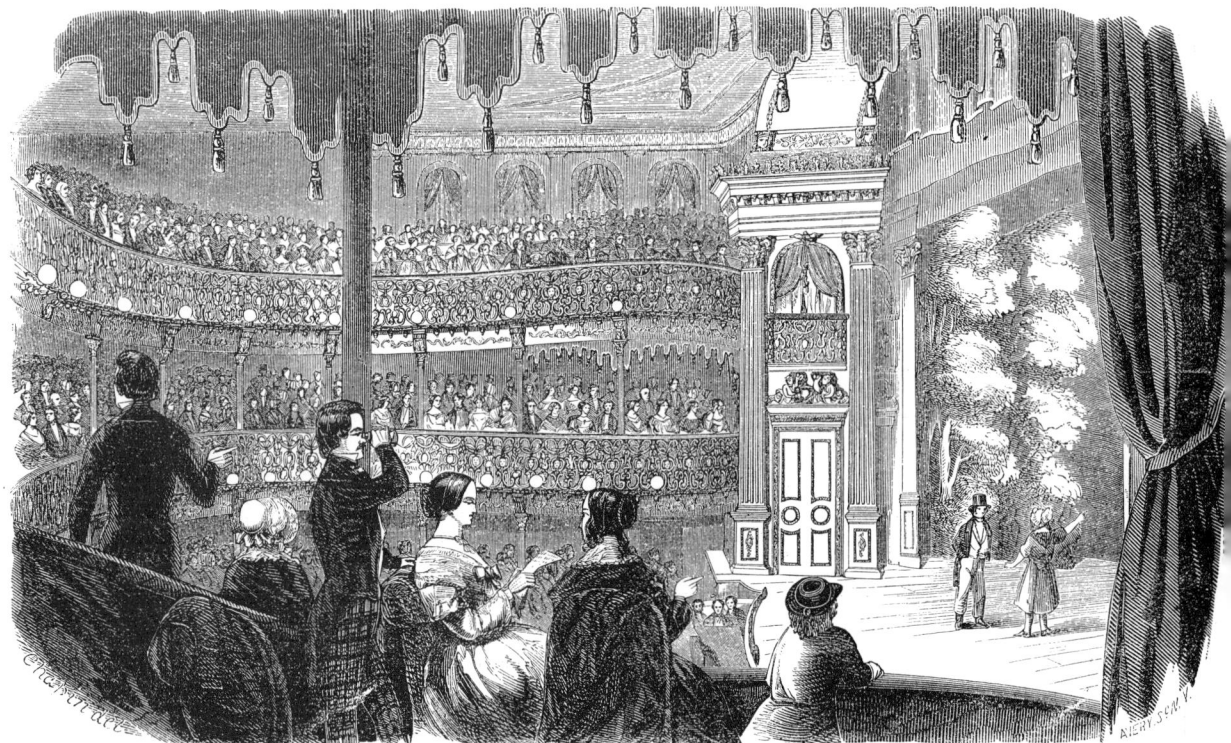

From *Gleason's Pictorial Drawing-Room Companion,* January 29, 1853

INTERIOR VIEW OF THE LECTURE ROOM OF THE AMERICAN MUSEUM, NEW YORK

The finest operatic performances, viewed by over four thousand music lovers, could be enjoyed at New York's Academy of Music.

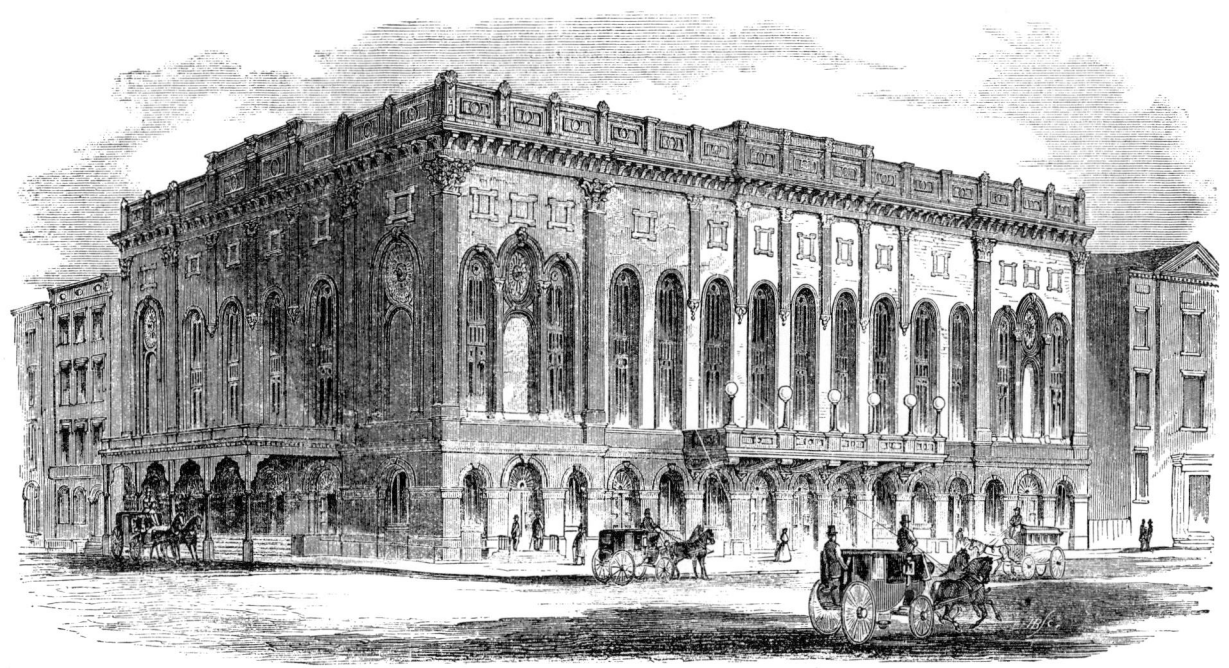

NEW YORK ACADEMY OF MUSIC

From *Ballou's Pictorial Drawing-Room Companion,* March 24, 1856.

NEW YORK ACADEMY OF MUSIC—INTERIOR VIEW

"Four times grand opera had attempted to obtain a permanent domicile in New York, and four times the effort had ended in quick failure. When in 1854, however, the Academy of Music was built at the corner of Fourteenth Street and Irving Place, the city at last obtained a house which proved to be a continuous home of at least moderately successful opera for a long term of years. The Academy, with a seating capacity of four thousand six hundred and an immense stage, was one of the largest theaters in America. At the outset the house was under the management of James H. Hackett, who opened it with Bellini's *Norma,* October 2, 1854. In April, 1855, a new group took over the management and produced *William Tell* and *Il Trovatore,* both for the first time in America. Later managers were Max Maretzek, at one time conductor at the Academy, Maurice Strakosch, and Bernard Ullman. The house was destroyed by fire, May 21, 1866, but was rebuilt the following year. It continued as the center of grand opera in New York, during its later years under the direction of Colonel James H. Mapleson, until it was superseded in 1883 by the Metropolitan Opera House."

From *The American Stage, Pageant of America,* 1929.

For musical extravaganzas and superbly choreographed ballet performances, Niblo's Garden achieved fame as a New York landmark of outstanding theatricality.

Few places of popular amusement could vie with Niblo's Theater and Garden, which survived many upheavals during its long career. Originally built as the Sans Souci in 1827, it was located at Broadway and Prince Street. Completely burned out, in 1846 and 1872, it was rebuilt each time and continued with several long-run productions. Sensational novelties in theatrical fare had taken the city by storm. In 1866, *The Black Crook,* a musical spectacle of unparalleled splendor and unabashed sensuality, began its record-breaking run of nearly five hundred performances at Niblo's Garden. "It was a daring ballet-show, as nearly unclad as possible, exploiting a large aggregation of *coryph*ées and four lovely *premières danseuses,*" a sedate critic of the time reported. "All that gold and silver and gems and light and woman's beauty can contribute to fascinate the eye and charm the sense is gathered up in this gorgeous spectacle." From nearly all the city's pulpits there sounded dire warnings. "To see *The Black Crook* was to slide down the incline to Hell. Gilded youth, and young New York in general, paid little heed, while elderly gentlemen showed an alarming tendency to imperil their souls repeatedly. Here, for the first time, was a massive display of unveiled feminine beauty. Here was infectious gaiety, dazzling scenic effects, and an incomparable ballet. What could Wallack's offer, or the Academy of Music, or even the most brazen concert saloon, that rivaled the manifold attractions of *The Black Crook?* An enchanted public ignored the protests of moralists, and the market for men's opera glasses flourished as never before."

From *Incredible New York,* by Lloyd Morris, 1951.

INTERIOR VIEW OF NIBLO'S THEATRE, NEW YORK

From *Ballou's Pictorial Drawing-Room Companion,* March 6, 1852.

NIBLO'S GARDEN, BROADWAY, NEW YORK

New York could boast of a dozen of the finest hotels where appointments, meals, and services were the equal of anything European hostelries could offer.

EXTERIOR OF THE FIFTH AVENUE HOTEL ON MADISON SQUARE, NEW YORK — From *Harper's Weekly,* October 1, 1859.

From *Gleason's Pictorial Drawing-Room Companion,* March 12, 1853.

A FINE VIEW OF THE NEW MAMMOTH ST. NICHOLAS HOTEL, BROADWAY, NEW YORK

"The leading hotels of the city lie very close together, the majority of them being found in the vicinity of Union and Madison Squares. This is found to be an advantage, as strangers find it pleasant to visit friends who are staying at other nearby houses. Many of the most fashionable houses are conducted on what is called 'the European plan,' in which a separate charge is made for rooms, meals, and every service rendered. It is adopted by the Hoffman, St. Denis, Glenham, Brevoort, Coleman, St. James, Albermarle, Clarendon, Everett, Gilsey, and several other prominent houses. The large hotels like the Fifth Avenue Hotel, St. Nicholas, Metropolitan and others depend entirely upon transient guests for their success. This city has, perhaps, the largest floating population in America. Thousands come and go daily, even in the summer months, and these are mostly people who have money to spend. In the Spring and Fall, the Southern and Western merchants come to New York in great numbers to buy goods, and are among the best customers of the hotels. The smaller houses, while they compete with their great rivals for transient custom, rely chiefly upon their permanent guests. These are filled with families who have come to avoid the trouble of keeping house, and who remain all through the year. They are mostly persons of wealth and fashion. All first class hotels keep private detectives on duty at all hours. Suspicious persons are at once apprehended, and required to give an account of themselves. Some queer mishaps often befall guests of the house who are not known to the detectives."

From *Lights and Shadows of New York Life,* by James D. McCabe, 1872.

Elaborate dinner parties were "staged with unprecedented beauty, magnificence and costliness," as the wealthy vied with one another in extravagance.

The dining rooms of New York's leading hotels were noted for the exquisite service, elaborate silver service, and unsurpassed cuisine. In fact, the boast of their maîtres d'hôtel was that any dish that a patron ordered would be forthcoming and in the best of taste.

"Gotham's gourmets (and gourmands) flocked to Fifth Avenue and 26th Street trying hard to make up their minds whether to sample the famed cuisine of the Brunswick, or the titillating viands emerging from Delmonico's equally famed kitchens. No matter what dining room he selected, the gourmet was constantly making 'agonizing reappraisals' on subsequent visitations to New York's then most famed culinary spot. Lorenzo Delmonico had long conducted a restaurant in the Wall Street district, on South William Street, where prices were sufficiently high to discourage anyone but the wealthiest from patronizing it. At 26th Street, Delmonico catered to the wives and families of gentlemen of the financial district, and here the service was meticulous, the food superb."

From *This Was New York,* by Maxwell F. Marcuse, 1969.

From *Harper's Weekly,* October 1, 1859.

THE DINING-ROOM OF THE FIFTH AVENUE HOTEL, ON MADISON SQUARE

From an engraving by Frank Leslie (who later established his own newspaper), *Gleason's Pictorial Drawing-Room Companion,* September 18, 1852.

DINNER AT THE OPENING OF THE METROPOLITAN HOTEL, NEW YORK

Masked balls and grand receptions were popular charity affairs, the largest of which were staged in the huge ballroom of the Academy of Music.

201

From *Frank Leslie's Illustrated Newspaper*, January 17, 1880.

NEW YORK CITY—GRAND RECEPTION AND MASKED BALL GIVEN BY THE STOCKHOLDERS AT THE ACADEMY OF MUSIC, ON MONDAY EVENING, JANUARY 5TH

The giant ballroom of the Academy of Music was the largest in the city, and as such accommodated many of the greatest gatherings at balls, fetes, and events of civic interest. The opera house, although erected by subscription among the wealthiest citizens of the city, was built with strictly utilitarian views, not at all limited to operatic festivities. There were annual get-togethers of the Patriarchs, the Assembly, the Charity Balls, not to mention more democratic routs such as the Old Guard, The Arion, French Cooks, and Cercle de l'Harmonie. The high jinks at some of these latter caused much concern among the stockholders on the mornings after, the golden horseshoe being considerably tarnished by the revelers. There seemed always to be an annual deficit, no matter how many affairs were held in various parts of the Music Hall. The grand reception and masked ball given annually by the Academy's stockholders was always a gala occasion, certain to raise a vast sum toward paying off debts. The gay festivities of this special function did much to dispel, at least temporarily, any thoughts of deficits.

Walt Whitman, commenting upon the social scene in New York, noted that "beneath the surface glow and grandeur, was much flippancy and vulgarity, infidelity and low cunning...."

"The stretch of Broadway between Madison Square and Forty-second Street—'the Rialto,' as it was called—was a street of legend, and it had a romantic attraction for all Americans across the continent. This mile of the wide avenue was lined, on both sides, with luxurious hotels, glittering bars, the city's principal theaters. At night, the lobbies of the hotels and the facades of the theaters were beginning to be brightly illuminated by Edison's new incandescent lamps. By contrast with their glare, the gas-lights of the street-corner lampposts seemed feeble, but it was pleasant to watch the lamplighters making their rounds at dusk, using a long torchlike device to open the square glass lamps, turn on the gas jets and kindle them into flame. Long before eight o'clock, the sidewalks of the Rialto were jammed with crowds bound for the theaters, and a continuous procession of lacquered carriages would be drawing up in front of each of them," wrote Lloyd Morris in *Incredible New York*. The theaters included Daly's and Wallack's, on opposite sides of Broadway at Thirtieth Street, the Standard, the Park, and the Casino, opposite the new Metropolitan Opera House. During the 1860s, the most brilliant company in America was assembled under the banner of the Wallack Theater. It was noted for its lavish and varied productions, employing the most talented and experienced men and women of the stage. Some of these notable performers included John Gilbert, E. L. Davenport, Rose Eltynge, John Brougham, Rose and Charles Coghlan, and Dion Boucicault.

Engraved from a drawing by Charles Graham and Thure de Thulstrup, *Harper's Weekly,* January 7, 1882.

INTERIOR OF WALLACK'S NEW THEATRE—THE SCREEN SCENE IN THE "SCHOOL FOR SCANDAL"

Wallack's Theater was noted for the high quality of its dramatic offerings, lavish productions and the appearance of the stage's leading celebrities

203

From *Frank Leslie's Illustrated Newspaper,* February 26, 1887.

NEW YORK CITY—THE GRAND MASQUERADE BALL OF THE ARION SOCIETY, AT THE METROPOLITAN OPERA HOUSE, FEBRUARY 17TH—SCENE AT 2 A.M. LOOKING FROM THE DRESS CIRCLE

One of New York's major social events was the annual grand masquerade ball of the Arion Society, attended by notables of wealth, society, and the cultural arts. It attracted several thousand, and thus the facilities of a large ballroom were needed. The new Metropolitan Opera House, at Broadway and Thirty-ninth Street, offered this. It had been formed by an influential group including Jay Gould, J. P. Morgan, Cornelius Vanderbilt, William Rockefeller, George F. Baker, and others who felt that the old Academy of Music had been outgrown. Furthermore, their inability to purchase choice boxes held by the old-time aristocracy made them feel like outsiders. The newly built opera house opened its doors on October 22, 1883, when its entire seating capacity of over three thousand plus hundreds of standees inaugurated its first "S.R.O." performance with the production of *Faust*. The "Met" continued to offer the best from established European scores, but financial difficulties and managerial problems persisted. In 1892 fire destroyed the opera house, but it was promptly rebuilt and opened anew in November 1893. "The Goulds and the Vanderbilts and people of that ilk perfumed the air with the odor of crisp greenbacks," reported the *Dramatic Mirror*, in its account of the opening.

Carnegie Hall was opened to the public in 1891, providing, at long last, what the concert-loving New Yorkers had demanded for many decades.

For the lover of theatrical and musical entertainment, New York could offer a varied menu, more complete, or so it seemed, than any other city on earth. Yet the followers of the concert stage and the musical purists complained that no theater or concert hall offered a complete facility for their favorite form of entertainment. To answer this need, the New Music Hall, on Fifty-seventh Street and Seventh Avenue, was opened, in 1891. The structure, by architect William B. Tuthill, was designed in the modified Italian Renaissance manner, and before long came to be known as Carnegie Hall. To its stage came the world's leading symphony orchestras and chamber groups, as well as the Oratorio Society and other choral groups. There was an intimacy among musical devotees, and year after year saw the same people in the same seats. The list of eminent soloists, musical geniuses, and orchestral maestros would constitute a veritable "Who's Who" in music. The Carnegie Music Hall, after eighty-five years, still stands.

Engraved from a drawing by W. P. Snyder, *Harper's Weekly*, May 9, 1891.

THE CARNEGIE MUSIC HALL   1. THE ENTRANCE   2. THE LOBBY   3. THE INTERIOR

Selected Bibliography

ABBOTT, BERENICE. Text by Elizabeth McCausland. *Changing New York*. New York: E. P. Dutton & Co. and Federal Writers' Publications, 1939. Reprinted under the title *New York in the Thirties*. New York: Dover Publications, 1973.

ALBION, ROBERT G. *The Rise of the New York Port, 1815–1860*. New York: Charles Scribner's Sons, 1939.

ALLEN, FREDERICK LEWIS. *The Big Change*. New York: Harper, 1952.

———. *The Great Pierpont Morgan*. New York: Harper, 1949.

———. *Only Yesterday: An Informal History of the Nineteen-Twenties*. New York: Harper, 1931.

———. *Since Yesterday: The Nineteen-Thirties in America*. New York: Harper, 1939.

ALLEN, ROBERT S., ed. *Our Fair City*. New York: Vanguard Press, 1947.

ANDREWS, WILLIAM LORING. *The Iconography of the Battery and Castle Garden*. New York: Charles Scribner's Sons, 1901.

ASBURY, HERBERT. *The Gangs of New York*. New York, 1928.

BALDWIN, H. W., AND STONE, S. *We Saw It Happen*. New York: Simon & Schuster, 1938.

BEATON, CECIL. *Portrait of New York*. London: B. T. Batsford, Ltd., 1948.

BELDEN, E. PORTER. *New York: Past, Present, and Future*. New York: G. P. Putnam, 1849.

BERGER, MEYER. *City on Many Waters*. New York: Golden Griffin Books, 1955.

———. *The Eight Million*. New York: Simon & Schuster, 1942.

———. *Meyer Berger's New York*. New York: Random House, 1960.

Blue Water Views of Old New York. Scrimshaw Press, 1970.

BOBBE, DOROTHIE. *DeWitt Clinton*. New York: Minton, Balch & Co., 1933.

BOLTON, REGINALD PELHAM. *Washington Heights, Manhattan, Its Eventful Past*. New York: Dyckman Institute, printed for the author, 1924.

BONNER, WILLIAM T. *New York: The World's Metropolis, 1624–1924*. New York: R. L. Polk & Co., 1924.

BOOTH, MARY LOUISE. *History of the City of New York from Its Earliest Settlement to the Present Time*. New York: W. R. C. Clark & Meeker, 1859.

BOTKIN, BENJAMIN A., ed. *New York City Folklore*. New York: Random House, 1956.

———. *A Treasury of American Folklore*. New York: Crown Publishers, 1944.

BRIERLY, J. ERNEST. *The Streets of Old New York*. New York: Hastings House, 1953.

Brooklyn Eagle. Historic Brooklyn. Brooklyn, N.Y.: Brooklyn Eagle, 1947.

BROWN, HENRY COLLINS. *Brownstone Fronts and Saratoga Trunks*. New York: E. P. Dutton, 1935.

———. *From Alley Pond to Rockefeller Center*. New York: E. P. Dutton, 1936.

———. *Old New York, Yesterday & Today*. New York: Valentine's Manual, 1922 and various years.

———. *The Story of Old New York*. Illustrated by Frank Rennie. New York: E. P. Dutton, 1934.

BROWNE, JUNIUS HENRI. *The Great Metropolis: A Mirror of New York*. New York: American Publishing Co., 1869.

BURNHAM, ALAN, ed. *New York Landmarks*. Middletown, Conn.: Wesleyan University Press, 1963.

CALLENDER, JAMES H. *Yesterdays on Brooklyn Heights*. The Dorland Press, 1927.

CAMPBELL, HELEN; KNOX, THOMAS W.; AND BYRNES, THOMAS. *Darkness and Daylight: or Lights and Shadows of New York Life*. Hartford, Conn.: A. D. Worthington, 1892.

CENTRAL PARK ASSOCIATION. *The Central Park*. New York: Thomas Seltzer, 1926.

CHAMBERS, JULIUS. *The Book of New York: Forty Years Recollections*. New York: Book of New York Co., 1912.

CHILD, LYDIA MARIA. *Letters from New York*. New York, 1843.

CHURCHILL, ALLEN. *The Upper Crust*. Englewood Cliffs, N.J.: Prentice-Hall, 1970.

CLAPP, MARGARET. *Forgotten First Citizen: John Bigelow*. Boston: Little, Brown & Co., 1947.

COLLINS, FREDERICK L. *Money Town: The Story of Manhattan Toe, that Golden Mile which Lies Between the Battery and the Fields*. New York: G. P. Putnam's Sons, 1946.

COMSTOCK, SARAH. *Old Roads from the Heart of New York*. New York: G. P. Putnam's Sons, 1915.

DEFOREST, ROBERT W., AND VEILLER, LAWRENCE. *The Tenement House Problem*. New York: The Macmillan Co., 1903.

DE LEEUW, R. M. *Up Both Sides of Broadway*. New York: De Leeuw, Riehl Publishing Co., 1910.

DENSION, LINDSAY, AND FISCHEL, MAX. *Villages and Hamlets Within New York City*. New York: Press Publishing Company, 1925.

DEPEW, CHAUNCEY. *My Memories of Eighty Years*. New York: Charles Scribner's Sons, 1922.

DESPARD, MATILDA PRATT. *Old New York from the Battery to Bloomingdale*. New York: G. P. Putnam, 1875.

DE VOE, THOMAS. *The Market Book—a History of the Public Markets in the City of New York from Its First Settlement to the Present Time*. Printed for the author, 1862.

DICKENS, CHARLES. *American Notes*. New York: Harper & Brothers, 1842.

DUNSHEE, KENNETH HOLCOMBE. *As You Pass By*. New York: Hastings House, 1952.

EDMISTON, SUSAN, AND CIRINO, LINDA D. *Literary New York*. Boston: Houghton Mifflin Co., 1976.

ELLIS, EDWARD ROBB. *The Epic of New York City*. New York: Coward-McCann, 1966.

FEDERAL WRITERS' PROJECT. WORKS PROGRESS ADMINISTRATION, NEW YORK CITY. *New York City Guide*. New York: Random House, 1939.

———. *New York Learns: A Guide to the Educational Facilities of the Metropolis*. New York: M. Barrows & Co., 1939.

———. *New York Panorama: A Comprehensive View of the Metropolis, Presented in a Series of Articles*. New York: Random House, 1938.

FLEMING, ETHEL, AND KATES, HERBERT S. *New York*. New York: The Macmillan Co., 1929.

FLEXNER, JAMES THOMAS. *Steamboats Come True: American Inventor in Action*. New York: Viking Press, 1944.

FORD, JAMES, et. al. *Slums and Housing*. Cambridge, Mass.: Harvard University Press, 1936.

GILDER, RODMAN. *The Battery: Four Centuries on Manhattan Island's Tip*. Boston: Houghton Mifflin Co., 1936.

Glimpses of New York City. Charleston, S.C., 1852.

GREENE, ASA. *A Glance at New York*. New York: n.p., 1837.

HARLOW, ALVIN. *Old Bowery Days: The Chronicles of a Famous Street*. New York: D. Appleton & Co., 1931.

HARRISON, MRS. BURTON. *Recollections Grave and Gay*. New York: Charles Scribner's Sons, 1912.

HASWELL, CHARLES H. *Reminiscences of New York by an Octogenarian, 1816–1860*. New York: Harper & Brothers, 1896.

HAVENS, CATHERINE ELIZABETH. *The Diary of a Little Girl*. New York: Henry Collins Brown, 1920.

HEMSTREET, CHARLES. *The Broadway of Yesteryear*. New York: Cadwallader Publishing Co., 1905.

———. *Nooks and Corners of Old New York*. New York: Charles Scribner's Sons, 1899.

———. *The Pleasure Resorts of Old New York*, 1907.

———. *When Old New York Was Young*. New York: Charles Scribner's Sons, 1902.

HENDERSON, HELEN WESTON. *A Loiterer in New York: Discoveries Made by a Rambler Through Obvious Yet Unsought Highways and Byways*. New York: George H. Doran, 1917.

HILL, F. T. *The Story of a Street (Wall)*. New York: Harper and Brothers, 1908.

HONE, PHILIP. *Diary*. Ed. Allan Nevins. New York: Dodd, Mead and Company, 1927.

HORNUNG, CLARENCE P. *Wheels Across America*. New York: A. S. Barnes & Co., 1959.

HOWELLS, WILLIAM DEAN. *A Hazard of New Fortunes*. New York: Harper & Brothers, 1890.

HUXTABLE, ADA LOUISE. *Classic New York*. Garden City, N.Y.: Doubleday & Co., 1964.

JAMES, THEODORE, JR. *Fifth Avenue*. New York: Walker & Co., 1971.

JENKINS, STEPHEN. *The Greatest Street in the World: The Story of Broadway, Old and New, from Bowling Green to Albany*. New York: G. P. Putnam's Sons, 1911.

———. *The Story of the Bronx, from the Purchase Made by the Dutch from the Indians in 1639 to the Present Day*. New York: G. P. Putnam's Sons, 1912.

KELLEY, FRANK BERGEN, comp. *Historical Guide to the City of New York*. New York: Frederick A. Stokes Co., 1909. Includes bibliographies.

KING, MOSES. *King's Handbook of New York City*. Boston: Moses King, 1898.

KLEIN, ALEXANDER. *The Empire City: A Treasury of New York*. Rinehart & Co., 1955.

KOUWENHOVEN, JOHN A. *The Columbia Historical Portrait of New York*. New York: Doubleday & Co., 1953.

LAMB, MARTHA, AND HARRISON, MRS. BURTON. *History of the City of New York: Its Origin, Rise and Progress*. New York: A. S. Barnes & Co., 1896.

LANE, WHEATON J. *Commodore Vanderbilt: An Epic of the Steam Age*. New York: Alfred A. Knopf, 1942.

LANGSTAFF, B. MEREDITH. *Brooklyn Heights, Yesterday, Today, Tomorrow*. Brooklyn, N.Y.: Brooklyn Heights Association, 1937.

LANIER, HENRY WYSHAM. *A Century of Banking in New York, 1822–1922*. New York: George H. Doran Co., 1922.

LENG, C. W., AND DAVIS, W. T. *Staten Island and Its People: A History, 1609–1933*. New York: Lewis Historical Publishing Co., 1929–33.

LEONARD, JOHN W. *History of the City of New York, 1609–1909: From the earliest discoveries to the Hudson-Fulton celebration, together with brief biographies of men representative of the business interests of the city*. New York: Journal of Commerce, 1910.

LEVICK, M. B. "Last of Harlem's Country Seats," *New York Times Magazine*, 1923.

LEVINE, BENJAMIN, AND STORY, ISABELLE F. *Statue of Liberty, National Monument, Bedloe's Island, New York*. Washington, D.C.: National Park Service, 1952.

LEVINSON, LEONARD LEWIS. *Wall Street*. New York: Ziff-Davis Publishing Co., 1961.

LEVY, FLORENCE N. *Art in New York: A Guide to Things Worth Seeing*. 5th ed. New York: Municipal Art Society, 1935.

Little Old New York Illustrated. New York: Oxford Publishing Co., 1910.

LOCKWOOD, SARAH M. *New York: Not So Little and Not so Old*. New York: Doubleday, Page & Co., 1926.

LOSSING, BENSON J. *History of New York City, Embracing an Outline Sketch of Events from 1609 to 1830, and a Full Account of Its Development from 1830 to 1884*. New York: Perine Engraving & Publishing Co., 1884.

MCALLISTER, WARD. *Society as I Have Found It*. New York: Cassell Publishing Co., 1890.

MCCABE, JAMES D. *Lights and Shadows of New York Life*. New York: National Publishing Co., 1872.

———. *New York by Sunlight and Gaslight*. New York, 1882.

MCCULLOUGH, ESTER M. *As I Pass On, O Manhattan*. New York: Coley Taylor, 1956.

MCKAY, RICHARD C. *South Street: A Maritime History of New York*. New York: G. P. Putnam's Sons, 1934.

MANHATTAN COMPANY, THE. *"Manna-hatin," the Story of New York*. New York: Manhattan Company, 1929.

MARCUSE, MAXWELL F. *This Was New York!* New York: LIM Press, 1969.

MARSHALL, DAVID. *Grand Central*. New York: McGraw-Hill Co., 1946.

MARTIN, EDWARD S. *The Wayfarer in New York*. New York: The Macmillan Co., 1909.

MAURICE, ARTHUR BARTLETT. *Fifth Avenue*. Drawings by Allan G. Cram. New York: Dodd, Mead & Co., 1918.

MAYER, GRACE. *Once Upon a City*. New York: The Macmillan Co., 1958.

MONAGHAN, FRANK, AND LOWENTHAL, MARVIN. *This Was New York: The Nation's Capital in 1789*. New York: Doubleday, Doran & Co., 1943.

MORRIS, LLOYD. *Incredible New York*. New York: Random House, 1951.

MOSS, FRANK. *The American Metropolis, from Knickerbocker Days to the Present Time: An Histigraph of New York*. New York: Peter Fenelon Collier, 1897.

MOTT, HOPPER STRIKER. *The New York of Yesterday—A Descriptive Narrative of Old Bloomingdale*. New York: G. P. Putnam's Sons, 1908.

MUMFORD, LEWIS. *The Brown Decades*. New York: Harcourt, Brace & Co., 1931.

———. *The City in History*. New York: Harcourt, Brace & World, 1961.

———. *The Culture of Cities.* New York: Harcourt, Brace & Co., 1938.

———. *Sticks and Stones.* New York: Boni & Liveright, 1924. Rev. ed. New York: Dover Publications, 1955.

Mysteries and Miseries of the Great Metropolis. New York: D. Appleton & Co., 1874.

NEVINS, ALLAN. *Abram S. Hewitt, with Some Account of Peter Cooper.* New York: Harper & Brothers, 1935.

———. *John D. Rockefeller.* New York: Charles Scribner's Sons, 1940.

NEVINS, ALLAN, and KROUT, JOHN A., eds. *The Greater City: New York, 1898–1948.* New York: Columbia University Press, 1948.

NEVINS, ALLAN, and THOMAS, MILTON HALSEY, eds. *The Diary of George Templeton Strong.* New York: The Macmillan Co., 1952.

New York Daguerreotyped. New York: Putnam's Magazine, 1853.

New York the Metropolis. New York: The New York Recorder, 1893.

Old New York: Downtown. New York: Broun-Green Co., 1900.

OLMSTED, FREDERICK LAW, and KIMBALL, THEODORA, eds. *Frederick Law Olmsted, Landscape Architect, 1822–1903.* New York: G. P. Putnam's Sons, 1928.

OSBORN, GARDNER. *Streets of Old New York.* New York: Harper & Brothers, 1939.

OSTRANDER, S. M. *History of the City of Brooklyn and King's County.* Edited with introduction and notes by Alexander Black. Brooklyn, N.Y., 1894.

PASKO, W. W., ed. *Old New York: A Journal Relating to the History and Antiquities of New York City.* Published by the author, 1890.

PERINE, E. T. B. *Here's to Broadway.* New York: G. P. Putnam's Sons, 1930.

PETERSON, A. EVERETT. *Landmarks of New York.* New York: City History Club of New York, 1923.

PIERCE, CARL HORTON. *Harlem, Its Origin and Early Annals.* New York: James Riker, 1881.

POOLE, ERNEST. *The Harbor.* New York: The Macmillan Co., 1915, 1942.

PORTER, WILLIAM S. (O. HENRY). *The Four Million.* New York: Doubleday, Page & Co., 1909.

———. *The Voice of the City.* New York: Doubleday, Page & Co., 1908.

POST, JOHN J. *Old Streets, Roads, Lanes, Piers and Wharves of New York.* New York: R. D. Cooke, 1882.

POUND, ARTHUR. *The Golden Earth: the Story of Manhattan's Landed Wealth.* New York: The Macmillan Co., 1935.

PRITCHETT, V. S. *New York Proclaimed.* New York: Harcourt, Brace & World, 1964.

RICHARDS, T. ADDISON. *Guide to the Central Park.* New York: James Miller, 1866.

Rider's New York City. New York: The Macmillan Co., 1924.

RIIS, JACOB A. *How the Other Half Lives.* New York: Charles Scribner's Sons, 1890. Reprint. New York: Dover Publications, 1971.

ROGERS, AGNES, and ALLEN, FREDERICK LEWIS. *Metropolis.* New York, 1934.

RUSH, THOMAS E. *The Port of New York.* New York: Doubleday, Page & Co., 1920.

SHACKLETON, ROBERT. *The Book of New York.* New York: Penn Publishing Co., 1917.

SILVER, NATHAN. *Lost New York.* New York: Schocken Books, 1967.

SMITH, ARTHUR D. H. *John Jacob Astor, Landlord of New York.* Philadelphia: J. B. Lippincott Co., 1929.

SMITH, FRANCIS HOPKINSON. *Charcoals of New and Old New York.* New York: Doubleday, Page & Co., 1912.

SMITH, MATTHEW HALE. *Sunshine and Shadow in New York.* New York, 1868.

STEINMAN, DAVID B. *The Builders of the Bridge—The Story of John Roebling and His Son.* New York: Harcourt, Brace & Co., 1945.

STILL, BAYRD. *Mirror for Gotham.* New York: New York University Press, 1956.

STONE, WILLIAM L. *History of New York City.* New York: Virtue & Yorton, 1872.

TOCQUEVILLE, ALEXIS DE. *Democracy in America.* Edited by Phillips Bradley. New York: Alfred A. Knopf, 1945.

TODD, CHARLES BURR. *Story of the City of New York.* New York: G. P. Putnam's Sons, 1902.

TROLLOPE, ANTHONY. *North America.* London, 1862.

TULLY, ANDREW. *Era of Elegance.* New York: Funk & Wagnalls Co., 1947.

ULMANN, ALBERT. *A Landmark History of New York, Including a Guide to Commemorative Sites and Monuments.* New York: D. Appleton-Century Co., 1939.

———. *New Yorkers: from Stuyvesant to Roosevelt.* New York: Chaucer Head Book Shop, 1928.

VALENTINE, DAVID THOMAS. *History of the City of New York.* New York: G. P. Putnam, 1853.

———, comp. *Manuals of the Corporation of the City of New York, 1841 to 1870.*

VAN DYKE, JOHN C. *The New New York.* New York, 1909.

VAN PELT, DANIEL. *Leslie's History of Greater New York.* New York: Arkell Publishing Co., 1898.

VAN WYCK, FREDERICK. *Recollections of an Old New Yorker.* New York: Liveright, 1932.

VEBLEN, THORSTEIN. *The Theory of the Leisure Class.* New York: The Macmillan Co., 1899.

WARSHOW, ROBERT IRVING. *The Story of Wall Street.* New York: Greenberg, 1929.

WEITENKAMPF, FRANK. *Manhattan Kaleidoscope.* New York: Charles Scribner's Sons, 1947.

WHARTON, EDITH. *The Age of Innocence.* New York: Grosset & Dunlap, 1920.

———. *A Backward Glance.* New York: D. Appleton-Century Co., 1934.

WHITEHOUSE, ROGER. *New York: Sunshine and Shadow.* New York: Harper & Row, 1974.

WHITMAN, WALT. *Complete Writings.* Edited by R. M. Bucke, T. B. Harned, and H. L. Traubel. Camden edition. New York, 1902.

WILSON, JAMES GRANT, ed. *Memorial History of the City of New York from Its First Settlement to the Year 1892.* New York: History Co., 1892–93.

WILSON, RUFUS R. *New York Old and New: Its Story, Streets and Landmarks.* Philadelphia: J. B. Lippincott Co., 1903.

WILSON, RUFUS R., and OTILIE, BRICKSON. *New York in Literature: The Story of Landmarks of Town and Country.* Elmira, N.Y.: Primerva Press, 1947.

Wood's Illustrated Handbook to New York and Environs. New York: G. W. Carleton & Co., 1873.

ZEISLOFT, E. IDELL. *The New Metropolis.* New York, 1899.

Artists, Engravers, & Photographers

Abbey, E. A., 15
Anthony, E. and H. T., 42–43
Austin, William B., 34

Beard, D. C., 19
Berghaus, Albert, 134
Bidwell, 181
Bogert, J. A., 72
Bonwil, C. E. H., 86
Brown, J. G., 57

Cary, W. M., 20
Clement, J., 95
Cozzens, Fred S., 16

David, Theodore R., 124–125
Day, Ben, Jr., 106
Du Mond, F. V., 153

Eltinge, Sol, Jr., 123

Fox, Stanley, 12, 24, 118, 139, 176
Frenzeny, Paul, 149
Frost, A. B., 173

Graham, Charles, 19, 36, 48–49, 56, 64, 77, 92–93, 101, 108, 168, 203
Graham, Charles, and Thulstrup, de Thure, 36, 202
Gray-Parker, 151, 178–179
Gubelman, 92–93

Hawley, Hughson, 17, 52, 53, 187
Hitchcock, 42–43
Homer, Winslow, 80, 144–145, 148
Hopkins, L., 165

Inness, George, 166

Jackson, A. L., 194
Jewett, W. S. L., 29

Keetels, R. A., 5, 99
Klepper, Max, 123

Lagard, 63

Meeker, E. J., 4

Ogden, H. A., 109, 180

Pach, 50, 127
Perkins, Granville, 21, 194
Pilliner, 40
Pranishnikoff, Ivan, 6, 7, 14, 158, 164

Reinhart, Charles Stanley, 61, 190
Rockwood, 33, 45, 46, 160
Rogers, W. A., 65, 66, 68, 100, 111

Schell, F. H., 17, 26, 37, 97, 159, 175
Schell, F. H., and Hogan, 26, 37, 88, 90, 97, 150, 159, 175
Shelton, W. H., 186
Shults, A. B., 11
Smith, F. Hopkinson, 94
Snyder, W. P., 54, 55, 69, 128, 130, 146–147, 172, 188, 204

Tavernier, Jules, 22–23
Taylor, C. J., 128

Wade, W., 38
Wallin, S., 38
Waud, A. R., 8–9, 72, 177, 184–185
Waud, W. W., 140
Weldon, D. D., 73
Wells, J., 39
Worth, Thomas, 62, 121

General Index

Academy of Music, 197, 198, 201
Albion, Robert Greenhalgh, 4, 7, 12
American Architecture, 81
American Notes, 29, 64
American Scene, The, 71, 138
American Society, 147, 173
American Stage in Pageant of America, 197
Annals of American Sport, 191
Appleton Building, 160
Apthorpe Mansion, 52
Archery, 174
Arden, Jacob, House, 52
Arion Society, 201, 202
Arthur, President Chester, 90
As You Pass By, 41
Astor House, 30–31
Astor Place, 51, 186
Astoria, 100
Athletic clubs, 174
Atlantic Dock, 84
Atlantic Monthly, 174
Avenue A, 61

Baker, George F., 202
Ballou's Pictorial Drawing-Room Companion, 3, 18, 27, 32, 59, 85, 197
Bancroft, George, 136
Barclay Street, 31
Barges, 4, 5
Barnum's American Museum, 196
Barnum's Hippodrome, 160
Bartholdi, Frederic Auguste, 82, 104
Baseball, 174, 188, 189
Bathing scenes, 106, 107, 108, 110–111
Battery, The, 2, 15, 29, 78, 83, 108, 112, 114, 116, 124, 149, 161
Baxter Street, 64
Beach Pneumatic Tunnel, 114, 124, 127
Bedloe's Island, 82, 102, 105
Belmont, August, 157, 184
Bergh, Henry, 133, 166
Bicycles (Cycling), 174, 192–193, 195
Blackwell's Island, 100

Bloomingdale Road, 52, 174
Boathouses, 99
Book of New York, The, 19, 60
"Bottle Alley," 65
Bourget, Paul, 89
Bowery, The, 58, 63, 177
Bowling Green, 28
Brady, "Diamond Jim," 193
Brighton Beach, 82, 109
Broad Street, 52
Broadway, 27, 28, 29, 30–31, 32, 33, 37, 47, 54, 56, 70, 72, 77, 113, 114, 115, 120, 122, 149, 154, 160, 174, 185, 186, 193, 194, 196, 198, 202
"Broadway," in *Holiday Magazine,* 31
Broadway Overground Railway, 117
Bronx River, 97
Bronx, The, 98, 99
Brooklyn (Breukelen), 4, 16, 49, 79, 81, 82, 84, 85, 87, 88, 92–93, 112, 130, 168
Brooklyn Bridge, 79, 81, 86, 87, 88, 89, 90, 91, 92–93, 94, 95, 104, 168
"Brooklyn Bridge," in *Harper's Bazaar,* 87, 88, 93
Brooklyn Elevated Railway, 130, 167
Brown, Gene M., 34, 36
Brown, Henry Collins, 69, 111, 145, 146, 166, 169
Brown Decades, The, 91, 135
Bruce, Wallace, 95
Brunswick Hotel, 182, 200
Brush Electric Illuminating Company, 56
Bryant, William Cullen, 136, 139
Bryant Park, 41
Bull's Head Hotel, 177
Buttermilk Channel, 84
Buttonwood Agreement, 28

Cabot, John (Giovanni Caboto), 2
Canal boats, 4, 5, 10–11
Canal Street, 33, 60, 186
Carmine Street, 58
Carnegie Hall, 204

Carriages, 47, 116, 118, 151, 176, 177, 178, 186, 187, 196, 197
Central Labor Union (C.L.U.), 172
Central Park, 71, 74, 75, 136, 137, 138, 139, 140, 141, 142, 143, 144–145, 146–147, 148, 149, 150, 151, 152, 174, 176, 181, 183, 193
Central Park: A History and a Guide, 144
"Central Park, The," in *Harper's Magazine,* 152
Central Park West, 75
Central Park Zoo, 138, 139, 141
Chamber Street, 40
Chinatown, 58
City Hall, 28, 30–31, 33, 46, 47, 49, 58, 78, 155, 186
City Hall Park, 159
Claremont, 52
Claremont Inn, 183
Cleveland, President Grover, 75, 104, 105
Coaching, 150, 179, 180, 181, 182, 183, 184, 189
Coaching Club, 180, 182
Coenties Slip, 154
Columbus, Christopher (Cristoforo Colombo), 2
Columbus Avenue, 194
Coney Island, 83, 101, 106, 107, 108, 109, 110–111, 112
Cooper Institute (Cooper Union), 51, 114
Crane, Hart, 95
Cricket, 188, 190
Croquet, 174, 191
Croton Aqueduct, 96, 100, 101
Crystal Palace, 38, 39, 40, 41
Culver Road, 82
Custom's House, 28
Customs Inspection, 13, 14

Daily News, 157
Dakota Apartments, 146–147
Davidson, Marshall, 15
de Hauranne, Duvergier, 137
Delmonico's, 200

Depew, Chauncey M., 168
Diary of a Little Girl in Old New York, 149
Diary of George T. Strong, 113
Dickens, Charles, 29, 64
Dock scenes, 1, 4, 5, 6, 7, 8–9, 10–11, 12–13, 14
Downing, Andrew Jackson, 136
Draft, 157
Draft Riots, 154, 156
Dramatic Mirror, 202
Dreiser, Theodore, 58
Dressler, Marie, 193
Dunshee, Kenneth Holcomb, 41, 153
Dutch West India Company, 2, 82, 106

East River, 1, 2, 3, 4, 16, 42, 61, 81, 84, 85, 86, 87, 88, 89, 91, 92–93, 95, 121, 161
Edison, Thomas, 55, 203
Egyptian Obelisk, 151
Elections, 77
Elevated Railways, 115, 116–117, 118, 119, 123, 124–125, 126, 127, 128, 129, 130, 131
Eleventh Avenue, 58
Ellis, Edmund Robb, 55, 157, 168, 172
Emigrant in New York, The, in *The Nineteenth Century,* 66
Enjine! Enjine!, 153
Epic of New York City, The, 55, 157, 168, 172
Erie Canal, 4, 5
Evening Post, 139
Excursion boats, 100, 101, 105, 109, 112

Ferry-boats, 3, 16, 17, 86, 87, 92–93
Ferries, 82, 85, 92–93, 121
Field, Cyrus, 114, 127
Fifth Avenue, 28, 42–43, 50, 56, 58, 72, 137, 145, 174, 176, 183, 185, 186, 187, 200
Fire-boats, 161
Fire-fighting, 41, 153, 155, 158, 159, 160, 161, 162–163, 167
Fireworks, 76, 78, 79, 159
"Five Points," 58, 67
Flatiron Building, 77
Flower Market, 60
Forty-second Street, 44, 70, 203
Fourteenth Street, 45
Fourth Avenue, 134
Frank Leslie's Illustrated Newspaper, 13, 44, 51, 60, 67, 74, 104, 105, 107, 116–117, 134, 143, 152, 157, 189, 195, 201, 202
Fraunces Tavern, 52
French Travellers in the United States, 137
Fulton Market, 2, 18, 19, 21

Fulton Street, 33
Fulton Street Elevated Railway, 130
Fulton Street Ferry, 85

Garbage disposal, 69
Gardner, Albert Ten Eyck, 80
General Slocum disaster, 61
Genin's footbridge (Loew fotbridge), 114, 115
George, Henry, 172
German districts, 61
German street band, 57
Gilbert, R. H., 118
Gilbert Elevated Road, 114, 119, 127
Glance at New York, A, 33
Gleason's Pictorial Drawing Room Companion, 1, 3, 30–31, 38, 39, 40, 72, 78, 83, 84, 96, 115, 196, 198, 199, 200
Goulds, the, 202
Governor's Island, 84
Gowanus, Brooklyn, 82
Grain elevators, 5, 11
Grand Central Depot, 44, 114, 134
Grand Street, 58, 68, 170, 186
Grant's Tomb, 183, 184, 194
Greeley, Horace, 136
Green, Andrew H., 136
Greene, Asa, 33
Greenwich Street, 114, 116, 118
Greenwich Village, 58
Gridiron street plan, 124, 125, 127

Harlem, 58, 114
Harlem Lane, 136, 174, 184
Harlem River, 82, 96, 98, 99, 100, 101, 121, 174
Harper's Weekly, 3, 4, 5, 6, 7, 8–9, 10–11, 12, 14, 15, 16, 17, 19, 20, 21, 22–23, 24, 25, 26, 29, 33, 34, 35, 36, 37, 41, 42–43, 45, 46, 47, 48, 49, 50, 52, 53, 64, 65, 66, 70, 71, 73, 75, 76, 77, 79, 80, 86, 87, 88, 89, 90, 92–93, 94, 97, 98, 99, 100, 101, 102, 106, 108, 109, 110–111, 113, 118, 120, 121, 124–125, 128, 129, 130, 131, 132, 133, 137, 138, 139, 140, 141, 142, 144–145, 146–147, 148, 149, 150, 151, 153, 155, 156, 158, 159, 160, 161, 162–163, 164, 165, 166, 167, 168, 170–171, 172, 173, 175, 176, 177, 178–179, 180, 181, 182, 183, 184–185, 186, 187, 188, 190, 191, 192–193, 194, 200, 203, 204
Harse, Jacob, House, 52
Harvey, Catherine Elizabeth, 149
Hawkers and Walkers in Early America, 59
Hell Gate, 82, 99, 100
"Hell's Kitchen," 58

Hemstreet, William, 116–117
Here Is New York, 63
Hewitt, Abram S., 114, 172
High Bridge, 96, 97, 98, 100, 101
Holmes, Oliver Wendell, 174
Homer, Winslow, 136, 144–145, 148
Hornung, Clarence P., 25
Horsecars, 17, 19, 38, 44, 46, 48, 49, 77, 85, 118, 124, 126, 127, 128, 129, 132, 133, 134, 164, 165, 166, 168, 170–171, 172
Horses, 146–147, 148, 149, 150, 151, 162–163, 164, 173, 175, 176, 177, 178–179, 180, 182, 183, 184–185, 186
Hotels, 199, 200, 203
How the Other Half Lives, 58, 65, 67, 154
Howells, William Dean, 151
Hudson, Henry, 2
Hudson River (also North River, Mauritius), 2, 8–9, 16–17, 28, 43, 98, 121, 161, 192, 194, 195

Immigrants, 12, 66, 67
Impressions and Experiences, 151
Incredible New York, 70, 108, 109, 182, 185, 193, 199
Indians, 2, 82, 83, 106
Iron Steamboat Company, 108, 110
Irving, Washington, 136
Irving Place, 45, 197
Italian neighborhoods, 58, 67
Italian organ grinder, 57

Jerome, Leonard W., 181, 184–185
Jerome Park, 174, 181, 184–185
Jewish quarters, 58
James, Henry, 71, 138
Jockey clubs, 174, 181, 184–185
Jones' Wood, 100
Journal of Commerce, 157
Jumel Mansion, 52

Kazin, Alfred, 87, 88, 93
Kingsbridge, 97, 116

Lambert, John, 24
Lazarus, Emma, 103
Life and Liberty in America, 158
Life in America, 15
Life of Barnum, The, 196
Lights and Shadows of New York Life, 44, 181, 199
Lincoln, Abraham, 51, 154
Loew footbridge, 33
London Times, The, 50
Long Island Sound, 99
Lost New York, 52
Lower East Side, 58
Lyman, Susan Elizabeth, 51

McAllister, Ward, 185
McCabe, James D., 44, 181, 199
McComb, John, Jr., 155
McComb's Dam Bridge, 98, 146
Mackay, Charles, 158
Madison Square, 28, 55, 56, 70, 104, 174, 186, 199, 203
Madison Square Garden, 178
Mangin, Joseph, 155
Manhattan Athletic Club, 53
Manhattan Beach, 82, 108, 109
Manhattan Beach Hotel, 111
Manhattan Kaleidoscope, 26, 72, 73
Manhattanville, 28, 114, 183
Marcuse, Maxwell F., 195, 200
Marjoribanks, Alexander, 183
Mark Twain's Travels with Mr. Brown, 132
Market scenes, 2, 18, 19, 21, 22–23, 24, 25, 26, 60
Marshall, Walter G., 126
Meigs Elevated Railway, 125
Memorial History of the City of New York, The, 97
Metropolitan Milieu, The, 128
Metropolitan Opera House, 197, 202, 203
Michaux Club, 193
Minuit, Peter, 2, 28
Mirror for Gotham, 107, 120
Monaghan, Frank, Ed., 137
Monuments, 48, 146–147, 183, 184, 194
Morgan, J. P., 202
Morris, Lloyd, 70, 108, 109, 182, 185, 193, 199
Morrisania, 97
Moving Day, 62
Mulberry Bend, 58, 65, 67
Mulberry Street, 58, 67
Mumford, Lewis, 91, 92, 128, 135
Murray Hill, 28
Murray Street, 114, 122

Narrows, The, 2, 42–43
Nassau Street, 28, 48
New Amsterdam (Nieu Amsterdam), 28, 30, 82
New New York, 9
New York Athletic Club, 53
New York Central Railroad, 168
New York Circumnavigated, 83, 97
New York Elevated Railroad, 114, 127
New York Harbor, 82, 83, 86, 102, 104, 121
New York Herald, 164
New York Skating Club, 145
New York Steam Company, 54
New York Sun, 165
New York Times, 48

New York World, 48, 49, 102, 157
Niblo's Theatre and Garden, 198

O'Brien, Charlotte G., 66
Olmsted, Frederick Law, 136, 194
Omnibuses, 37, 47, 77, 113, 119, 120, 187, 196, 199
Outre-Mer: Impressions of America, 89

Panics, 35, 37, 124
Panoramic views, 3, 30–31, 42–43, 86, 87, 98, 102
Parades, 72, 73, 74, 75, 76
Park Avenue, 134
Park Row, 28, 47, 48, 167
Pearl Street, 52
Peck Slip, 82, 97, 99
Peddlers, street, 20
Penny lunch, 68
Perry, George Sessions, 139, 141
Plaza, The, 187
Police, 170–171, 172
Polo Grounds, 145, 174, 188, 189
Post Office, 28, 46, 47
Printing House Square, 48
Pulitzer, Joseph, 49, 102
Pulitzer Building, 49

Racing, horse, 176, 181, 184–185
Rapid Transit, 115, 116–117, 118, 119, 122, 123, 124–125, 126, 127, 128, 129, 130, 131, 134
Recollections of an Old New Yorker, 176
Reed, Henry Hope, and Duckworth, Sophia, 144
Restaurants, 68, 200
Rialto, The, 203
Richards, T. Addison, 83, 97, 152
Riis, Jacob, 58, 67, 154
Riots, 154, 156
Rise of New York Port, The, 4, 7, 12
Riverside Drive, 75, 183, 192, 193, 194, 195
Rockaway, 101
Rockefeller, William, 202
Rodgers, Cleveland, and Rankin, Rebecca B., 127, 130
Roebling, John A., 82, 87, 88, 121
Roebling, Washington, 82
Roosevelt, Theodore, 172
Russell, Lillian, 193

Sailing vessels, 1, 3, 4, 5, 6, 7, 8–9, 15, 19, 84, 86, 87, 88, 92–93, 94, 95, 99, 104
St. Paul's Church, 28, 33, 113, 120
St. Patrick's Cathedral, 187
St. Thomas's Church, 187
Saturday Evening Post, 139, 141

Schuyler, Montgomery, 87
Scientific American, 81, 91, 103, 118, 119, 122, 123, 126, 127, 135, 169
Seymour, Governor Horatio, 157
Shackleton, Robert, 19, 60
Shanties, 142, 143
Sheepshead Bay, 82, 109
Shopping, 29, 30–31, 80, 186
Silver, Nathan, 52
Sixth Avenue, 124–125
Sixth Avenue El, 129, 169
Skating, 144–145, 174
Sleighing, 146–147, 148, 149, 173, 175
Slums, 64, 65, 66, 67
Smith, Matthew Hale, 27
Smith's Mansion, Colonel, 52
Snow-storms, 164, 165, 166, 167, 168, 169
Society for the Prevention of Cruelty to Animals, 132, 166
Soldiers' and Sailors' Monument, 75, 194
South Ferry, 84
South Street, 1, 2
Spring's Brick Church, 42–43
Spuyten Duyvil, 82, 97, 98, 99, 168, 194
Stanley, Edward, 31
Staten Island, 3, 42–43, 82, 83, 168
Staten Island Cricket Club, 190
Staten Island Ferry, 169
Statue of Liberty, 82, 102, 103, 104, 105
Stephenson, John, 130, 133
Sticks and Stones, 92
Still, Bayrd, 107, 120
Stock Exchange, 28, 36, 50
Stone, General Le Roy, 119, 130
Story of New York, The, 51
Street Cleaning Department, 69
Street crowds, 29, 33, 34, 35, 37, 38, 70, 71, 72, 73, 76, 77, 78, 80, 115, 118, 120, 170–171
Street hawkers, 59
Street scenes, 6, 8–9, 24–25, 27, 30–31, 32, 33, 34, 37, 38, 44, 45, 46, 47, 48, 49, 54, 56, 57, 60, 61, 67, 72, 73, 74, 75, 79, 80, 113, 115, 116–117, 118, 119, 120, 124–125, 128, 129
Striker Homestead, 52
Strikes, 170–171
Strong, George Templeton, 156
Sunshine and Shadow in New York, 27

Tammany Hall, 45
Tavern-on-the-Green, 139, 141
Tenements, 64, 65, 66, 67
Tennis, lawn, 174, 190, 191
Teresina in America, 14

Theatres, 196, 197, 198, 203
Thérèse Yelverton, 14
Third Avenue, 156
Third Avenue El, 129
This Was New York, 195, 200
Through America; or Nine Months in the United States, 126
Times Square, 31
Toboggan slide, 145
Tompkins, Governor Daniel D., 61
Tompkins Square, 61
Towle, George M., 147, 173
Traffic scenes, 6, 8–9, 10–11, 16–17, 19, 24, 25, 26, 32, 33, 37, 44, 48, 49, 77, 115, 120, 121, 128, 164, 166, 168
Travels in South and North America, 163
Travels through Canada and the United States of North America, 24
Travers Island, 53, 184
Tribune, The, 48, 51
Trinity Church, 27, 28, 31, 34, 37
Twenty-third Street, 77

Underground Railway, 122

Union Course, 184
Union Square, 55, 70, 199
United States Treasury, 27, 37

Valentine's Manual of the City of New York, 69, 111, 145, 146, 166, 169
Van Cortlandt Manor, 52
Van den Heuvel House, 52
Vanderbilt, Commodore Cornelius, 50, 136, 176
Vanderbilt, William H., 50, 146
Vanderbilt family, 187, 202
Vanderbilt homes, 50
Van Dyke, John C., 9
Van Wyck, Frederick, 176
Vaux, Calvert, 136, 194
Verrazano, Giovanni da, 2
Vesey Street, 30–31

Wall Street, 27, 28, 30–31, 34, 35, 154
"Wall Street: Men and Money," in *Park Magazine,* 34, 36
Wallack's Theatre, 203
Wallabout Bay, 82

Warren Street, 114, 122
Washington Heights, 97, 100
Washington Market, 2, 19, 21, 22–23, 24, 25, 26
Washington Square, 176
Waterfront, the, 1, 2, 3, 4, 6, 7, 8–9, 10–11, 15, 154
Weitenkampf, Frank, 26, 72, 73
West Farms, 97
West Street, 8, 9, 133
Westchester, 53
Westminster Kennel Club, 178
Wheels Across America, 25
White, E. B., 63
Whitman, Walt, 6, 8, 32, 38, 39, 42, 77, 86, 106
Winslow, Homer, An American Artist: His World and His Work, 80
Winter sports, 144–145, 146–147, 148, 149
Wolfe, Thomas, 95
Wood, Fernando, 157
World's Capital City, The, 127, 130
Wright, Richard, 59

Yorkville, 58, 61, 114